THE
PURPOSE
OF
IT ALL

Msgr. Behrmann

Nov. 1996

Books by the same author

Les tendances nouvelles de l'ecclésiologie

The Relevance of Physics

Brain, Mind and Computers
(Lecomte du Noüy Prize, 1970)

The Paradox of Olbers' Paradox

The Milky Way: An Elusive Road for Science

*Science and Creation: From Eternal Cycles
to an Oscillating Universe*

*Planets and Planetarians: A History of Theories of the Origin
of Planetary Systems*

The Road of Science and the Ways to God
(Gifford Lectures, University of Edinburgh, 1975 and 1976)

The Origin of Science and the Science of its Origin
(Fremantle Lectures, Oxford, 1977)

*And on This Rock: The Witness of One Land
and Two Covenants*

Cosmos and Creator

Angels, Apes, and Men

Uneasy Genius: The Life and Work of Pierre Duhem

Chesterton, a Seer of Science

The Keys of the Kingdom: A Tool's Witness to Truth

Lord Gifford and His Lectures: A Centenary Retrospect

Chance or Reality and Other Essays

The Physicist as Artist: The Landscapes of Pierre Duhem

The Absolute beneath the Relative and Other Essays

(continued on p. 295)

THE PURPOSE OF IT ALL

Stanley L. Jaki

REGNERY GATEWAY
Washington D. C.

Copyright © 1990 by Stanley L. Jaki

LIBRARY OF CONGRESS CATALOGING-IN-PUBLICATION DATA
Jaki, Stanley L.
    The purpose of it all / Stanley L. Jaki.
        p.   cm.
    Includes bibliographical references and index.
    ISBN 0-89526-740-3
    1. God—Proof, Teleological.   2. Natural theology.   3. Religion and science—1946–   4. Philosophy, Modern.   5. Man.   6. Evolution.   7. Free will and determinism.   I. Title
    BT102.J34   1990
    210—dc20
                                                          90-44307
                                                          CIP

Published in the United States by
Regnery Gateway
1130 17th Street, NW
Washington, DC 20036

Distributed to the trade by
National Book Network
4720-A Boston Way
Lanham, MD 20706

Printed on acid free paper
Manufactured in the United States of America
Designed by Irving Perkins Associates

10   9   8   7   6   5   4   3   2   1

CONTENTS

FOREWORD

The eight chapters of this volume are the enlarged form of the eight lectures which the Farmington Institute for Christian Studies, Oxford, and the Farmington Trust asked me to deliver in November 1989. It is my pleasure to express my appreciation to the Hon. Robert Wills, Chairman of the Trust, and to its Board of Trustees, for the invitation.

The lectures were delivered in Corpus Christi College, Oxford. As a Visiting Fellow I would like to thank the President and Fellows of Corpus Christi College for their kind hospitality.

INTRODUCTION

Among the various ways of demonstrating the existence of God, ways very different from the art of convincing, the design argument has always had a special appeal. Few features of existence seem to point so effectively to a cause beyond them as is their appearance of being designed for some purpose. Would it not therefore be safe to conclude that if the universe shows a design, then logic demands that one should trace it to the purposeful act of the Creator of all? For if the universe is the totality of all things, God alone is to be found in that "beyond" which is not physical but metaphysical.

This line of reasoning seems to have received in recent years powerful support in physical research relating to what is now called the anthropic principle. Has not therefore the stage been reached where one can assert with an eye on exact science that matter has been designed from the very start so that man may eventually appear on the scene? If so, a perfect ground would be available for the theologian to repeat the old claim that the purpose of man is to be the conscious voice of Nature's silent testimony about her having been created for the glory of God, the highest purpose of it all.

Actually, this line of reasoning is not altogether worthy of what reason can say in the matter. First, design is not the same as purpose. In fact, designs have been registered before anything specific could be ascertained about their function, let alone the purpose of their functioning. The purpose remains in fact often in the dark, while more and more scientific light is shed on the specifics of the function. This in itself may suggest that not a few formulations of the design argument may in fact be but versions of the cosmological argument. In the latter, consistently co-ordinated specifics

are to be established about the universe in order to justify
the raising of the question: why this and not something else?

Apart from this closeness of the design argument to the
cosmological argument and at times plain identity with it,
forms of the design argument can be very defective in coming to grips with the notion of purpose. Hardly ever is
attention paid to the fact that the very source of our knowledge of purpose relates to our own personal consciousness
of acting for a purpose. Clearly then one cannot read, without further ado, purpose into mere biological processes in
which there is no evidence of a conscious aim at work.
Seeing purpose at work in the purely biological domain
demands therefore a careful philosophical consideration,
which, so it is argued in this book, comes only from the
doctrine of the analogy of being.

Such a doctrine is very alien to prevailing ideas about the
reality of purpose at large. This intellectual alienation is part
of a cultural malaise to which more than one factor has
contributed. A most conspicuous of them is the loss of
credibility suffered by the idea of progress which so many
took, during the Enlightenment and the Industrial Revolution, for the very purpose of human existence. Darwinism
dealt another blow at belief in progress which was not
shored up by philosophies whose proponents banked heavily on some quasi-metaphysical reinterpretation of biological evolution.

It is argued in these lectures, in which a detailed analysis
is given of these mistaken and at times crudely misguided
efforts to specify the purpose of existence, that the clue lies
in a close look at the origin of man's firm belief in his free
will. This firm belief, which the Greeks of old themselves
lacked, to say nothing of other great ancient cultures, has its
source in the far-reaching alternative which the biblical revelation offered from its very start to man. The choice between life as prosperity and death as doom, which then

gradually emerged as a choice between an eternal personal life and a no less eternal failure, has been the prime cause of a vivid consciousness about the reality of purpose and of profound reflections on it.

The present-day rise in the Western World of cults, so strange after so many centuries steeped in Christianity, is a proof of the need for religious considerations if the question of purpose is to be seen in its breadth and depth and if an abiding sense of purpose is to be recovered.

The need for that recovery should be very evident to sober observers of the modern scene. A runaway technology brings daily illustrations of the growing split between intrinsically sane means and increasingly maddening motivations. The psychiatric diseases especially rampant in affluent societies form another proof that our post-Christian age will have to look in a direction which is religious, and in a sense far transcending the shallows of mere estheticism.

In the concluding pages of this book the cult centered on Christ is held high as the supreme terminal point of that direction. The main body of the book is devoted to two tasks. One is to portray the failure of efforts that sought true sense of purpose in directions other than genuinely religious. The other is to marshal the cultural, scientific, and philosophical reasons that point, indirectly and directly, toward Christ as the ultimate answer to man's search for the purpose of it all.

THE
PURPOSE
OF
IT ALL

Chapter One

PROGRESS FOR
SCANT PURPOSE

From Utopia to the Land of Promise
In coming to grips with the problem of the purpose of it all,
modern man would readily fall back on his faith in progress.
He takes that progress above all for a business of science as if
science automatically assured its own purpose as well as the
purpose of mankind. A most recent case in point is the
euphoria sparked by the performance of spaceprobe Voyager
2. Of course, as a scientific feat Voyager 2 deserved the
highest encomiums. After having covered, in 12 years and
five days, 2.75 billion miles on its way to Neptune, Voyager
2 was only 20 miles off course. Such accuracy corresponds
to marksmanship which misses by only a thousandth of a
millimeter a hairline about 1 km away. No less accurate
was the timing. Voyager 2 reached a mere 1.4 seconds late its
closest approach, 1900 miles, to that until now most mysterious planet.

While experts alone could savor the full extent of the
technological marvel, there was much in it to astonish the
layman. The 12-foot disk antenna of Voyager 2 worked as a
22 watt bulb, a rather weak source of illumination even

when at arm's length. The signals of that antenna as received from Neptune's distance were 20 billion times weaker than the electrical power in an ordinary digital wristwatch. The decoding of such incredibly faint signals into pictures revealed stunningly new details about the surfaces and atmospheres of Jupiter, Saturn, Uranus, and Neptune. Saturn's rings turned out to be an intrically composite affair, and rings, however narrow, were found to exist around the other planets as well.

Such details and the total of 24 new moons discovered around those planets could but prompt the kind of reaction in which admiration grows into a renewed sense of purpose. This seemed to be the gist of a brief letter, sent on August 25 to the editor of *The Times* (London) and published there the next day: "Sir, Tennyson's Ulysses says it well '. . . my purpose holds to sail beyond the sunset and the baths of all the western stars until I die'. Farewell, then, heroic Voyager 2."[1] Voyager 2 fared indeed so well as to suggest that its Grand Tour of the outer planets heralded even greater tours across cosmic spaces. Underlying that expectation is the belief that science would penetrate all puzzles and provide man thereby with a sense of abiding purpose.

The belief that science, and science alone, can provide man with a sense of purpose took on an unparalleled intensity as the 19th century approached its midpoint. Science suddenly seemed to be possessed with the ability to deliver its promises in tantalizingly tangible forms. Seeing progress under one's very eyes took the place of belief in it, a belief previously stated in portrayals of Utopias or at best in abstract reasoning. As he held high the idea of progress, in the closing decade of the 18th century, Condorcet could not have boasted of technological progress even if he had been really interested in it. He might have been dumbstruck on learning that the Middle Ages had provided all the major technological innovations on which rested almost all the crafts of his time, displayed by his friend Diderot in two sumptuous volumes.[2] Condorcet struck a note less characteristic of a philosopher, even less of a scientist, than of a political visionary as he consoled himself in his hiding with a view of the human race

> emancipated from its shackles, released from the empire of fate and from the enemies of its progress, advancing with a firm and sure step along the path of truth, virtue and happiness. It is the contemplation of this prospect that rewards him for all his efforts to assist the progress of reason and the defence of liberty. . . . Such a contemplation is for him an asylum, in which the memory of his persecutors cannot pursue him; there he lives in thought with man restored to his natural rights and dignity . . . ; there he lives with his peers in an Elyseum created by reason and graced by the purest pleasures known to the love of mankind.[3]

A generation or so later Heinrich Heine added "free industrial institutions" to the political ones through which "mankind is destined to happiness" and long before, as the Christian religion would have it, "only on the Day of Judgment, in Heaven."[4]

By then more and more people saw progress mainly concretized in the steam engine. Its coming in the form of locomotives gave to many the impression of moving from one world into another. Thackeray, for one, felt that as a child he had lived in the old world of "stage coaches, more or less swift, riding-horses, pack-horses, highway-men, knights in armour, Norman invaders, Roman legions, Druids, Ancient Britons painted blue, and so forth." By the time he had reached middle age, it was the new world of railways: "Your railroad starts the new era, and we of a certain age belong to the new time and the old one. We are of the time of chivalry as well as the Black Prince of Sir Walter Manny. We are the age of steam."[5] He did not live long enough to see much of the fast-coming new age of electricity.

In concrete terms the railroad increased in two short decades (1825-1845) by 400 percent the speed of land travel, that is, from 12 miles to 50 miles per hour, at least in some lucky stretches of Britain. The Continent still lived in the old world, as old indeed as the world of the Roman Empire. When in 1841 Robert Peel received in Rome Queen Victoria's call to form a new government, his journey to London took thirty days. No more time was needed, almost two thousand years earlier, by Emperor Vespasian to rush from Rome to his province of Britain.

This parallel was pointedly recalled by Winston Churchill as he portrayed the progress that had taken place during the three generations following Queen Victoria's accession to the throne.[6] Very correctly, Churchill saw more progress in that period than all the progress that had accumulated during the thirty generations prior to Louis XIV. The bathrooms of the palaces of Minos were superior, Churchill mischievously noted, to those of Versailles. In a facetious manner he prognosticated the mass production, within fifty years, of chicken breasts separately from entire chickens and, in a serious vein, the tapping of fabulous supplies of energy on the basis of Einstein's relativity.

If Churchill was seized for a moment with a Utopian vision of progress, he merely echoed those many who in the 1830s took the railroad as a concrete conveyance into the Promised Land. About that time the *Illustrated London News* carried the following encomium of rail travel:

> Lay down your rails, ye nations near and far—
> Yoke your full trains to Steam's triumphal car.
> Link town to town; unite in iron bands
> The long-estranged and oft-embattled lands.
> Peace, mild-eyed seraph—Knowledge, light divine,

Shall send their messengers by every line. . . .
Blessings on Science, and her handmaid Steam!
They make Utopia only half a dream.[7]

By mid-century things seemed to move within striking
distance of the Promised Land as Britain was quickly turning into a vast network of rails. Otherwise it would not have
been possible for six million Britons and tens of thousands
of foreigners to visit the Great Exhibition in the Crystal
Palace between its opening day, May 1, 1851, and its closing
day five months later.

The Great Exhibition
The Crystal Palace was in itself a stunning evidence of
progress. With its dimensions—600 meters long, 130 meters wide and 30 meters high in its transepts where it covered some of the tallest elm trees in Hyde Park—it was the
largest unit construction in the world. Its glass walls, a
million feet of glass panels, signaled the availability of a
material that only years earlier had still heavily been taxed as
a luxury item. It was prefabricated. All its 2,300 girders,
3,310 columns, rows upon rows of gutters and sash bars had
been identical and therefore interchangeable.

Progress was further symbolized by the fact that Joseph
Paxton, the architect, was a self-made man. He had already
been one as chief-gardener of the Duke of Devonshire. His
design of the Crystal Palace, that won out over 254 other
designs, mostly drawn up by professionals, was an enlarge-
ment of a glass house he had built for the Duke. Progress
blared forth in the speedy construction. Paxton drew up the
blueprints in just one month, from June 11 to July 15, 1850.
The ground was handed over to him on July 30th and by
September 26 the first columns were standing. Within sev-
enteen weeks all the glass panels were in place.

Then came the opening which, in the words of the editorial in the *Illustrated London News*, had "the characteristics of a national holiday."[8] That editorial, which has been conspicuously ignored in the vast literature on the Crystal Palace, contains all the principal reflections evoked by the Great Exhibition. First came the remark that "ten years ago it [the Great Exhibition] would have been reckoned a thing possible, but not probable." Of course, even in 1841 enough technical know-how was on hand to build a cast iron structure with glass walls and roofs. It was then that the great French architect, Henri Labrouste, began to build, along similar plans, the main reading room of the Bibliothèque Sainte Geneviève in Paris, a picture of which hardly fails to appear in serious art histories.

If the Crystal Palace was to be "an Exhibition of the Arts and Industry of all Nations," the editorial went on, distances among the nations of the earth had to shrink first in the physical sense. The shortening of physical distances through railroads, steamships, and electric telegraph made it possible "to make Europe one large country" together with "the realisation of that great idea—a friendly rivalry in the arts of peace." What in 1841 could appear "possible but not probable," would have appeared in 1830 "the over sanguine expectation of a too credulous philosopher or poet," and in 1820 "the dream of a lunatic."

The dream implied much more than technological progress. Such progress appeared worth pursuing because it seemed to generate and fulfill an overriding sense of purpose pivoted in a civilized peaceful life for all. This prospect appeared especially glittering when drawn against a dark background, "the most furious and desolating war recorded in European history," a war very much yet in memory around 1851. The Napoleonic wars' two main legacies, one "an enormous national debt," the other a "no less enormous amount of international jealousy and even of hatred," now appeared to be items that could be turned into a blessing, and largely through science: "Trade had done much, but Science began to feel her strength to discover new worlds in nature for the exercise of her power and ingenuity, and to take the first steps towards drawing into closer and more indissoluble union the long-estranged brethren of the great human family."

Such belief in progress was not only distinctly religious in character, but now presented itself as the fulfillment of Christian religion. No one put this more memorably than the Rev. Charles Kingsley, soon to be appointed chaplain to the Queen. As one of the thirty-thousand or so who had the opportunity to see the Exhibition in its opening day, he was moved to tears. Not, of course, because he heard the Archbishop of Canterbury hint, in his official prayer, at the Gospel's warning about the possible loss of one's soul at the price of gaining the whole world. Kingsley wept because on entering the Crystal Palace he felt he was moving into the Promised Land. The sermon he preached four days later, a Sunday, was the proof of his seeing the Crystal Palace and the arts and crafts exhibited within it in a "spiritual" light:

> If those forefathers of ours could rise from their graves this day they would be inclined to see in our hospitals, in our railroads, in the achievements of our physical science, confirmation of that old superstition of theirs, proofs of the kingdom of God, realizations of the gifts which Christ received for men, vaster than any of which they had dreamed.[9]

This new, more "spiritual" religion found a hilarious expression in the phrase "Paxton vobiscum," as if the spiritual peace carried by the hallowed greeting, "Pax vobiscum" could now be obtained through engineering skill. The same idea could be detected even in that solemn editorial. With industrial progress came, so it was claimed there, first the elimination, or at least the mitigation, of brutish impulses: "The hatred of the French, and of all other foreigners, which a bygone race of Englishmen had nurtured, not wisely but too well, was gradually consigned to oblivion, and replaced by a more sensible, a more humane, and a more Christian principle." Christian principles and the purpose they stood for meant, however, no more than the pursuit of a civilized and refined way of life.

Once more the railroads, these sooty vehicles of progress, were given the lion's share of credit: "The railway system has removed a whole world of difficulties. It has made us all understand one another better than we did before; broken down the ancient barriers of jealousy and exclusiveness; obliterated the rancourous remembrances of bygone wars; softened the lingering asperities of traditional hatreds."

If all this, that would have called for tens of thousands of alter egos of Francis of Assisi rather than for a similar number of puffing engines, had not been enough, something far more was claimed in the same editorial. Had the railroad system been on hand "fifty or sixty years" earlier, there would, in all likelihood, have been "no battles of Nile, the Baltic, or Trafalgar, and no carnage of Aboukir, Marenge, Jena, Leipsic, Moscow, Saragossa, or Waterloo." But what then would have become of Wellington and Napoleon? In answering this admittedly speculative question, the author of that leader made recourse to the Crystal Palace by turning it into a crystal ball:

> Who shall say, if we had a railroad system pervading Europe in 1780, and steam-ships plying between New York and Liverpool at the same period, whether Napoleon Bonaparte might not have become a great sculptor or a great cotton-spinner in 1810? whether Wellington, the mighty Captain, might not thirty years ago have been a philosopher greater and more

genial than Bentham, or a Lord Chancellor more potent and profound than Eldon?

That Napoleon might have turned into a "great sculptor"
should have appeared most doubtful to anyone familiar with
the unpredictable rise of artistic genius. More than plain
common sense, of which Wellington had an ample share, is
needed for becoming a great philosopher whatever the dubious messages of so-called great philosophers contemptuous of common sense. At any rate, if railway systems
were supposed to tame even the fiercest warriors, the supposition that science would bring about heaven on earth,
and fulfill thereby the highest purpose man could think of,
had to seem a most plausible prospect.

Indeed the editorial came to a close with a glorious view
of the future based on the present, a view that reflected
views that had already been voiced in England, and with an
eye on the science of the day, a hundred and two hundred
years earlier. In 1664 Henry Power, a member of the nascent
Royal Society, claimed that with the method of science in
hand "there is no Truth so abtruse, nor so far elevated out of
our reach, but man's wit may raise Engines to Scale and
Conquer it."[10] In 1771 Joseph Priestley predicted, with an
eye on that same scientific method, the coming of a new and
final age of mankind, an age "glorious and paradisiacal
beyond what our imagination can now conceive."[11]

In the context of both prognostications one would look in
vain for as much as a touch of hesitation, let alone of fore-
boding. The same is true about the editorial which graced
the May 10, 1851, issue of the *Illustrated London News*. Its
author compared favorably the Crystal Palace with the
wonders of the ancient world—the pyramids, the Colossus
of Rhodos, the gates and walls of Thebes. He did so not so
much because of the physical prowess of the Crystal Palace
as because "of the true nobility of the purpose for which it

was created" and because "it is sanctified by a high purpose, the highest indeed known to that practical religion, which, including all objects of human interest, preaches not simply love of God, but good-will to men."[12]

By failing to say "love of God, but *also* good-will to men" the author of that editorial endorsed a religious ideal which shortly afterwards, under the label of "Social Gospel," swayed many Christians. They came to think that good will toward men was a good substitute for the love of God and that promotion of material well-being would not fail to generate sense of purpose. It was in that perspective that the author of that editorial saw the Crystal Palace as a symbol. Whatever the relative fragility of its construction, "its idea will remain to all coming ages, a living fact, endowed with a fecundity that shall produce the mere outward form of similar or still more splendid monuments of human progress in every quarter of the globe, whenever they may be required for a purpose so exalted."

A fragile connection

On a cursory look this contrast supported that inner core over a mere external form, or a progress replete with purpose over its purely external expression. Even in this case it could seem doubtful that the Great Exhibition was "the most remarkable event in the modern history of mankind." Of course, the Crystal Palace quickly became a model for similar exhibitions. A huge exhibition in New York in 1853 boasted of its own "Crystal Palace." Two years later Paris was the scene of a celebration of progress through a grandiose exhibition which closed in a financial loss just as the one in New York did. This may have been symbolic of the failure of such celebrations of progress to strengthen man's sense of purpose. Progress would hardly issue in a sense of purpose as long as the idea of progress remained a dubious mixture of shallow empiricism and hollow optimism. In that mixture material items were the first ingredients, to be followed hopefully by some spiritual factors. This order was explicitly endorsed in that editorial: "In the history of nations as in that of individuals, physical facts always take precedence of, and are the forerunners of moral and spiritual facts."

This kind of empiricism could but suggest that physical actions invariably preceded their spiritual counterparts instead of being at some crucial junctures propelled by the latter. The view that the physical was, for all practical purposes, a harbinger of the spiritual, supported that reasoning which, so Herbert Spencer declared in the very year of the Great Exhibition, assured that "progress is not an accident but a necessity." To add to the irony he stated this in a chapter entitled "The Evanescence of Evil" which contained axioms such as that

> The ultimate development of the ideal man is logically certain—as certain as any conclusion in which we place the most implicit faith; for instance, that all men will die. . . . As surely as the tree becomes bulky when it stands alone . . . as surely as a blacksmith's arm grows large and the skin of the laborer's thick . . . so surely must the things we call evil and immorality disappear; so surely must man become perfect.[13]

That Spencer's claims were very unoriginal can easily be gathered by a look at that editorial in which the physical was, for all practical purposes, the sure anticipation of the spiritual. It mirrored an optimism which could not see the fragile connection between two steps. One was to "do physical work in concert," the other to follow it up "with moral and religious work."

Had this fragility, so patently obvious, been suspected by the author of that editorial, he would have put the emphasis not on the fourth but on the very first word in his great conclusion: "When they [the workers of the world] take *that* step a new era will begin and Utopia will no longer be an idle dream but will take the form and substance of a possible fact." Only by ignoring the question about the timing of that momentous *when* could the author of that editorial assure its readers that the Crystal Palace was not to carry ever on its facade some ominous words: "Once again there is a handwriting upon the wall—not in the warning characters of *Mene tekel upharsin* but in the hopeful words which seem to come spontaneously from all lips, and to shape themselves into the divine accents, *peace on earth, and good-will to men.*"

A century and a half later one can still ask about the moment *when* the workers of the world, blue-collar and professional, would not only take the step of working in concert but also follow it up, on their own accord, with moral and religious actions. Around 1851 not a few had already thought that workers should be "forcefully" organized to act in concert and "enlightened" about religion as the opiate of the people. An ominous handwriting kept filling sheet upon sheet on a reader's desk in the British Museum Library where Karl Marx was spending long hours in collecting data on behalf of his economic theory of progress and purpose. In a sense he tried to give a vast framework to an essay which Engels had published in 1840 on the conditions of working men in Great Britain, the most industrialized nation. Against that background, largely unnoticed at that time, rather ironic had to appear a report in the June 28 issue of the *Ilustrated London News*. It reported, with smug satisfaction, that farmers and workers, in large numbers, visited on the preceding Saturday and Sunday the Exhibition at the expense of their landlords and employers.[14]

One paid holiday spent at the Exhibition was not much more than the proverbial lone swallow that does not make a summer. The leisured class in Britain saw an endless day ahead with no sun setting on it. Its members could be almost perverse in deploring small inconveniences produced by progress. W. R. Greg's essay, "Life at High Pressure," appeared in 1875 and contained the plaintive admission that his contemporaries felt they were living "without leisure and without pause—a life of *haste*—above all a life of excitement, such as haste inevitably involves —a life so full . . . that we have no time to reflect where we have been and whither we intend to go . . . still less what is the value, and the purpose, and the *price* of what we have seen, and done, and visited."[15] A few years later, Frederic Harrison, another enthusiastic apostle of progress through technology, complained that now "we are whirled about, and hooted around, and rung up as if we were all parcels, booking clerks, or office boys."[16]

Such were some of the unintended symptoms of progress. Cumbersome as they could be, they were not to cause second thoughts about belief in progress, especially when that belief took its strength from the "cult of science."[17] The cult could take on at times a most defiant aspect in a truly cultic sense. A case in point was Kingsley's *Yeast* where the hero, Lancelot Smith, writes to his Roman Catholic cousin:

> When your party compare sneeringly Romish Sanctity, and English Civilization, I say, 'Take you the Sanctity, and give me the Civilization! . . . Give me the political economist, the sanitary reformer, the engineer; and take your saints and virgins, relics and miracles. The spinning-jenny and the railroad, Cunard's liners and the electric telegraph, are to me, if not to you, signs that we are, on some points at least, in harmony with the universe; that there is a mighty spirit working among us, who cannot be your anarchic and destroying Devil, and therefore may be the Ordering and Creating God'.[18]

Those Christians for whom the devil and his pomp remained a reality to reckon with had no choice but to take the immensely unpopular stand of denouncing faith in necessary progress, especially as it meant that knowledge would automatically generate upright behavior. Progress in that Spencerian sense was a target of the much misunderstood Syllabus of errors issued by Pius IX in 1864: "Anyone who says that the Roman Pontif may and should reconcile and align himself with progress, with liberalism, with modern civilization, let him be anathema."[19] Yet, the idea that material progress and diffusion of knowledge automatically strengthened man's morals had been by then for decades attacked by John Henry Newman who, again in 1876, minced no words:

> The temptation is to think that . . . the time will come when in the enthusiastic sanguineness of some about the future, the science of medicine will be so perfect that all diseases will be cured. All these wonderful elements of power which we have seen in the last fifty years, I mean like steam and the power of electricity, and so on, lead men to think that other discoveries may be made which will make the world a sort of heaven, that in this way we should destroy evil, and we should be a happy land. As for ourselves, these men say, let us enjoy what we have, and they make a Divinity of the world and worship it.[20]

In 1876 Newman was still three years away from being raised to the cardinalate which assured him of admiration though of no real hearing in his country. Not much attention was paid there to the contrast he had drawn in the mid-1850s, in his *The Idea of a University*, between the essentially non-progressive character of the humanities, above all of theology, natural and supernatural, and the progress, mostly a process of accumulation, of the sciences.[21] Society at large rather relished the same parallel as drawn in 1840 by Macaulay, a parallel slightly contemptuous of perennial truths. [22] Not much was left by the 1870s of the nostalgia for a pre-industrial past which Macaulay had already strictured as the first railroads began to criss-cross the English countryside. [23] Just as little was left by the 1870s of that High-Tory cum High-Church sensitivity on which Newman still could count when in 1841 he upheld to ridicule, in the pages of *The Times*, Henry Brougham, Sir Robert Peel and other heralds of a better future to come through science popularization. [24] Society applauded T. H. Huxley as he insisted in 1865 against Matthew Arnold on the superior merits of scientific over literary education. [25]

Victorian society, engrossed and intoxicated with technological progress, could not believe that evil would come, and in a volume unimaginable, through science. As Victorian times headed toward their completion, a heady confidence could be sensed everywhere. In 1887 T. H. Huxley gave a glowing report about scientific progress during the previous half a century. [26] Two years later Frederic Harrison greeted in a memorable address, delivered in Manchester, the center of British industrial power, the advent of a "New Era." [27] Then came Alfred Russell Wallace, the co-proponent of evolution through natural selection, with his book *The Wonderful Century* in which he drew a balance sheet between its successes and failures, the former heavily outweighing the latter. [28] The farce could be best measured by Wallace's counting among the few failures the introduction of compulsory vaccination!

More farce, though truly tragic, was to come both in ideas and in deeds, both of which went largely unnoticed. Nietzsche was taken for an eccentric when he celebrated the Superman (Uebermensch) in his book, *On the Genealogy of Morals*. It contained the kind of realistic account of the true nature of progress which in retrospect should strike one as supremely prophetic also in its relevance to Social Darwinism:

> True progress always appears in the form of will and way to *greater power* and is always enforced at the expense of a large number of lesser powers. The amount of "progress" is, in fact, measured by the mass of all that had to be scarificed in order to bring it about: mankind *en masse* sacrificed in order to insure the growth of a single, *stronger* species of man—that *would be* progress. [29]

The "wonderful" century had not yet run its course when Hiram Maxim began to entertain European Royalties, Prime Ministers, and General Staffs with his newly constructed machine gun. Two decades later the machine gun made possible in a single morning a carnage on which the atom bomb dropped on Hiroshima could improve only in respect to speed. Internal combustion engines appeared as deadly tanks in the same war, the first to be known as World War. Chemistry helped introduce a new type of war, silent attack with poisonous gases. It was science again, through the production of synthetic nitrate, that made possible the extension of the War from four months to four terribly long years. No comfort could be gained from Einstein's writing, in a private letter in 1917, the epitaph of progress through science: "Our much vaunted progess in technology, generally of civilization, is like the axe in the hand of a pathological criminal." [30] Clearly, the progress witnessed by three generations had been for scant purpose; it was certainly very effective in promoting a most purposeless behavior. Yeats had more than enough reason to register, in the wake of World I, an almost universal loss of sense of purpose:

> Things fall apart; the centre cannot hold
> Mere anarchy is loosed upon the world,

The blood-dimmed tide is loosed, and everywhere
The ceremony of innocence is drowned;
The best lack all conviction, while the worst
Are full of passionate intensity.[31]

By 1919 Bolshevism had already given ample glimpses of what its passionate intensity was to achieve. The malaise grew passionate in defeated Germany where the two heavy volumes of Spengler's *Decline of the West*, that saw print after print following the first edition in 1918, were taken for a proof that belief in Progress served no real purpose. The fact now loomed large that quantitative growth, which alone could be delivered by science and technology, did not necessarily bring about purposive improvement in the qualitative sense. A long nurtured and mistaken trust in quantities readily provoked its opposite extreme, a blind celebration of instincts. Those who should have showed cool thinking, leading physicists to wit, began to celebrate a non-causal nature. They did so a few years before young Heisenberg provided a glitteringly misleading scientific justification for this orgy in reasoning.[32] Such was the broader cultural soil which the fledgling Nazi movement found very useful for its further progress and ugly purposes.

Progress unmasked

Cultural and social upheavals were not indispensable for perceiving the hollow ring in the idea of progress. John Bagnell Bury, professor of history in Cambridge from 1902 on, began his work on his book, *The Idea of Progress*, sometime before World War I made its dispiriting impact felt even within the academic comforts of Imperial Britain. That Bury unsparingly analyzed the idea of progress had much to do with his resolve to take not only political history, but conceptual history too for "science, no more no less,"[33] that is, for a process with clear logical structure. Such an approach could not, of course, issue in a runaway bestseller like Spengler's work. Yet the brief epilogue of Bury's *The Idea of Progress* contained more instructiveness than Spengler's thousand rambling pages or even the three hundred or so carefully documented pages that preceded that epilogue in Bury's book.

For in that Epilogue Bury faced up to the inexorable logic contained in the assumption that led to the rise and broad espousal of the idea of progress. He made no secret of the fact, all too evident in the writings of the 18th- and 19th-century champions of progress, that it was not so much a reasoned conclusion derived from facts than a dogma largely independent of them. Further, Bury also faced up to the fact that as a secularist dogma or belief, the idea of progress based itself on a refutation and rejection of an earlier idea of progress: a divine providential guidance with a primarily supernatural purpose. Most importantly, the various forms of that refutation had one basic point in common, namely, that the idea of absolute finality was an illusion. But, Bury asked with commendable candor,

> if we accept the reasonings on which the dogma of Progress is based, must we not carry them to their full conclusion? In escaping from the illusion of finality, is it legitimate to exempt that dogma itself? Must not it, too, submit to its own negation of finality? Will not that process of change, for which Progress is the optimistic name, compel Progress too to fall from the commanding position in which it is now, with apparent security, enthroned?[34]

While these questions should have called for an unhesitating yes, Bury hesitated to give it. He sought an escape hatch from his own logic in the evolutionary process by viewing it as an implementation of purpose insofar as it is still to be attained by an already mature organism. What he declared in the Introduction of his book, namely, that "the principle of duty to posterity is a direct corollary of the idea of progress,"[35] he repeated as the conclusion in his book's last chapter on "Progress and Evolution." There he put the capstone on his appraisal of Darwinian and Spencerian evolution as a purposeful process with a recall of Frederic Harrison's address on "The New Era." The address, Bury wrote, had for its dominant note "the faith [in] human progress [on earth] in lieu of celestial rewards of the separate soul."[36]

But with the emphatic elimination of personal immortality and the fulfillment of purpose it alone could bring about, there remained only a purpose vested in humankind as a purely biological species. The only purpose that could be valid for individuals within that species was their serving the well-being of the species itself insofar as it wanted to perpetuate itself:

> Consideration for posterity has throughout history operated as a motive of conduct, but feebly, occasionally, and in a very limited sense. With the doctrine of Progress it assumes, logically, a preponderating importance; for the centre of interest is transferred to the life of happiness denied to us, but which our labours and sufferings are to help to bring about.[37]

Purpose deposited in the progress of posterity could appear far worse than a weak panacea. It could conjure up the specter of biological fatalism which Bury hastened to dissipate: "If the doctrine is held in an extreme fatalistic form, then our duty is to resign cheerfully to sacrifices for the sake of unknown descendants, just as ordinary altruism enjoins the cheerful acceptance of sacrifices for the sake of living fellow-creatures." From that stifling specter he offered as an escape a reference to man's ability to act freely for a purpose, and in this case, for the purpose of promoting "for good or

for evil the destinies of the race." He further tried to sweeten
matters by conjuring up the perspective of being connected
with many more individuals than our contemporaries:
"Our duties towards others reach out through time as well
as through space, and our contemporaries are only a negligible fraction of the 'neighbours' to whom we owe obliga-
tions."[38]

As countless other devotees of the Darwinian view of
evolution, Bury too chose to ignore the question of how in
that view it was possible to account for the emergence of
genuine free will. He also chose not to consider an all too
obvious difference between the behavior of man and other
species. While animals do not care for their aged but leave
them behind when gravely ill, humans very much care for
them, a difference hardly explainable in strict Darwinian
terms. Moreover, that specifically unique human care for
the sick and the aged received a special stimulus through
those very supernatual considerations for which Bury had
no use.

Apart from that Bury's unquestioning reliance on Darwinism contrasted with doubts widely voiced about it in
the best scientific circles around the turn of the century.[39]
Many of the first readers of Bury's book could not fail to
notice its stark contrast with a very different appraisal of
Darwinism as an assurance of progress, an appraisal that
resounded from the stage where George Bernard Shaw's
play, *The Heartbreak House*, was being performed to over-
flow audiences. In its Preface the famous playwright and
social critic excoriated precisely that half a century, postdating the Great Exhibition, which Bury held high as the
crowning touch, together with Darwin's theory, on the idea
of progress. The same theory, which reduced mankind to
the animal level where ruthless competition reigned, appeared to Shaw in a very different light. With an eye on the
devastations brought about by World War I, he saw in that

theory a new-fangled religion, invented by the English and taught by them to Prussia where the councils of the General Staff echoed with references to the principle of the survival of the fittest. The plain truth was, Shaw minced no words, that

> Prussia bettered our instruction so effectively that we presently found ourselves confronted with the necessity of destroying Prussia to prevent Prussia destroying us. And that has just ended in each destroying the other to an extent doubtfully reparable in our time[40]

Shaw could, of course, be written off as a mere wit, good but in verbal swordplay. The Reverend William Ralph Inge had by then earned the epithet "gloomy dean" to be taken seriously for sounding off time and again as a latter-day Cassandra. Not that in his lecture, "The Idea of Progress," he denied the cumulative nature of scientific work. Still only the converted nodded in agreement on hearing him state that all the feats of science and technology "do not constitute real progress in human nature itself, and that in the absence of any real progress these gains are external, precarious, and liable to be turned to our own destruction, as new discoveries in chemistry may easily be."[41] He obviously had gas warfare in mind. One wonders what sort of wisdom did he really have in mind as he recalled the condemnation of progress by Pius IX, and noted that "only one great Church, old in worldly wisdom, knows that human nature does not change, and acts on the knowledge."[42]

With a touch of hesitation Gilbert Murray, classical scholar and cultural pontif, also spoke negatively of the Spencerian idea of progress in his *Religio grammatici*, a testimonial to noble paganism: "You will perhaps say that I am still denying the essence of human Progress; denying the progress of the human soul, and admitting only the sort of

progress that consists in the improvement of tools, the discovery of new facts, the recombining of elements. As to that
I can only admit frankly that I am not clear, I believe we do
not know enough to answer."[43] For all that he clung to
Progress as a "real fact." But in his own admission the truth
of Progress rested on its being an indispensable part, nay, the
very root "of our Religion," or the religion of Reason writ
large.

Progress aflame
That as a harbinger of destruction chemistry was to be far
outpaced by physics remained for a while unsuspected even
by physicists, let alone by such distinguished humanists as
Shaw, Inge, and Murray. All three lived long enough to
register with utter dismay the explosion of atomic bombs.
Before that they saw the sky bathed in a red glow in the early
night of November 30, 1936. By 8 o'clock that evening
flames enveloped the Crystal Palace, which since 1854 stood
in a much enlarged form in Sydenham, southeast London.
There it was the scene in 1913 of the grandiose Empire
Festival, apart from its ordinary use as a museum of sculpture, paintings, and architecture. It also served as the place
for band concerts and the annual Christmas circus. It had
just been refurbished for a large Summer Exhibition under
the managership of Sir Henry Buckland who was the first to
note the fire as he left the place at 6:15 p.m. Later he was seen
clutching the hand of his little daughter, called Crystal, as he
watched with hundreds of thousands of Londoners the
greatest conflagration in London since the Great Fire of
1666. It culminated shortly after 9 p.m. as the Crystal Palace
collapsed with three thunderous explosions. The Duke of
Kent, soon to become George VI, was on the scene until
after midnight when the fire began to die out.

Not everybody seemed to be crestfallen though. In the
weeks before quite a few of the glass panels were broken

with bricks thrown by the unemployed. No mention of this was made in *The Times*. Its next morning's editorial catered to esthetic and philistine emotions: "All kinds of interests must mourn its end—music, drama, statuary, fireworks, dog lovers, cat lovers . . . and many more besides."[44] Only a handful of readers knew enough biblical Latin to see in the very next phrase, *simul omnes collacrimabunt*, an allusion to the Book of Revelations with its repeated mentions (18: 9, 15, 19) of the weeping of kings, merchants, and sailors over the great Babylon "when they see the smoke arise as she burns."

Most likely the allusion was not fully intended by the editorial writer himself, although a series of events that was just coming to a head, would have more than justified a view in depth perhaps even a hint that the sun itself might be setting over the Empire. That it might have been rash to write in 1851 that an ominous handwriting would never appear on the Crystal Palace, did not occur to the editor of the *Illustrated London News* who proudly recalled the wide coverage given there to the dedication of the Crystal Palace in 1851. Soon its issues were dominated by a potentially far more serious crisis, the abdication of Edward VII and the accession of George VI to the throne. If this was a progress, it was a progress in ethics, which, unlike material or technological progress, is not necessarily cumulative, let alone inevitable.

At any rate, more realistic was the perception about the fate of the Crystal Palace from a distance, the other shores of the Atlantic. "In a way," went the editorial of *The New York Times*,

> it was the bonfire of an epoch, of the England of the glorious Reign, of Dickens and Disraeli, of the Empire and what not, of Home Rule debates and never setting sun. That England is no more. A good many stones

have lately been thrown at the big glass house and the impact has marred the solid glaze, the ineffable aplomb of a people who never before felt vulnerable in their many-windowed domicile. The Crystal Palace burns at a dark moment.[45]

The moment's true darkness found its most revealing portrayal ten years later when H. G. Wells, already seventy-nine, came out with his last book or rather booklet, *Mind at the End of Its Tether*. There at midway he referred to a "series of events" that had forced on him ("the intelligent observer") some new insights which he argued throughout that booklet. The insights should have been all too obvious to such a champion of progress through biological evolution as H. G. Wells had been for all his life. It took such "series of events," as the the flash of atomic conflagration that ended World War II and the grim political and social realities that followed in its wake, to make H. G. Wells suddenly see the true logic of that evolution of which more in the next chapter. Here let it suffice to recall H. G. Wells' declaration that modern man's state was worse than bankruptcy: "*Our* universe is not merely bankrupt; there remains no dividend at all; it has not simply liquidated; it is going clean out of existence, leaving not a wrack behind. The attempt to trace a pattern of any sort is absolutely futile."[46]

An unconvincing phoenix

Just as tragic events could call forth dark clouds from behind the silvery linings of evolutionary process, the reverse was equally possible. No sooner had those events begun to fade in memory than the optimistic facade of evolutionary progress once more dominated the intellectual scene. Belief in progress came alive as a phoenix reborn from the ashes though not too convincingly. The change came rather fast, possibly because science produced not only the nuclear bomb but also the burgeoning marvels of semiconductor devices that gave an unexpectedly new life to capitalist productivity. Tellingly a memorable new defense of progress came from a prominent economist of liberal market policy. In his *The Constitution of Liberty*, published in 1960, Hayek deplored the antiprogressivist mood prevailing among intellectuals: "Though the great mass of the people in most parts of the world still rest their hopes on continued progress, it is common among intellectuals to question whether there is such a thing, or at least whether progress is desirable."[47] Yet in support of his offensive on behalf of progress Hayek offered but a circular definition of it: "The preservation of the kind of civilization that we know depends on the operation of forces which, under favorable conditions, produce progress."[48] This meant that civilization was progress and progress was civilization.

Another freshly established spokesman of progress, Jacob Bronowski, could offer but a distinction which begged the question. Undoubtedly there was a difference between the tools created by science and their misuse by non-scientists.[49] Apart from the fact that scientists too could be guilty on that score, the disctinction did not answer the question why scientific technology did not necessarily serve a constructive progress. Similar inconsistency burdened Medawar's stricture of philosophers who failed to inspire faith in progress.[50] He should have rather concentrated on his own failure to ask about what makes certain philosophies incapable of accommodating any talk about purpose. Nor did Medawar consider the question why in his own circles no hearing whatever is given to philosophers who keep insisting that the idea of purpose must first be clarified in order to obtain a clear idea of progress.

Those philosophers have kept saying in times past as well as during the mad 1960s that the very idea of progress, to say nothing of a progress for abiding purpose, is rooted in religion that genuinely cares for the sacred.[51] They received, in the secularist West, far less hearing than Andrei D. Sakharov who for all his criticism of the Soviet system refused to abandon Marxist tracks and their materialist directives. The best known proof of this is Sakharov's prescription for the future, published in English as *Progress, Coexistence, and Intellectual Freedom*.[52] He remained so Marxist as to foresee a necessity for a multiparty system in the Soviet Union only in the case if "a ruling Communist party refuses for one reason or another to rule by the scientific democratic method required by history."[53]

Sakharov remained a genuine Marxist even in coming up with a timetable of progress as if it could be handled in the form of a forty-year variation on a Five Year Plan. The timetable, which stretched from 1960 to 2000, was to be implemented in four stages. From the vantage point of late 1989 when these lecture were delivered[54] (let alone of mid-1990 when they are being prepared for publication), Sakharov's prognostications should seem to reveal an astonishing measure of naiveté and misjudgment. The only exception to this is his account of the first stage, 1960-1980. In the second half of the 1960s it required no special crystal ball to characterize that stage as a conflict between rigid Communist ideologues (Maoists in particular) and advocates of a realistic outlook. There were too many dire realities in the Soviet Union and its satellites to allow a look other than a very realist one.

The second stage (1972-1985), which included the first five years of the Reagan years, turned out to be the very opposite to what Sakharov expected it to be, "the victory of the leftist reformist wing of the bourgeoisie."[55] In the third stage (1972-90) Sakharov expected "the Soviet Union and the United States, having overcome their alienation, to solve the problem of saving the poorer half of the world." One wonders whether Sakharov had ever ventured inside shops not reserved for Party members. One ironic aspect of this Utopistic view turned out to be the need for the Soviet

Union to reveal its underdeveloped status in order to be rescued from it by massive investments from capitalist countries, from the United States and West Germany in particular. Only these countries could think even now of the means, the taxing of 20 percent of their national income, by which Sakharov wanted to finance a task to be completed by 1990:

> Gigantic fertilizer factories and irrigation systems using atomic power will be built [in the developing countries], the resources of the sea will be used to a vastly greater extent, indigenous personnel will be trained, and industrialization will be carried out. Gigantic factories will produce synthetic amino acids and synthesize proteins, fats, and carbohydrates.[56]

In the fourth stage (1990-2000) Sakharov foresaw a vast expansion of nuclear energy and a space exploration with "thousands of people to work and live continuously on other planets and on the moon, on artificial satellites and on asteroids whose orbits will have been changed by nuclear explosions." It was certainly not the Soviet Union that was to be the place "of an all-encompassing scientific and technological revolution" which, as the very precondition of all that progress, Sakharov described as follows:

> The synthesis of materials that are superconductors at room temperature may completely revolutionize electrical technology, cybernetics, transportation, and communications. Progress in biology (in this and subsequent periods) will make possible effective control and direction of all life processes at the levels of the cell, organism, ecology, and society, from fertility and aging to psychic processes and heredity.[57]

A succinct judgment on this came on June 13, 1989, when former President Reagan, on receiving honorary membership in the Order of the Garter, delivered in Guild Hall a speech which contained the memorable phrase: "The Goliath of totalitarianism will be brought down by the David of the microchip."[58] Institutionalized communism met its defeat in terms of its basic contention that the tools of production determine the outcome of history. Yet those on the victorious side may wonder whether their triumph is not laden with the kind of heavy losses that prompted the remark of Pyrrhus, king of Epirus, "One more such victory and I am lost."

It is not at all sure whether the runaway productivity made possible by the computerization of industrial techniques can find an effective restraint in human nature. Progress may very well be choked in pollution or, what is even more sinistrous because less tangible, in sophisticated complacency. The latter set the tone both of Francis Fukuyama's Hegelian claim that liberal capitalism is the goal of history and its termination,[59] as well as of the glib comment that "after late capitalism comes more capitalism."[60]

This secularist apotheosis of progress, which still finds voluble advocates among prominent men of science,[61] finds a powerful disclaimer in religious revivals spilling over the most industrialized nations, and in cults both traditional and weirdly innovative. Most revealingly, the Soviet Union witnessed a resurgence of the Christian sense of the sacred which for champions of progress like Sakharov would make no sense whatever. His numerous admirers in the West, so eager to keep him in the forefront, undoubtedly in order to distract attention from the "mystical" Alexander Solzhenitsyn, should have rather focused on a most dubious aspect of progress. It is the exponential rise of crime in increasingly prosperous times[62] which flies in the face of the secularist dogma of progress as an inevitable outcome of more knowledge and know-how.

In view of this obvious debacle of secularism, nothing

would be more tempting than to turn to the sacred as the true foundation and safeguard, historically as well as conceptually, of belief in progress. But in order to see the true nature of those foundations one must first unmask some illusory supports of that belief. They are mostly dressed in references to natural science and steeped in naturalistic philosophies. The most conspicuous of them is Darwinian evolution with its latter-day variations to which we must now turn in order to see whether it offers a purpose which is more than a mere word.

Chapter Two

PURPOSELESS EVOLUTION

Eclipse or eclipses?

In speaking about evolution, it has become impossible not to think of Darwin. His views on evolution, appropriately called Darwinism, are unique in more than one respect. Although Darwinism is all too often taken for the definitive theory of evolution, it definitely has not provided answers to not a few salient facts of the "evolutionary" record. Darwinism is among all major scientific theories the one that claims the most on the basis of relatively the least. But this is to anticipate. Darwinism also has, among major scientific theories, the dubious distinction that its opponents did not die out with their first generation. The contrast is particularly strong with physics, and modern physics in particular. Max Planck proved to be very much a prophet when he noted in the 1920s that the first-generation opponents of quantum theory would be its last ones. [1]

That the pattern is very different with respect to Darwinism is a fact which Darwinists have always been all too ready to overlook. Thus R. S. Lull, professor of biology at Yale, assured countless readers of his textbook, *Organic Evo-*

lution, first published in 1917, that "since Darwin's day, Evolution has been more and more generally accepted, until now in the minds of informed, thinking men there is no doubt that it is the only logical way whereby the creation can be interpreted and understood."[2] This is, of course true, but only on the strict condition that one does not, unlike Lull, take evolution for its Darwinian mechanism and materialism.

Opposition to the Darwinian theory of evolution was very noticeable among first-rate biologists as they celebrated, a few years before Lull's book was published, the half-centenary of the publication of the *Origin of Species*. Scholarly dissent from Darwinism grew about that time to such extent as to correspond to an almost total eclipse of a once bright body in the scientific sky. It was indeed appropriate to give to a study of that development the title, *The Eclipse of Darwinism*.[3] About a generation after Darwin had been honored with burial in Westminster Abbey, the British Association for the Advancement of Science heard, in 1914, its President declare: "To us Darwin no longer speaks with philosophic authority."[4] The one who uttered these words, that had a devastating ring only in ears tuned to the art of British understatement, was none other than William Bateson. Apart from having been among the first to rescue Mendel's work from oblivion and the first to speak of genetics, Bateson was the first occupant of a chair for genetics at Cambridge University.

Three years earlier Thomas Dwight, Parkman professor of anatomy at Harvard, had already said much the same, though in the no-holds-barred style characteristic of the New World: "Beyond question just at the time when the uneducated are prating about the triumph of Darwinism, it is fast losing caste among men of science."[5] That his science and not his Catholicism prompted Dwight to speak as he did, can be easily gathered from a mere recall of a book, which Félix Le Dantec, an avowedly materialist professor of physiology at the Sorbonne, published about the same time on the crisis of "transformisme," the French word for evolution.[6] Somewhat later came the voice of the leading French biologist, Lucien Cuénot, a pantheist: "It is pretty clear that we must wholly abandon the Darwinian hypothesis."[7] Germany's philosopher-biologist, Hans Driesch, minced no words: "For men of clear intellect Darwinism has long been dead."[8]

The volume and weight of anti-Darwinist (though not anti-evolutionist) voices at that time was best registered by a contemporary, V. L. Kellogg, professor of biology at Stanford University. In the last few years, he wrote in his *Darwinism To-day*, first published in 1907, scientific criticism of Darwinism

> reached such proportions, such strength and extent, as to begin to make itself apparent outside of strictly biological and naturo-philosophical circles. Such older biologists and natural philosophers as von Baer, von Kölliker, Virchow, Nägeli, Wigand, and Hartmann, and such others writing in the nineties and in the present century as von Sachs, Eimer, Delage, Haacke, Kassowitz, Cope, Haberlandt, Henslow, Goette, Wolff, Driesch, Packard, Morgan, Jaekel, Steinmann, Korschinsky, and de Vries, are examples of the anti-Darwinian ranks. Perhaps these names mean little to the general reader; let me translate them into the professors of zoology, of botany, of paleontology, and of pathology, in the universities of Berlin, Paris, Vienna, Strasburg, Tübingen, Amsterdam, Columbia University, etc . . . One does not come to be a professor of biology in Berlin or Paris or Columbia solely by caprice of ministers of education or boards of trustees . . . To working biologists the names . . . mean even more than positions. They are mostly associated with

recognised scientific attainment and general intellectual capacity.[9]

Such was a telling admission about the formidable array
of anti-Darwinists. Kellogg's counterattack did not amount
to much more than a long chapter in which he summarized
the pro-Darwinian arguments of Ludwig Plate, a German
biologist. To those in the know Kellogg's armour displayed
some chinks with respect to truthfulness. In recalling a pro-
Darwinian point made by George Romanes, he made much
of the fact that he was "conspicuous as the only pupil and
disciple of Darwin personally advised and aided by the
master himself, and one of the most brilliant upholders and
expositors of Darwinism."[10] While this was certainly true,
it was no less true that Romanes, who originally planned to
become a clergyman and parted with the Christian faith
under the influence of Darwin, returned to it towards the
end of his life and for reasons touching at the very foundations of Darwinism as an ideology. Darwinism, Romanes
wrote in a posthumously published essay, destroys trust in
human nature and whatever purpose it may have.[11]

Most biologists doubtful of the merits of Darwinism kept
their misgivings to themselves. It fell to no less a biologist
than Thomas Hunt Morgan to register this behavior hardly
born in good faith:

> I venture to prophesy that if anyone will undertake to
> question modern zoologists and botanists concerning
> their relation to the Darwinian theory, he will find
> that, while professing *in a general way* to hold this
> theory, most biologists have many reservations and
> doubts which they either keep to themselves or, at any
> rate, do not allow to interfere either with the teaching
> of the Darwinian doctrine or with the applications
> which they make of it in their writings. The claim of
> the opponents' of the theory that Darwinism has be-

come a dogma contains more truth than the nominal
followers of the school find pleasant to hear.[12]

Dwight himself felt impelled to speak of the "tyranny of the
Zeitgeist" which few dared to oppose "absolutely and un-
qualifiedly."[13] What this meant was that although many saw
the eclipse, only a few were ready to admit its taking place.

Eclipses and closed eyes
Long after the centenary celebrations of *The Origin of Species*
began to fade in memory, the endurance of that tyranny was
authoritatively registered by the Nobel-laureate biologist,
Sir Ernst Chain, co-discoverer of the curative properties of
penicillin:

> To postulate that the development and survival of the
> fittest is entirely a consequence of chance mutations
> seems to me a hypothesis based on no evidence and
> irreconcilable with the facts. These classical evolution-
> ary theories are a gross oversimplification of an im-
> mensely complex and intricate mass of facts, and it
> amazes me that they are swallowed so uncritically and
> readily, and for such a long time, by so many scientists
> without a murmur of protest.[14]

The celebrations of the centenary of *The Origin of Species*
provided sundry instances of this attitude, as much suspect
ethically as intellectually. As a leading figure of those celebrations, Julian Huxley, a great-grandson of T. H. Huxley,
Darwin's "bulldog," did not care to recall, let alone to
discuss in detail, what he had called a few years earlier a
"major concern to general biological theory."[15] His refusal
to air that concern during those celebrations was all the more
curious because he, more than anyone else among Darwinists, had to take note of it. It was his book, *Evolution in
Action*, that prompted the noted zoologist, James Grey of

Cambridge University, to sound the jarring note of dissent: "No amount of argument, or clever epigram, can disguise the inherent improbability of orthodox [evolutionary] theory; but most biologists feel it is better to think in terms of improbable events than not to think at all."[16]

Tellingly, the center of the centenary celebrations was not the orthodox theory but the so-called synthetic theory, whatever the difficulties of distinguishing it from its orthodox counterpart. If the synthetic theory appeared to its proponents a celestial body in full brightness, it was only so because they deliberately ignored those for whom it appeared very much eclipsed. In fact it was exactly as it has always been with eclipses. Unless the observer is located in a particular region of the earth, he will not see the eclipse of the moon or of the sun. Or perhaps in some regions observers prefer to shut their eyes whenever their pet ideas suffer an eclipse.

With respect to the periodic eclipses of Darwinism, the Anglo-Saxon world seems to be the very region from which they are looked upon with eyes closed. This was admitted in a roundabout way by no less a modern Darwinist than George G. Simpson as he reported his impressions about an international congress on paleontology held in Sabadell, Spain, in July 1954. "The fact is," he wrote, "that many European evolutionists, just as accomplished as any in America, do not consider those questions closed and give quite different answers from those of the American majority."[17] The questions touched on precisely those points where Darwinism or evolutionism turns from science into an ideology.

If an Anglo-Saxon Darwinist could not help noticing an eclipse in the Darwinist sky, he could still resort to means far less expensive than moving into another part of the globe in order not to be bothered. The means consisted in shoving the anti-Darwinian evidence under the rug. That such has

indeed been a favorite procedure among Darwinists received its telling admission from none other than a Huxley,
Sir Andrew. Darwinists, he noted in his presidential address
to the Royal Society, have "too often swept under the carpet
the biggest problem of biology, the existence of consciousness."[18] He also recalled the problem of the origin of life as
the target of a similar underhanded procedure on the part
of Darwinists. Sir Andrew failed to speak of some non-
scientific motivations that alone could prompt procedures
even more disreputable than the using of carpets for foil. Yet
it had to be all too clear that answers to those two problems
very much decide the most important question, namely,
whether there is purpose at all properly so called.

That the synthetic theory was not immune to being subject to a major eclipse was admitted by no less an early
enthusiast than Stephen J. Gould who turned into the most
publicized dissenter from it. He described himself as one of
those unsuspecting graduate students of the mid-1960s
whom the synthetic theory "beguiled with its unifying
power." As the years went by, he was compelled to watch it

> slowly unravel as a universal description of evolution.
> The molecular assault came first, followed quickly by
> renewed attention to unorthodox theories of speciation
> and by challenges at the level of macroevolution itself. I
> have been reluctant to admit it—since beguiling is
> often forever—but if Mayr's characterization of the
> synthetic theory is accurate, then that theory, as a
> general proposition, is effectively dead, despite its per-
> sistence as text-book orthodoxy.[19]

The same orthodoxy was the implicit target of a conclusion
reached five years earlier, in 1975, by Steven M. Stanley of
Johns Hopkins University:

> Contrary to the prevailing belief, natural selection
> seems to provide little more than the raw material and

fine adjustment of large-scale evolution. The reductionist view that evolution can ultimately be understood in terms of genetics and molecular biology is
clearly in error. We must turn . . . to studies of specia-
tion and extinction in order to decipher the higher-level
process that governs the general course of evolution.[20]

At that time the word extinction could not help but sound
evocative of vast eclipses of life, soon to dawn with brute
force on Darwinists. But this is to anticipate. When set
against such admissions about the eclipse of synthetic theory, the counterattack of some older stalwarts of it should
seem loaded with that ideological motivation which they
tag on those who keep their eyes open as the eclipse unfolds.
One cannot help feeling that the shoe is on the other foot
when reading, say, E. Mayr's claim that attacks on the
notion that "all evolution is due to the accumulation of small
genetic changes . . . are either based on ignorance or are
motivated ideologically."[21]

Those mindful of the many books, old and new, whose
authors presented evolution as a purposeful process,[22] could
see more than what meets the eye in the title, "Evolution:
Explosion, not Ascent," of an essay which Gould published
in 1978 in *The New York Times*.[23] If explosion meant anything it was the very opposite to that gradualism on which
Darwin and Darwinists have always set so great a store.
Further, Gould's essay contained enough evidence to suggest that his purpose in writing it was to cover up the deeper
purposes of the champions of orthodox and synthetic evolutionary theory.

Gradualism or something more
That such purposes or motivations had been at work since
Darwin's days, and in fact in Darwin himself, could be
gathered from Gould's recall of a letter which T. H. Huxley
wrote to Darwin on November 23, 1859, the eve of the

publication of the *Origin of Species*. The letter was a classic of contradiction, a point not mentioned by Gould. For if it was true that, as Huxley stated, Darwin had "demonstrated the true cause [natural selection] for the production of species," then it could not also be true that Darwin merely loaded himself "with an unnecessary difficulty in adopting *Natura non facit saltum* so unreservedly."[24] The difficulty, represented by a very gradual or practically imperceptible rate of evolution, was a very necessary part of Darwin's theory. It was also its most debilitating part, in addition to being a part most shrewdly contrived for purposes far beyond the legitimate purport of any scientific theory.

Huxley did not suspect that he prophesied something most ominous to emerge in the distant future as he cited his second objection: "It is not clear to me why, if continual physical conditions are of so little moment as you suppose, variations should occur at all." By 1859 the idea of geological evolution as riddled with major catastrophes had for some time been fallen into disrepute, largely through the work of Lyell, an early supporter of Darwin. Huxley merely noted that the idea of very gradual change was incompatible with the fossil record. Four generations later Gould could only add that

> the fossil record still proclaims it [very gradual change] false, after more than a century of diligent search . . . Paleontologists have documented virtually no cases of slow and steady transformation, foot by foot up the strata of a hillslope—not for horses, not for humans.[25]

Behind that brief reference to horses lay a long story, which culminated in the early 20th century with the setting up, in the American Museum of Natural History in New York, of a large display of the fossil record of the evolution of the modern horse. For decades it served as the trump

evidence of the truth of the Darwinian mechanism of evolution, a mechanism based on the gradual accumulation of
minute changes, for a long-term purpose, over very long
periods of time. The display was not the first of its kind but
the largest, preceded by smaller exhibits, such as the one set
up by O. C. Marsh at Yale University in the 1870s. It
prompted Lull to introduce, in his book already quoted, the
chapter on horses with a minor panegyrics:

> The evolution of the horse has for humanity a very
> deep interest because of the debt of gratitude which
> man owes to this humble servitor and comrade and
> because of the fact that, largely through the unweary-
> ing efforts of Professor Marsh of Yale University, a
> collection of fossil horses was there assembled which
> was to prove the first documentary record of the evo-
> lution of a race. This classic collection was studied by
> Huxley, who pronounced it conclusive evidence in fa-
> vor of evolution. Darwin was so impressed with its
> importance that he would have visited it had his health
> permitted, but he died without having seen such a
> culminating proof of the theory of evolution.[26]

The quiet downgrading of that display at Yale did not
make the headlines, nor did similar steps at the American
Museum of Natural History. Darwinists have always enjoyed a good press. Newspapers, always on the lookout for
scandals and ready to unveil frauds, did not find it newswor-
thy that countless visitors to that display in New York had
been kept in the dark for over half a century about an all
important deception built into it: The data were presented as
a proof of an orthogenetic evolution of horses, which, of
course, turned out to be phylogenetic. In respect to size
alone, as a grim Darwinist was forced to admit, "horses had
now grown taller, now shorter, with the passage of time."[27]
The display found its way into countless textbooks as an

illustration of *the* proof of evolution, although it was a rank manipulation of scientific data. One cannot help therefore suspecting that some murky purposes gave rise to it in the first place and sustained it for over so many decades.

The purposes of Darwinism

In order to unveil those purposes, a good starting point can be found in Gould's essay. Its ultimate purpose is to make it appear that Darwin espoused the idea of a most gradual change because he was part of his times, dominated by social and economic liberalism. Spokesmen of liberalism, Gould argued, wanted, by invoking gradualism in nature, "to preserve the social order against increasing threats (and practices) of revolutions."[28] But if Darwin, as Gould put it, "did not see gradualism [that is, fossil evidences of biological evolution] in the rocks," was the socio-political climate a sufficient motivation for him to see in gradualism a major factor of paramount importance for his scientific purposes? Or did he have even more important purposes?

The very fact of Darwin's lack of interest in politics and society, let alone in social reforms, should warn against making much of that socio-political explanation. The publication of his early Notebooks removed any doubt about some markedly non-scientific motivation at work in him when he jotted down his first ideas on evolution, within a year or two after he had stepped ashore from the *Beagle*. In those Notebooks there is no trace of the one who a few years earlier lectured, with references to the Bible, the officers of the *Beagle* on the evil of swearing and cursing. Rather, the Notebooks contain more than one scoff, revealing in their crudeness, at a theistic outlook on existence in general and human nature in particular.

Darwin felt antagonistic to the doctrine of creation in a far deeper sense than the special creation of every species. His real target was the primeval creation. No wonder that he felt ashamed for having "truckled to public opinion" by speaking, in the conclusion of the *Origin*, of the evolutionary process as ultimately due to the Creator. [29] In stating, around the centenary celebrations of that book, that "Darwinism removed the whole idea of God as the creator of organisms from the sphere of rational discussion," Julian Huxley tried to strike at primeval creation by aiming first at the special creation of each and every species. [30]

Darwin's remark in those Notebooks that "if all men were dead, then monkeys may make men," [31] reveals his thorough conviction that man's origin and therefore his end too were exclusively animal. The same conviction was coupled with a contempt for anything spiritual in the following remark: "Origin of man now proved—Metaphysics must flourish—He who understands baboon would do more toward metaphysics than Locke. . . . Our [simian] descent then is the origin of our evil passions!—The Devil under form of Baboon is our grandfather." [32] This remark was no less pitiful as far as reasoning went than the question: "Why is thought, being a secretion of brain, more wonderful than gravity, a property of matter?" [33] This and similar utterances of Darwin, among them his call for an "evolutionary" conquest of that citadel of theism which is the mind, [34] point at some primitive instincts at work for some patently nonscientific purposes.

Clearly, if Darwin had been just a scientist, how could he feel an overriding urge to conquer that citadel for a purpose which had to do more with crude materialism than with science? Most importantly, if he had but a scientific purpose to implement, why did he feel it necessary to set dissimulation as his policy? His biographers mention on occasion that, following his marriage in 1845, he did his best to hide from his pious wife the measure of his agnosticism and materialism, if not plain atheism. Years before that, the Notebooks are the proof, he had set it for himself not to reveal his materialist views: He would merely say that "emotions, instincts, degrees of talent, which are hereditary, are so because the brain of a child resembles parent stock."[35] He knew that not a few among the best contemporary minds, to say nothing of the religious establishment, would have denounced him as an intellectual charlatan had he plainly claimed a full biological determinism of all mental processes. He did not wish to be cast in a martyr's role, although he held high, with an eye on the early astronomers, in the same Notebooks, the duty of scientists not to conceal their convictions: "Must remember that if they believe and do not openly avow their belief, they do as much as retard [scientific progress]."[36] He must have taken the view that in the successful pursuit of his purpose, the end, or the final discrediting of divine purpose, justified the means, be that means a plain dissimulation.

Darwin himself wondered about the eagerness with which the public grabbed up copies of the *Origin*, a long and often unentertaining book. The total number of copies so far published in English and in translations may be well over a million. The number of those who had it in their hands possibly a hundred million. The number of those who really read it may be a small fraction of all the copies printed, a point made already by Chesterton.[37] If it was a satisfactory feeling just to hold that book in hand, it must have answered to some aspiration and therefore must have conveyed some badly wanted assurance. The aspiration, always a pursuit of a purpose, aimed at barring any purpose that pointed beyond this life. Darwin himself noted this as he registered the overwhelmingly favorable reception of *The Descent of Man*.[38] One explanation of this, not suggested by Darwin, was that in the conclusion of that book Darwin presented evolution as the vehicle of man's ascent. He did so by speaking there of "the inheritance of virtuous tendencies,"[39] a prospect that must have appealed to Victorian upper and

middle classes, still not burdened with taxes of inheritance.

In view of what has since been revealed about some deeply suppressed aspirations in that society, often pagan to the
core, but almost invariably Christian to outward appearances, an admission of Aldous Huxley may seem much to
the point. It is part of his reminiscences about the 1920s
which saw many of the Victorian pretensions swept away.
He and many of his young contemporaries welcomed the
resulting vacuum of meaninglessness as an "instrument of
liberation" in two respects:

> The liberation we desired was simultaneously libera-
> tion from a certain political and economic system and
> liberation from a certain system of morality. We objec-
> ted to the morality because it interfered with our sex-
> ual freedom; we objected to the political and economic
> system because it was unjust. The supporters of these
> systems claimed that in some way they embodied the
> meaning (a Christian meaning, they insisted) of the
> world. There was one admirably simple method of
> confuting these people and at the same justifying our-
> selves in our political and erotic revolt: we could deny
> that the world had any meaning whatsoever. [40]

The reliance on Darwinism as a means of legitimizing those
purposes was clear though somewhat indirectly. In the same
long paragraph Aldous Huxley contrasted the new vacuum
with "Victorian passion for respectability" which discour-
aged the overt use of either Positivism or of Darwinism "as
a justification for sexual indulgence."[41]

Evolutionism at cross purposes
So much for the broader context of the impact which Darwinism as an ideology, which it certainly is, can have on
man's choice among purposes available to him in his strictly

personal pursuits. That the two objectives as specified by Aldous Huxley are logical implications of Darwinian theory should seem to be obvious if one recalls two prominent statements, one now a hundred years old, the other made half a century ago. The former comes from T. H. Huxley, a most authentic interpreter of orthodox Darwinism. In the Prolegomena to his Romanes Lecture of 1893, that sent a shockwave through Darwinist circles, Huxley described civilization taken for progress as "a process of an essentially different character from that which brings about the evolution of species."[42] In the Lecture itself he stated that biological evolution "has no sort of relation to moral ends."[43] With that Huxley firmly separated whatever purposes biological evolution could assure from those that relate to cultural and ethical goals. Not only that. Huxley put at cross purposes those two sets of purposes. The ethical purpose of society "depends not on imitating the cosmic process . . . but on combating it."[44]

And if all this had not already been revealing enough, Huxley called attention to the difference between the investigation of the *how* as the business of science and of the *why* or for what purpose about which science in general and the science of evolution in particular cannot teach anything. "The cosmic evolution may teach us," he noted, "how the good and evil tendencies of man may have come about." In the same breath he also warned that the same teaching would remain "incompetent to furnish any better reason why what we call good is preferable to what we call evil than we had before."[45] What Huxley did not reveal, at least in this context, related to the deeper purposes of the upholders of classical Darwinian theory as they avidly pursued their line of investigation of a process that could have no purpose.

The utter irrelevance of the synthetic theory of evolution for an appraisal of purpose should seem very clear from the emphatic remark which brings to a close George G. Simpson's *The Meaning of Evolution*: "Man is the result of a purposeless and materialistic process that does not have him in mind. He was not planned."[46] Clearly, the synthetic theory of evolution left, with respect to purpose, matters exactly there where John Dewey had found the orthodox theory about which he declared: "*The Origin of Species* foreswears inquiry about absolute origins and absolute finalities."[47]

Neither Simpson, nor Dewey tried to answer the question: How a process void of plan can issue in a being, man, whose very nature is to plan, which is always a pursuit of purpose. Much less were they willing to fathom the question: If there was no absolute finality or purpose, in what sense could purpose be spoken of and with a reliable meaning? Answers to these questions should seem to have been all the more imperative in view of the wide acceptance among Darwinists of Julian Huxley's remark: "At first sight the biological sector seems full of purpose. Organisms are built as if purposely designed. . . . But as the genius of Darwin showed, the purpose is only an apparent one."[48]

It has often been stated that the evidence of free will should cause nightmares to a consistently materialist determinist or, for that matter, to anyone who stakes all on a chance carefully left undefined. Much the same is true about purpose as far as the Darwinist biologist, orthodox or synthetically reformed, is concerned. As a Darwinist the biologist cannot countenance purpose, but as a biologist he cannot live without it. Consequently, the Darwinist has to live with purpose, or its study, teleology, in a clandestine manner. The heyday of orthodox Darwinism saw the biologist, E. von Brücke, make the observation that "teleology is a lady without whom the biologist cannot live but with whom he would not appear in public."[49]

Morphology and Teleology

It is an old story that clandestine liaisons thrive on half-
truths, studied evasions, and at times on something even
worse. Patently weak reasonings, let alone sheer verbalisms,
such as the specious distinction between purposive and purposeful,[50] should be taken for what they really are, a super-
ficiality cultivated for the purpose of keeping something
under the surface. The airing of such points should have
occupied Darwinists from the very moment there appeared
in *Nature*, in 1874, Asa Gray's article, "Charles Darwin." A
prominent botanist and one privy to Darwin's mind, Gray
stated that in view of "Darwin's great service to Natural
Science . . . instead of Morphology versus Teleology we
shall have Morphology wedded to Teleology."[51] Darwin
hastened to congratulate Gray: "What you say about teleology pleases me especially, and I do not think any one else has
ever noticed the point."[52]

Darwin had not noticed that point before, most likely
because he did not wish to face up to the obvious. Morphology, or the study of the shape of bones in particular, is a
pointer in two directions. Similarity of bones of the same
organs in different species strongly suggests their common
descent, a point obviously to the liking of Darwin. Yet the
particular shape of a bone evokes no less powerfully the idea
of its being designed for a very special purpose, a point that
could not please Darwin at all, or Darwinists for that matter. To cope with the difficulty, they purposefully emptied
the word purpose of its obvious meaning while using it
profusely.

Thus it quickly became customary in Darwin's circles to
see his "most remarkable service to the philosophy of biology" in "the reconciliation of it [teleology] with morphology." This statement of T. H. Huxley in 1887, a part of his
contribution to Francis Darwin's *The Life and Letters of
Charles Darwin*,[53] was a follow-up to earlier similar remarks

of his.[54] He hastened to add that the teleology in question does not weaken the destruction by Darwin's theory of the view that any organism, however, intricate, evolved for the purpose of making possible its very functioning. To drive the point home, Huxley took the eye for his example: "The teleology which supposes that the eye, such as we see it in man, or one of the higher vertebrata, was made, with the precise structure it exhibits, for the purpose of enabling the animal which possesses it to see, has undoubtedly received its death-blow."[55]

Clearly, the celebration by Darwinists, among them by Francis Darwin himself,[56] of the saving of teleology by Darwin, could only mean a not at all sophisticated encomium of mechanism. The biologist must assume a primordial arrangement of molecules that gave rise ultimately to all phenomena in the universe. But the more the biologist demonstrates that mechanism in his own field, Huxley continued, "the more completely is he thereby at the mercy of the teleologist, who can always defy him to *disprove* that this primordial molecular arrangement was *not* intended to evolve the phenomena of the universe"[57] (italics added). Yet if anyone did not feel to be at the mercy of the teleologist's insistence on an overall design, it was Huxley, the agnostic.

For the purposes of Huxley's agnosticism it was enough to eliminate the specter of particular, empirically verifiable purposes about which Darwinists and most teleologists failed to note that they were not and could not be a matter of empirical observation. Darwin certainly failed to perceive this all-important point as he wrote in 1870 to J. Hooker: "I cannot look at the universe as a result of blind chance. Yet I can see no evidence of beneficent design, or indeed any design of any kind, in the details."[58] Darwin was much too shortsighted philosophically to realize that in order to see design one needed, in addition to physical eyes, mental eyes.

They alone can make a philosophical inference equivalent to registering the presence of a design.

In addition to disclosing philosophical myopia on Darwin's part, his statement also bespoke of a short memory. In the *Origin of Species* he had already stated that "natural selection works solely by and for the good of each being, all corporeal and mental endowments will tend to progress toward perfection."[59] There he also described "innate tendency towards progressive development" as something that "necessarily follows . . . through the continued action of natural selection."[60] Moreover, he saw in the innovative power and boldness of the Anglo-Saxon people the supreme progressive form which had until then been achieved by the evolutionary process.[61]

As one consistent with the materialist underpinnings of his science, Darwin echoed, now and then, purposes dear to racists and warmongers. Darwinism was honored in the breach when R. A. Wallace, the co-proponent of evolution through natural selection, conjured up the biological future in the form of a "single homogeneous race, no individual of which will be inferior to the noblest specimens of existing humanity." Anyone believing in such a future could foresee "as bright a paradise as ever haunted the dreams of seer or poet"[62] being eventually achieved on earth.

Actually, exactly the opposite followed on Darwinian principles. Apart from the dubious identification of purpose with a tendency towards some pleasurable state, the ultimate state for mankind had to appear a most fearsome matter to consistent Darwinists. Only one of them, H. G. Wells, dared to note that the species known as *homo sapiens* could derive no lasting assurance from its being endowed by evolutionary forces "with a tenacity of self-assertion." He did so in a chapter with a dispiriting title, "The End Closes in upon the Mind." The writer, Wells wrote of himself, "is convinced that there is no way out or round or through the impasse. It is the end."[63] The only certainty man's reason could register related to the eventual replacement of mankind by a "new modification of the *hominidae*," a modification "certainly not to be human." Wells did not put into any category of reason the other certainty, namely, the macabre wish "to be in at the death of Man and to have a voice in his final replacement by the next Lord of Creation, even if, Oedipus-like, that successor's first act be parricide."[64]

Such was plain talk about the plain impossibility of accommodating purpose within Darwinism. In speaking of purpose Darwinists could offer but its purely verbal shadow, conveniently brought to the stage through the back door or through some make-belief. Such a make-belief was the exceedingly slow and steady rate at which Darwin expected evolution to work. He needed that rate, which implied the absence of geological catastrophes over billions of years, for two reasons. One was his inability to specify the mechanism that gave rise to variations on which natural selection was supposed to work. It was a supposition because, as Darwin himself admitted shortly after the publication of the second edition of the *Origin*, "in not a single case" could he prove "that it [natural selection] changed one species into another."[65]

Darwin's other reason for postulating that very slow rate related to the question of purpose. An exceedingly, that is, imperceptibly slow evolutionary change could make it appear that there was at work some purpose although it could not be seen. Those who let themselves be drawn into this make-believe, could then easily be rebutted if they insisted on seeing purpose in particulars. As to their seeing purpose in general, it therefore rested on no more evidence than a vague undefined process. The tactic was a transparent sleight of hand. It would have deserved the same unsparing exposure which James Martineau offered, a year after the publication of the *Origin*, with respect to the working of natural selection: "A logical theft is more easily committed piecemeal than wholesale. Surely, it is mean device for a philosopher to crib causation by hairs-breadths, to put it out at a compound interest through all time, and then disown the debt."[66]

Catastrophes for no purpose

Martineau's stricture of Darwinian logic was couched in terms of a financial catastrophe to come. Since as applied to Darwinism the catastrophe meant a bankruptcy in logic, only logical minds, very rare among Darwinists, could appreciate its force. Quite sensitive was Darwin to more tangible forms of catastrophes that threatened his theory. He did not seem to be concerned about the threat those catastrophes posed to his theory as a support of purpose. Nor did F. Jenkin see in this light the calculations he submitted in 1867. They showed that the few "useful" mutations were bound to be swamped out by the much more numerous "useless" ones. Jenkin could not have turned the tables more effectively on Darwin than by noting that Darwin's references to chance implied a chain of "successive creations,"[67] the very idea which his theory meant above all to discredit. That statistics did not favor the "useful" mutations meant, however, a rebuttal of the Darwinist claim that an imperceptibly slow evolution implemented some unseen purpose. Purpose, of course, received no sound support when in the late 1920s mathematical analysis of genetic mutations offered an escape from Jenkin's conclusion.

Darwin was no less upset by the calculations of William Thomson, the future Lord Kelvin, who showed in the 1860s that there was not enough geological time for an imperceptibly slow evolution. Thomson showed that on the basis of physics one could not assign more than a few hundred million years to the age of the sun. He also argued, along a different line, that the earth could not have solidified earlier than a few hundred million years, whereas Darwin demanded billions of years for his evolutionary mechanism to work. Darwin had been dead for some time when the discovery of radioactivity assured to the sun as well as to the earth those billions of years.

What should have caused real puzzlement to Darwin was the disappearance of many species and the appearance of many new ones at geological "moments" that marked the transition from one major geological epoch to the next. He should have insistently asked himself whether this phenomenon could be reconciled with the very slow evolutionary rate of change he postulated. He should have pondered whether those gigantic transitions did not indicate something very different from a catastrophe-free geological past he held indispensable for the working of that very slow rate of change. Had he done so, he would have proposed his views as a theory and not as a verity. Furthermore, he might have anticipated views that, theories perhaps in his time, would have become prophecies.

As if by supreme irony, the first major evidence of global geological catastrophes was spotted within a few years of the centenary of the publication of the *Origin*. In 1967, the Nobel-laureate physicist, W. Alvarez and his associates, who included his son, L. Alvarez, began to test their theory about periodic geological upheavals, through a field work in the precipitous mountainsides rising above the Italian town of Gubbio. There they found at the K-T boundary, that separates the Cretaceous from the Tertiary period, a pencil-thin layer very rich in iridium. Since iridium is very rare on earth but very abundant in meteors, it appeared logical to place the source of iridium, that was later found elsewhere on the globe in the same layer, in the earth's collision with an asteroid ten kilometers or so in diameter.

While the idea created at first considerable controversy, it is now generally conceded that among the factors that brought about the end of the Cretaceous period and the extinction of the dinosaurs (among other things), there was one collision with a huge body from outer space. The cataclysm triggered thereby is best given in the words of the younger Alvarez:

> In the first days after the earth was hit, dust blanketed the entire world. It grew pitch-dark from one to three months. If the impact was on land, it probably got bitter cold. If it hit at sea, the water vapor could have created a greenhouse effect, making things hot. Hot nitric acid would have rained out of the atmosphere life-threatening rain that would have dissolved the shells of organisms.[68]

This apocalyptic scenario has become even more so with further details emerging from the analysis of the iridium from that layer. Associated with that iridium were large amounts of soot which can only be explained if much of the earth was enveloped in fire. According to E. Anders, a cosmochemist at the University of Chicago,

> even if it [the asteroid] hit in the ocean, the impact would have created a crater 300 kilometers across. A huge plume would have pushed the atmosphere aside. The fireball would have had a radius of several thousand kilometers. Winds of hundreds of kilometers an hour would have swept the planet for hours, drying trees like a giant hair dryer. Two-thousand-degree rock vapor would have spread rapidly. It would have condensed to white-hot grains that could have started additional fires.[69]

The feverish research in historical biology sparked by the discovery of Alvarez has now completely discredited the idea of a slowly changing geological past. Instead, we have not only a geological past pockmarked with global catastro-

phes, but also a biological past riddled with extinctions of
life-forms on a giant scale and at a periodic rate, roughly 26
million years.[70] As to the extent of extinction a few data may
tell a great deal. At the boundary of the Ordovician and
Silurian epochs 75% of all living forms perished. There was
a similar rate of loss at the boundary of the Devonian and
carboniferous epochs. The sudden transition from the Per-
mian to the Triassic corresponds to a 90% loss, while there
appears a 75% loss through the K-T transition.

All this has major challenges for the Darwinian (orthodox and synthetic) theory of evolution. For in a sudden
catastrophic transition most features, apparently advantageous for survival, can become major liabilities. Mam-
mals owed their rapid development to the very small size
they had when the K-T catastrophe occurred which put an
end to all large animals such as the dynosaurs, in addition to
finally eliminating the ammonoids, once a major phylum.
Or to quote David Jablowski of the University of Chicago:
"Mass extinctions change the rules of evolution. When one
strikes, it's not necessarily the most fit that survives; often
it's the most fortunate."[71]

Of course, even before 1978 evolutionary theories were
full of pointers toward mere luck. Its continual presence
over billions of years should seem to discredit any effort to
see purpose in the evolutionary process in terms of Darwinian theory, orthodox or synthetic. Not that David M. Raup,
curator of Field Museum in Chicago, and possibly the foremost expert today on those biological catastrophes, implied
this as he registered the plain fact:

> Instead of finding the gradual unfolding of life, what
> geologists of Darwin's time and geologists of the pre-
> sent day actually find is a highly uneven or jerky re-
> cord; that is, species appear in the sequence very
> suddenly, show little or no change during their exis-

tence in the record, then abruptly go out of the record.[72]

Stephen Gould ventured closer to the heart of the matter as he registered the number, a mere two thousand or so species, that could survive in a geological catastrophe causing the extinction of 96 percent of species. In this case, he remarked,

> some groups probably died and others survived for no particular *reason* at all. There are few defences against a catastrophe of such magnitude, and survivors may simply be among the *lucky* four per cent; . . . our current panoply of major *designs* may not represent a set of *best* adaptations but *fortunate* survivors.[73]

The words to which emphasis has been added should speak clearly about a roundabout admission that there in no purpose to be sought in the evolutionary process as interpreted by Darwinism. With the return in full force of the catastrophic picture purpose can no longer retain its furtive place in evolutionary discourse. Can any purpose be seen in the impacts of huge asteroids on earth even if they hit with fair regularity? Darwinists would be the last to see behind any such impact God's guiding hand who, of course, and who alone, can make any catastrophe work for a purpose in a deeper sense. Buffon's idea that a comet hurled by God toward the sun turned it into a solar system, did not prove convincing even for that very limited purpose.

The saving of some purpose was certainly not in the mind of Gould as he collaborated on the new theory of evolution, called punctuated equilibrium. Its main purpose is to make it appear credible that the few species that survive global catastrophes will rapidly proliferate and variegate owing to the absence of competition. The theory may amount to a mere registering of sudden changes in the rate of development without really accounting for them. At any rate, the theory is a radical abandonment of the view of evolution as an ascent, that is, something that achieves a long term purpose, such as the rise of intelligent beings.

It would indeed be difficult to outdo Gould in his denial of purpose to the human race. He did not try to be less than a full-blooded Darwinist as he protested, three years ago, in the name of evolutionary biology, the putting of a moral label on the origin and spreading of AIDS. Tellingly, the elimination of morality once more turned into a flouting of all purpose. Mankind could appear but a mere flotsam and jetsam on unfathomable dark waters if one was to take, with Gould, for a "normal" event of biological evolution the possible elimination by AIDS of as much as one half of the entire human race.[74]

Clearly, the Darwinist flouting of purpose can issue in grim prospects, in addition to presenting one with that primarily academic spectacle which is best rendered by Whitehead's inimitable remark: "Those who devote themselves to the purpose of proving that there is no purpose constitute an interesting subject for study."[75] The immediate target of their absurd devotion is the specific pattern of each and every organism. Although each of those patterns appears to be a design, they claim all of them to be the product of a purposeless process and to serve no larger purpose whatever.

These are, of course, profoundly philosophical claims, however counter-philosophical at first look. The latest presentation of this intellectual counterrevolution in Darwinian garb is Gould's *Wonderful Life*, through which all wonder would be taken out of life if its anti-Darwinian Darwinist author had cared to define what he means by contingency. It is on this term, left by Gould in a conceptual limbo where it can mean a chance which is a "cause" though it does nothing, that rests not so much his story as his message. Once more he gives a most entertaining story, this time centered on the discovery and rediscovery of weird life-forms shown in the famed Burgess Shale in British Columbia. The sudden proliferation of life in the early Cambrian epoch into a wild variety of forms, now most of them extinct, is for Gould a proof that the origin of *homo sapiens* is merely the case of a "tiny twig on an improbable branch of a contingent limb on a fortunate tree." It therefore proves Darwin's scheme that "we are a detail, not a purpose or embodiment of the whole."[76]

If predictability, which justifies the ever imperfect tools of the scientist, sets limits to ontological cause, let alone to its teleological counterpart, then almost everything becomes unpredictable, that is, uncaused. To Gould this means an "exhilarating prospect" together with a "sense of freedom and consequent moral responsibility."[77] The kind of morality which can derive from that exhilaration should be clear from his dicta on AIDS. Freedom, as will be seen in a later chapter, is again a far more serious matter than Darwinists would imagine. Its Judeo-Christian provenance can but shock pundits like Gould, ready with anti-Christian slurs, the only kind of antisemitism now left for some liberals. Of course, not a few Christians are only to blame themselves for not making the most of the philosophical resources available to them. The principal fault with Darwinism is, as put so concisely by Whitehead, not so much scientific as philosophical. No different is the principal fault with the eagerness whereby each and every pattern is taken for a specific design, the very topic to which we must now turn.

Chapter Three

PATTERN VERSUS DESIGN

A watch in the meadow
The idea of design in Nature insofar as it reveals the purposes of the Author of Nature inevitably brings up the name
of the Reverend William Paley. A graduate of Cambridge,
he taught there for a decade before taking up an ecclesiastical
career in 1776. Paley had already been for three years Archdeacon of Carlisle when he published in 1783 his *Principles of
Moral* and *Political Philosophy*. This book, which went
through 15 editions before Paley's death in 1805, certainly
kept his memory alive in Cambridge classrooms. He greatly
furthered his reputation within ecclesiastical circles with
two works of Christian apologetics. One, the *Horae Pau-
linae*, dealt with the historical truth of Paul's ministry, the
other, which he published in 1794, was his celebrated *View of
the Evidences of Christianity*.

His name became a household work all over the intellectual world, during the 19th century and beyond, through
his *Natural Theology, or Evidences of the Existence and Attributes
of the Deity Collected from the Appearances of Nature*, published
in 1802. Hardly a book written in the 19th century on the

59

proofs of the existence of God fails to contain a reference to that book's opening paragraph centered on that hallowed timekeeping device, the watch:

> In crossing a heath, suppose I pitched my foot against a *stone*, and were asked how the stone came to be there; I might possibly answer, that, for any thing I knew to the contrary, it had lain there for ever: nor would it perhaps be very easy to show the absurdity of this answer. But suppose I had found a *watch* upon the ground, and it should be inquired how the watch happened to be in that place; I should hardly think of the answer which I had before given,—that, for any thing I knew, the watch might have always been there. Yet why should not this answer serve for the watch as well as for the stone? Why is it not as admissible in the second case, as in the first? For this reason, and for no other, viz. that, when we come to inspect the watch, we perceive (what we could not discover in the stone) that its several parts are framed and put together for a purpose, *e. g.* that they are so formed and adjusted as to produce motion, and that motion so regulated as to point out the hour of the day; that, if the different parts had been differently shaped from what they are, of a different size from what they are, or placed after any other manner, or in any other order, than that in which they are placed, either no motion at all would have been carried on in the machine, or none which would have answered the use that is now served by it.

After surveying in detail the parts of the watch Paley concludes: "The inference we think is inevitable, that the watch must have had a maker; that there must have existed, at some time, and at some place or other, an artificer or artificers who formed it for the purpose which we find it actually to answer; who comprehended its construction, and designed its use."[1]

In drawing this inference Paley offers a rather complex set of claims, each fairly clear though not sufficiently disentangled from one another. In claiming that the watch points at a cause of its existence, Paley evokes the cosmological argument. That the watch also suggests that it could not have *always* been there was a claim germane to the idea of creation in time. Most explicit is, of course, Paley's third claim, namely, that the watch bespeaks its having been made for a purpose. Last but not least, Paley emphatically claims that stumbling upon a stone in the middle of a meadow would not have justified such reflections.

Instead of clarifying those claims, Paley turns to answering eight objections. One of them is that the watch is a product of chance, which Paley considers unacceptable to "any man in his senses." In two other objections the watch is attributed to "some principle of order" and "to the laws of *metallic* nature." Paley's answer is that mere ideas do not produce concrete things. This commonsense feel for the tangibly real helps Paley brush aside the more subtle objection whose aim is to derail the argument into a subjectivist if not sceptical dead-end. According to that objection "the mechanism of the watch was no proof of contrivance, only a motive to induce the mind to think so." Paley's answer that the objection is "unbelievable" certainly proves his impatience with subtleties. He would have done better had he noted that the objection, in order to have intrinsic demonstrative value, is to be proposed first as something more than a mere motive. In his unbounded trust in common sense, Paley fails to see that it may get uncommon help from plain logic whereby one can turn the tables on one's opponents.

Again, common sense, which Paley does not articulate, supports his answer to four objections that are variations on a single theme, namely, the bearing on the argument of partial or total unfamiliarity with watches. Any of these objections would, Paley insists, carry weight only if man could be totally ignorant about things designed for purpose. Man, whoever he may be, "knows the utility of the end: he knows the subserviency and adaptation of the means to the end." Undoubtedly no opponent of the design argument would have argued that his rebuttal of it, say in book form, was not a means to an end. But it could still be objected that this did not justify one in seeing in entities, however complex, that did not, in all evidence, owe their origin to deliberate manufacture, so many means designed for a purpose.

This indeed was the objection that, two generations after Paley's death, appeared to many as being fatal to his argument. The objection was all the more effective because, as principally set forth by Darwin in *The Origin of Species*, it united philosophical vagueness with graphic observations of the animal world. Further, Darwin invested the objection with a high degree of elusiveness. He did so by postulating an immense number of intermediate steps, none of them distinctly useful, for the production of an obviously useful organ.

Paley should not be faulted for not anticipating Darwin's objections. He was, however, very much behind the times by failing to see the possible relevance of time to his argument. The debate between Vulcanists and Neptunists had already agitated the world of geologists for some time. Many more years than the few thousand implied for the age of the world in biblical chronology had already been urged by Buffon. Paley was behind the times with respect to the evolutionary ideas set forth in the mid-1790s by none other than a Darwin, Erasmus, the grand-father of Charles. But perhaps the most reprehensible as well as most defensible was Paley's falling behind the times in respect to philosophy. By the time Paley published his *Natural Theology*, Kant's onslaught on the design argument, which contained an explicit reference to a watch, had already been more than two decades old.

A watch in Königsberg

Paley could not, of course, be expected to take into consideration a philosopher who did not become really known in the British Isles until the second half of the 19th century. Since anecdotes travel fast, Paley might have heard about Kant's punctuality in setting out for his afternoon walk, used by neighbourhood citizens to set their clocks. At any rate, in Paley's time British philosophical thought was dominated by two trends, both unreceptive to what could appear not so much an insistence on logic as on logic chopping, a characteristic often exuding from the pages of the *Critique of Pure Reason*. Those two trends were the Scottish commonsense philosophy and a probabilism which Bishop Butler offered less as a strict demonstration than as a gentle persuasion.

Kant's objections to the design argument have an eerie relevance for Paley's argumentation. Kant fully acknowledged, and indeed seemed to recommend, the "authority of the argument" or what he called the "physico-theological proof."[2] Paley did not suspect that his praises of the design argument were so many echoes of an entire paragraph in the *Critique* that began with a reference to that very common sense by which Paley was to set so great a store:

> This proof always deserves to be mentioned with respect. It is the oldest, the clearest, and the most accordant with the common reason of mankind. It enlivens the study of nature just as it itself derives its existence and gains ever new vigour from that source. It suggests ends and purposes, where our observation would not have detected them by itself, and extends our knowledge of nature by means of the guiding-concept of a special unity, the principle of which is outside nature. This knowledge again reacts on its cause, namely, upon the idea which has led to it, and so strengthens the belief in a supreme Author [of nature] that the belief acquires the force of an irresistible conviction.[3]

But in the same breath Kant made clear that all the comfort and assurance to be derived from the design argument did not justify an "unconditional submission" to it. The reason for this was, according to Kant, that the design argument offered but a version of the cosmological argument, which did not, in substance, differ from the ontological proof of the existence of God. While Kant's rejection of the ontological argument rested on well trodden grounds, his analysis of the cosmological argument rested on new-fangled sophisms, similar to the ones characterizing his antinomies of reason.[4] The unsatisfactory character of Kant's analysis of the design argument came to a head on precisely that point where, as will be seen, Paley's argument too reveals itself as lacking solid foundations.

The point is whether the parallel between the complex coordination of parts in human artifacts and in purely natural products implies a mere similarity or a genuine analogy. By rejecting the old metaphysics, to which he failed to do justice if he knew it at all, Kant could admit only a similarity and he found it wanting. He did not even feel it necessary "to criticize natural reason too strictly in regard to its conclusion from the analogy between certain natural products and what our human art produces." He felt that the conclusion rested on the mere "similarity of those particular natural products with houses, ships, watches."[5] In short, the similarity justified nothing more than the registering of coherent specificities or patterns. They merely showed that the products, limited as they were to particular specifics, however complex in their coordination to be explained by chance, might very well have been otherwise and therefore contingent. One could therefore at best argue that their existence rested on an act, which, however creative, did not necessarily bespeak of design expressive of purpose.

Design or mere complexity

Paley followed the strategy of physico-theologies produced in large numbers throughout the 18th century. Their authors aimed at establishing the "designed" character of some natural products in order to conclude that if there was really a design on hand in some part of Nature then the whole of Nature had to be the result of an intelligent design. The strategy does not lack in a lasting appeal as shown not only by the continued proliferation of booklets on the design argument but also by some heavy tomes. Thus in the late 1920s F. R. Tennant, a divine philosophically far more sophisticated than Paley, argued that "if trustworthy evidence of design in the limited portion of the universe that we know were forthcoming, a world-Designer would be 'proved,' and our ignorance as to other parts would be irrelevant."[6] The crucial point is, however, not so much the limitedness of data about specific co-ordination but the specifics of the philosophical grounds on the basis of which an inference of universal validity can be made. In view of Paley's obvious shortcomings in matters philosophical, irony is not missing in one of his better-grade epistemological dicta: Man's "consciousness of knowing little, need not beget a distrust of that which he does know."[7]

Philosophy, however much needed for a construction of the argument from design, was of no major concern for Paley. This is suggested by the fact that only two of the objections considered by him, the ones relating to the alleged effectiveness of mere ideas, have a bearing on ontological causality. Further, in coming to grips with them Paley does not note that such causality can be considered in its own right, that is, with no immediate insistence on its purposeful nature. Had Paley been aware of this, he might have grasped the very special nature of the design argument insofar as it is about purpose and not merely about contingent existence which is the object of the cosmological argument.

Paley's offering a design argument which is not different from the cosmological argument, and in fact something much less, is noteworthy partly because it inspired further similar offerings. They culminated in the famed Bridgewater Treatises, published in the 1830s.[8] Even more noteworthy is Paley's failure to see that something went very wrong as he gave lopsided attention to the designed character of things over their ontological provenance. A reason for this is that Paley showed awareness of the difference between the cosmological and the design argument as he further explained the lessons that can be drawn from considering a watch.

First he makes one find a watch which contains also its machinery of production, such as moulds, lathes, files, and so forth. "The argument from design," Paley notes, "remains as it was." All parts of that machinery reveal a "subserviency to an end" and "imply the presence of intelligence and mind." In considering the case of an infinite series of such watches, Paley, as if by intent, touches but lightly on the inadequacy of a regress to infinity in looking for the ontological cause of concrete things. He merely mentions two series of terms, one tending towards a limit, the other not, and adds that "a chain composed of an infinite number of links can no more support itself, than a chain composed of a finite number of links." Rather, he insists that "contrivance is still unaccounted for. We still want a contriver. A designing mind is neither supplied by the supposition, nor dispensed with. . . . Contrivance must have had a contriver." Paley takes pains to note that we do not deal merely with the question of "how came the first watch into existence." Such might be the whole question "if nothing had been before us but an unorganized, unmechanized substance, without mark or indication of contrivance."[9]

Here we come to a little noted but crucial point in Paley's justification of his design argument. About that nondescript thing or substance he makes three points. One is that it would be difficult to show that such a substance could not have existed from eternity. One wonders whether Paley really saw the difference between creation out of nothing and creation in time. Paley's second point is no less revealing inasmuch as he takes a stone for a nondescript substance. Long before the advent of atomic theory and solid state physics, microscopes revealed more than enough of the complexity of any stone. The third is that the case of a watch, evidently the outcome of design, involves, according to Paley, no metaphysics. It should now be clear that the very starting point of Paley's book, or his insistence on the difference between coming upon a stone or a watch in a meadow, may hide an ulterior and very important aim on his part. He seems to be intent on constructing a design argument that works independently of an ontological or metaphysical foundation.

This suspicion becomes even stronger as one considers his last illustration of the design argument which he takes from astronomy. There at the very start he presents astronomy as "not the best medium through which to prove the agency of an intelligent Creator," that is, of a Creator who works for a purpose. The reason, as given by Paley, is the "very simplicity" of celestial bodies. "We deduce design from relation, aptitude, and correspondence of parts. Some degree therefore of *complexity* is necessary to render a subject fit for this species of argument." Complexity presupposes parts, but, Paley noted, "the heavenly bodies do not, except perhaps in the instance of Saturn's ring, present themselves to our observation as compounded of parts at all."[10]

It is not difficult to guess what sort of argument Paley would have forged had he known about the extreme complexity of the ring around Saturn. He could not easily be unfamiliar with Herschel's observation of the thinness of that ring and of its being divided into two parts,[11] but he seems to have required a far greater complexity to be on hand. Had the hundreds of concentric rings which fly-by satellites showed a few years ago around Saturn, been known to him, he would have argued as follows: The very complex structure of Saturn's rings reveals their manufactured character which, since the science of mechanics cannot account for it, should be credited to the divine artificer who wanted to enhance man's opportunities for admiring the work of creation. Paley forges the same kind of arguments from the various aspects of the solar system as a coherent whole of parts. [12] It is also an argument that recurs countless times in the main body of the book in which Paley lists well over a hundred examples of design from the organic world.

Design or mere gaps

Paley's summary of those many cases begins on firm philosophical footing and ends in a loss of firm grounds. He takes his final stand by evoking gaps in knowledge about mechanical contrivances so that he may fill them with references to God's direct action:

> In all cases, wherein the mind feels itself in danger of being confounded by variety, it is sure to rest upon a few strong points, or perhaps upon a single instance. Amongst a multitude of proofs, it is *one* that does the business. . . . For my part, I take my stand in human anatomy; and the examples of mechanism I should be apt to draw out from the copious catalogue which it supplies are, the pivot upon which the head turns, the ligament within the socket of the hip-joint, the pulley or trochlear muscles of the eye, the epiglottis, the bandages which tie down the tendons of the wrist and instep, . . . the knitting of the intestines to the mesentery, . . . the course of the chyle into the blood. . . . To these instances, the reader's memory will go back; . . . there is not one of the number which I do not think

decisive; not one which is not strictly mechanical: nor have I read or heard of any [mechanical] solution of these appearances, which, in the smallest degree, shakes the conclusion that we build upon them.[13]

Clearly, Paley's argumentation is all too often a case of argument from the gaps of scientific knowledge. In Paley's England few if any looked with suspicion at this type of reasoning. It had received scientific aura through the Scholium which Roger Coates appended to the third edition of Newton's *Principia* with its author's full approval.[14] There half a dozen features of the solar system, unexplainable in terms of the *Principia*, were listed as so many evidences of a directly divine design. Just before the publication of Paley's *Natural Theology* a memorable vote had been entered against the reliability of such arguments and with a reference to the mechanism of the solar system. To heighten the irony, no less a British man of science than William Herschel witnessed, in the presence of Napoleon, Laplace's boasting that his nebular hypothesis did not need a hypothetical intervention by God.[15]

This is not to suggest that either the science of Laplace or today's science have a satisfactory explanation of the formation of the solar system.[16] Many of the small and big contrivances in plant and animal life far surpass the skills of the best of late 20th-century engineers.[17] Still a great many gaps have been filled by science since Paley's day and at an increasingly accelerated rate. Therefore his, or anyone else's insistence on the absence of scientific explanation of sundry contrivances in nature runs the risk of turning the argument from design into an argument from gaps. An argument overshadowed by such a suspicion will not inspire that very confidence which Paley wanted to assure by his insistence on another burden of the design argument. It was also to reveal the Designer of nature as having a *benevolent* design in view.

Design as benevolence
According to Paley, Nature witnessed its benevolent design
in two principal ways. The first is that in the vast plurality of
cases, in which contrivance is perceived, the contrivance
reveals itself to be beneficial. The second is that animal
sensations carry with them more pleasure than what is necessary for the function of their organs. From there Paley
rushes to a paeon about the purpose of it all:

> It is a happy world after all. The air, the earth, the
> water, teem with delighted existence. In a spring
> noon, or a summer evening, on whichever side I turn
> my eyes, myriads of happy beings crowd upon my
> view . . . A bee among the flowers in spring is one
> of the most cheerful objects that can be looked upon.
> Its life appears to be all enjoyment; so busy and so
> pleased. . . . The *whole-winged* insect tribe, it is prob-
> able, are equally intent upon their proper enjoy-
> ments. . . . Plants are covered with *aphides*, greedily
> sucking their juices, and constantly, as it should seem,
> in the act of sucking. It cannot be doubted that this is a
> state of gratification. What else should fix them so
> close to the operation and so long? . . . If we look to
> what the *waters* produce, shoals of the fry fish frequent
> the margins of rivers, of lakes, and of the sea itself.
> These are so happy that they know not what to do
> with themselves. . . . If any motion of a mute animal
> could express delight it was this: if they had meant to
> make signs of their happiness, they could not have
> done it more intelligently. Suppose then, what I have
> no doubt of, each individual of this number to be in a
> state of positive enjoyment; what a sum, collectively,
> of gratification and pleasure have we here before our
> view![18]

Undoubtedly many a bee would have immensely enjoyed
stinging Paley's head, an outcome that would not have

made Paley jump with joy. Conversely, no fish or lamb could find any enjoyment in ending up on Paley's dinner table. At any rate, before not too long Darwin cast a long shadow on Paley's portrayal of the animal world as if it had been designed for experiencing endless raptures of happiness. In one of his few utterances about his loss of faith, Darwin referred to the enormous measure of suffering in the animal world.[19] He meant explicitly the absence of a *benevolent* design as he stated his inability to see design in any detail.[20] Once more it became very clear that it is very difficult, if not almost impossible, to become convinced about design in nature without demonstrating some purpose deeper than the satisfaction of sensory enjoyment.

Paley reasoned in his *Natural Theology* as if 18th-century optimism had not been dealt a fatal blow through the earthquake that, together with the conflagration touched off by it, had devastated Lisbon on All Saints' Day, 1755. Within a few weeks all Europe was reading about the calamity grim reports that made a lasting impression on old and young. Among the latter was Goethe, still a child of mere seven. From a distance of half a century, the reports stood out vividly in his memory together with the fact that for the first time in his life he felt his peace of mind to have been deeply disturbed:

> On the 1st of November, 1755, the earthquake at Lisbon occurred, and spread a mighty terror over the world, long accustomed to peace and quiet. A great and magnificent capital, at the same time a trading and maritime city, is smitten, without warning, by a most fearful calamity. The earth trembles and totters, the sea rages, ships are dashed together, houses collapse, churches and towers on the top of them, the royal palace is in part swallowed by the waters, the cleft earth seems to vomit flames, since smoke and fire are seen everywhere amid the ruins. Sixty thousand per-

sons, a moment before in ease and comfort, are annihi-
lated at once, and he is to be deemed most fortunate
who was not allowed time for thought or consciousness of the disaster.[21]

The greatest calamities lose much of their harshness when
seen from a great geographical distance and, what is even
more important, from a distance of almost half a century.
Paley did not recall what could have been remembered even
from those distances. Nor did he seem to suspect that his
arguments were threatened by that celebrated and biting
scepticism which Voltaire had offered in *Candide* about benevolent design in nature, a work inspired by the Lisbon
earthquake. In writing *Candide* Voltaire aimed at showing
that it was useless to find wider purposes for existence. If
life had any purpose it amounted to no more than performing the daily toil necessary to sustain life: Such is the gist of
that book's often quoted conclusion: "But we must cultivate
our garden."[22]
Paley's performance cannot be explained by the fact that
Carlisle, where he lived in peace and comfort, was far away
from the great troubles of contemporary world, even from
the threat of the invasion of Britain planned by Napoleon.
The latter, let it be recalled, was spoken of in Britain in
terms even worse than the ones accorded there to Hitler a
century and a half later. Not that the Archdeacon of Carlisle
was not a compassionate man. Among his works there is, in
addition to a collection of often moving sermons, also a
book, half as long as the *Natural Theology*, with the title: *The
Clergyman's Companion in Visiting the Sick*. Its third part is a
collection of "prayers for the sick and unfortunate in extraordinary cases."[23]
If Paley's eyes were closed to that chief objection to purpose which is human suffering on a colossal scale, those
eyes were not the Christian clergyman's but of the philoso-

pher who did not really philosophize as a Christian. Otherwise he would have spotted something most crucial, to be discussed in another chapter, for an utterly honest, and therefore effective, articulation of the design argument. It is the support which Christian revelation and cult bring to one's perception of an overall design with a purpose while leaving intact the rationality of that perception.

One should not, however, be too harsh on Paley. Two generations later, such a profoundly Christian thinker as John Henry Newman saw an escape from Paley's predicament only by shifting emphasis to the argument from consciousness. Newman gave his reasons for that shift in a letter to W. R. Brownlow who expressed surprise over the fact that Newman's just published *Grammar of Assent* did not contain the proofs of the existence of God "from the testimony of visible creation."[24] In his reply Newman referred to a short paragraph in the *Grammar* where order in the physical universe was presented as indication of purpose.[25] But the order he had there in mind was the perception of the working of a deliberate cause and not of the sequences established by science. Exclusive attention to the procedures of science, so Newman warned, could prompt one "to confuse causation with order." Unlike cause, order as mere sequence did not, so Newman argued, impress itself on the mind with a "logical force."[26]

The same difference, so Newman thought, existed between the design argument and the argument from consciousness. Further, in aiming at his contemporaries, Newman wrote to Brownlow, he had to focus on what they admitted or at least were familiar with. It was not the argument from design but the reality of consciousness: "Half the world knows nothing of the argument from design—and, when you have got it, you do not prove by it the moral attributes of God—except very faintly. Design teaches me power, skill and goodness—not sanctity, not mercy, not a future judgment, which three are of the essence of religion."

There was still another reason, and a most revealing one as it related to the weak point in Newman's philosophy. By "logical force" Newman could mean mere psychological impressiveness. The latter factor operated effectively, in respect to the design argument, only in the biblical context. Newman, never a systematic student of Aquinas, let alone of medieval philosophy on the relation of reason to revelation, should have anticipated Gilson in order to see the rationality of Christian philosophy in spite of its being steeped in Revelation.[27] Newman then might not have written to Brownlow: "And to tell the truth, though I should not wish to preach on the subject, for forty years I have been unable to see the logical force of the argument myself. I believe in design because I believe in God; not in a God because I see design."[28]

Those severed from the context of Revelation could but pour scorn on the design argument as presented by Paley. Thus Darwin recalled his reading of Paley's *Natural Theology* as one of those schoolbooks that were "of the least use to me in the education of myself."[29] Darwin's recollection might have been colored by his loss of faith, which he carefully kept to himself. Shelley's atheism was too open to doubt its impact on his brushing aside, in the Preface to *Prometheus Unbound*, Paley's reasonings: "I had rather be damned with Plato and Lord Bacon, than get to heaven with Paley and Malthus."[30] What Shelley and others, in whom the anti-exorcist and the non-scientist were closely united, failed to suspect was something about the scientific heaven. Those really familiar with its workings could not exorcize the evidence which their mental eyes showed about design and purpose in countless objects of their investigations. Most persuasive among those objects were their very physical eyes.

The eye's witness

The force of persuasion weighed heavily on Darwin but its effectiveness was thwarted by a very different consideration that dominated his thinking. Being preoccupied with the *how* or mechanistic *why* underlying the origin of a biological pattern, he was unable to appreciate the question about its *designed* or *purposeful* character whatever his many references to its usefulness. The brief section on "Organs of Extreme Perfection and Complexity" in *The Origin* illustrates this all too well. There Darwin states repeatedly that each step in the millions of gradations in the formation by natural selection of countless forms of eyes had to be useful. But he was not to engage in a philosophical reflection on design insofar as it reveals purpose. His sole concern was to show that it was not "absurd in the highest degree" to suppose that "the eye with all its inimitable contrivances for adjusting the focus to different distances, for admitting different amounts of light, and for the correction of spherical and chromatic aberration, could not have been formed by natural selection."[31]

It seemed to Darwin, and not without reason, that others, unable to share his views on the unlimited efficacy of natural selection, were preoccupied with the same alternative. This may be the gist of his admission later in that section: "I have felt the difficulty far too keenly to be surprised at others hesitating to extend the principle of natural selection to so startling a length." It does not seem that Darwin perceived something beyond that alternative when years later he recalled "the time when the thought of the eye made me cold all over, but I have got over this stage of the complaint and now small trifling particulars of structure often make me very comfortable."[32] As will be seen shortly, the number of such particulars is literally countless, although not the number of cases when biologists feel acute intellectual discomfort as they see them under their very eyes.

The alternative could turn into a myopia that was overcome but on occasion by such biologists who did not sys-
tematically stifle their philosophical sensitivities. One such
rare occasion came half a century after Darwin when Lucien
Cuénot, the great French biologist, reserved a central place
for his reflections on the eye in his book on finality in
biology. If one considers, he wrote, the most specific inter-
connections involved in the structure of the eye which can be
vitiated "by the smallest deviation, the idea of a finalist
direction is born invincibly. . . . It is not daring to believe
that the eye is made for seeing."[33] These two statements
enclose Cuénot's expression of philosophical despair. Its
cause is his seeing an irresolvable conflict between the finalist direction, which "amounts to explaining the obscure by
the more obscure" and the impossibility "to forgo a guideline in the train of [biological] events." Despair or not, he at
least registered the difference between two very different
perspectives.

Clearly, as long as a guideline leads somewhere, it means
goal-directedness, the very concept which the Darwinian
biologist cannot justify on the basis of his method, a method
of sheer mechanism. The Darwinian biologist also finds, to
continue with Cuénot, "that each type of eye from the most
rudimentary to the most developed is complete in itself. . . .
When one examines an animal, one does not hesitate for a
moment to identify the eyes." Then the question, "How
could one assign to chance variations the recurring origin of
such complexes with multiple interconnection?,"[34] becomes an expression of despair about that method. The
despair can indeed become so annoying as to make the
Darwinist biologist explode: "That damned eye—the human eye!"[35]

Such a reaction makes sense only if it betrays at least a tacit
admission on the part of the Darwinist biologist that natural
selection is not a wholly satisfactory explanation of the for-

mation of the eye. That it is such an explanation is the conviction underlying Ernst Mayr's approach to the problem whether the eye can evolve with any probability on that basis: "The evolution of the eye is not at all that improbable. In fact whenever eyes were of any selective advantage in the animal kingdom, they evolved."[36]

Of course, all that the biologist can do is to register the number (given by Mayr as forty or so) of such independent occurrences. But the biologist offers a mere speculation, when he takes, as Mayr does, "selective advantage," which can only work through natural selection, for an explanation. In doing so he constructs a glorified tautology similar to the one that the fittest survive. It is precisely the eye, which is either accurately formed or utterly useless, that shows the futility of thinking about transitional forms which, though inseparable from the alleged process of natural selection, offer no selective advantage.

Moreover, it is precisely against the background of this lesson provided by the eye that one shall best appreciate a penetrating remark about natural selection which, by definition, works for no end or design:

> Natural selection is a negative factor; it can account for the non-survival of those forms which have died out. Its work of elimination can be seen in operation in neglected gardens or waste land anywhere. There is nothing directional about it. The way it works depends on circumstances. If the climate changes from wet to dry, characters that were a handicap in the wet climate become an asset, and vice versa.[37]

Such a rigorous as well as unsentimental definition of natural selection should at least help the biologist in avoiding references to usefulness, let alone to design and purpose and similar philosophically loaded terms. Of course, most biologists dealing with evolution will make, as Darwin did,

continual references to the
ignore the philosophical bu
start cavorting in mental s
does, that a mere word, su
questions of philosophy: "
What good is five percent
possessor of such an incip
sight."[38]

The witness of other organs
If other organs, such as th
the same lesson, it is onl
cannot be investigated witl
titative precision. A math
most impossible to the pl
the males of three species
themselves differently fr
males as they copulate. Tl
to distract the female, ar
cocoon, and still another
viously these different pel

 ail Mary, full of grace. The Lord is with thee. Blessed art thou among women and blessed is the fruit of thy womb, Jesus. Holy Mary, mother of God. Pray for us now, and at the hour of our death. Amen

consummately purposeful action which is cunning. Whatever there is in those spiders that makes that cunning possible (neuronal circuits, muscles, tentacles, cuticles, etc.), it is a very special endowment that serves a very specific purpose.

Sufficiently impressive should, however, seem the measure of that precision that could be achieved, say, in evaluating the fitness of the feathers of birds to their manifold arts of flying. Apart from various types of take-off and landing, the flight can be soaring, gliding, hovering, diving, flapping or any combination of these—all of them still to be replicated by aircraft designers. The adaptation implies varieties in the structure of the feathers, in their waterproofing, and in their being covered with very thin heat-conducting layers. In fact, according to W. Thorpe, a leading animal behaviorist, "almost every one of the 6800-odd species of birds in the world could ultimately be found to possess special adaptations of feather and down to the particular ecological niche to which it has become adapted."[41]

A fair measure of mathematical precision could also be achieved in evaluating the adaptation of the mouth-parts of thousands of species of flies which have particular ways of obtaining the special type of food they need. The task is more complicated in connection with the ability of the insect cuticle "to allow for moulting and renewal and to resist desiccation where such resistance is essential, as in a climate or micro-climate with an atmosphere at less than saturation; yet to be selectively permeable to water in certain aquatic insects where such permeability is required."[42]

Such and countless other cases can, with an overwhelming force, impose the realization that, in addition to patterns one has under one's very eyes a design at work. To say as most Darwinists do that there ought to have been an infinite number of transitional patterns is but throwing a red-herring in the way of philosophical reflection. That in no case can those countless transitions be verified should reveal something of the strange fragrance of that unphilosophical herring. But this is not the real issue on hand. The real issue is not even a choice between natural selection and special creation, although all too often one is bombarded with this misguided missile.

The dispute about the bombardier beetle is a case in point. Its undoubtedly most skillful defense mechanism can no more be taken for an *empirical* proof of special creation than the whole universe can be taken for *such* a proof of an initial creation of all. In the former case the proof, if any, has to be a special revelation, while in the latter case the proof has to rely on metaphysics. It is that metaphysics, or at least sensitivity to it, that should evoke the presence of a design at work when one's eyes are fixed on the bombardier beetle's defense mechanism:

> When the beetle senses danger, it internally mixes enzymes contained in one body chamber with concentrated solutions of some rather harmless compounds, hydrogen peroxide and hydroquinons, confined to a second chamber. This generates a noxious spray of caustic benzoquinons, which explodes from its body at a boiling 212°F. What is more, the fluid is pumped through twin rear nozzles, which can be rotated, like a B-17's gun turret, to hit a hungry ant or frog with bull's eye accuracy.[43]

This summation of the bombardier beetle's defense mechanism is part of a widely read weekly magazine's report, characteristic of the media's reluctance to ask truly philosophical questions on a strictly philosophical issue. The latter is present even when the Darwinist expert on bombardier beetles, interviewed on the subject, finds no reason to choose Darwin at the expense of the Creator.[44] He merely sidetracks the issue as he insists in the same breath on the transitional stages among various types of bombardier beetles. He therefore should not complain for being challenged by creationists to show those extremely numerous and finely graduated transitions. Both sides are actually one in having no use for a philosophy that alone can cope with patterns that are also designs expressive of a purpose that mere mechanism cannot account for and of a purpose that does not supplement mechanical steps.

At any rate, philosophical sensitivity for design can be of great heuristic value for the biologist as he focuses his eyes on mere patterns in order to see in them a design for a purpose. A memorable instance of this is connected with that epoch-making break-through in biology, Harvey's discovery of the circulation of the blood. The only conversation which Robert Boyle had with the ageing Harvey included Boyle's question about "the things that induc'd him to think" of that circulation:

He answer'd me, that when he took notice that the
Valves in the Veins of so many several parts of the
Body, were so plac'd that they gave free passage to
the Blood towards the Heart, but oppos'd the passage
of the Veinal Blood the Contrary way: He was invited
to imagine, that so Provident a Cause as Nature had
not so Plac'd so many Valves without Design: and no
Design seem'd more possible than that, since the
Blood could not well, because of the interposing
Valves, be Sent by the Veins to the Limbs; it should be
Sent through the Arteries, and Return through the
Veins, whose Valves did not oppose its course that
way.[45]

The next major discovery about the blood, the difference
between red and white cells, is part of a most telling witness
of all living cells about the way in which patterns can be
evocative of design.

The witness of cells

The most universally valid statement about living forms is
that they have cells as their basic building blocks. To illustrate briefly what a cell is biologists usually speak of a
chemical factory or of a laboratory of immense complexity.
And if the biologist has, like Charles Sherrington, an evocative power, his portrayal of the cell will have a vibrating
quality:

It is a scene of energy-cycles, suites of oxidation and
reduction, concatenated fermentations. It is like a
magic hive the walls of whose chambered spongework
are shifting veils of ordered molecules and rend and
renew as operations rise and cease. A world of surfaces
and streams. We seem to watch battalions of specific
catalysts like Maxwell's 'demons', lined up, each waiting, stopwatch in hand, for its moment to play the part

assigned to it, a step in one or other great thousand-linked chain process.[46]

Less than ten years after Sherrington, another biologist, Stuart Mudd, of the University of Pennsylvania put the matter in a more scientific vein:

> Cells of many kinds of bacteria, furnished only with water, salts, glucose and simple sources of carbon and nitrogen, can synthesize proteins, complex carbohydrates, lipids, ribose and desoxyribose nucleic acids, growth accessories and enzymes, all organized into characteristic and reproducible protoplasmatic systems. The cell can reproduce itself and divide within an hour at body temperature. These feats of chemical synthesis and organization which cannot be duplicated by the finest chemical laboratories in existence, are accomplished within a cell a few microns in length and less than half a micron in diameter. The plain facts would seem fantastic if they were not so familiar. The simultaneous occurrence of the complex reactions involving energy utilization, synthesis and organization of the materials elaborated implies means of keeping the reactions in proper temporal and spatial relation to each other, and implies organization equivalent to an efficient system of transport and logistics.[47]

Still another ten years later Thorpe wrote: "The cell is a chemical laboratory of immense complexity. The cell itself could not possibly function without cell membranes which contain and selectively isolate the working parts of this laboratory."[48]

Such descriptions of cells are tantamount to suggesting that their complexities reveal an unmistakable design. Yet, none of those biologists who penned those descriptions stated that cells could come about only if they were specially produced by an extracosmic designer or creator. The reason

for their not saying this is that they are biologists whose
method can have no room for the assumption of any special
creation, let alone for a large number of them.

Method, as suggested by its etymology, is the restriction
of one's steps of investigations to a specific line or avenue.
About those avenues it is not true what has been stated
about roads, namely, that they all lead to Rome, that is, all
extend to the same final point of destination in the general
intellectual pursuit. The method of exact science is a road
that stretches from one empirical or quantitative configuration to another. In itself that road cannot even lead to a
stretch where statements of ontology are in order, not even
the kind of virtually ontological statement that there may be
a strict limit to the numerical succession of empirical steps.
Much less can that road logically include a stretch where
statements about purpose are in order.

The principal purpose of evolutionary biology consists in
establishing as many mutually connecting empirical steps as
possible. In their pursuit of this most commendable aim,
not a few biologists have suggested that so many of those
steps have been ascertained as to raise the theory of evolution to the level of scientific fact. Undoubtedly, evolutionary
research has demonstrated a great many groups of organisms that show a much greater similarity to one another than
Paley would have thought conceivable. Darwin's observations of slight graduated differences among various species
of finches of the Galapagos[49] was only the first of a great
many similar results in many different areas of biology. But
apart from extremely minute cases, best exemplified by the
industrial melanism of moths, biologists have not suceeded
in demonstrating scientifically, that is, in satisfactorily
quantitative details, the steps of transition that issue in the
variations of species. In other words, evolutionary theory is
still a theory, however plausible for the most part, and not a
scientific demonstration. This fact is acknowledged when-

ever the biologist, in an apparently unguarded moment, states that evolution is a fact although its mechanism is not sufficiently known.[50]

Unfortunately, by saying that they know the fact of evolution, which is a process, biologists imply that they know it scientifically which is to know the manner or mechanism of the process, together with all its phases. Admittedly they don't know the latter. Therefore their knowing the fact of evolution remains markedly non-scientific, indeed plainly metaphysical. That knowledge of theirs is an intellectual act of induction or generalization, and even more so when that act has to be very bold.

The measure of such boldness can readily be gathered from a brief recall about an all-important aspect of the evolutionary study of cells. Although cells are the basic building blocks of life, they are far from being uniform. They have a large set of varieties, each set serving a very special purpose. And if the cells special to liver, kidney, lung, heart, etc., fail to perform those special functions, the whole organism is bound to perish.[51] Yet in some other sense those basic blocks are very far above in complexity from a potentially basic level, or the level of "primeval soup," which in itself is a most hypothetical entity. What Thorpe stated about that difference twenty-five years ago is still valid:

> The 'life' which might have formed in this so-called 'primeval soup' has yet to be linked to life which reduplicates itself, leaving offspring to carry on the race. The crux of the whole problem, as we understand it, is to envisage the origin of the cell; for all the life which we now study, from bacteria to man, is cellular in almost all its stages. . . . Biologists have long hoped to find a really 'primitive' acellular life and life as we know it now. But there seems little doubt today that there are no primitive cells living on earth.

> All the cells that we know are of fantastic complexity. I
> believe that no biologist or physicist has yet been able
> to propose even the outlines of a theory as to how such
> a cell might have been 'evolved'. [52]

Today a biologist specializing in the study of the evolution
of the cell can say nothing essentially more than what was
stated in the conclusion of a major monograph on it published a hundred years ago. Of course, in view of the widespread dogmatic conviction that natural selection has
explained everything, the biologist will have to be just as
apologetic as was Edward B. Wilson, professor of inverte-
brate zoology at Columbia University, in warning that "we
cannot close our eyes to two facts." One was that we are
"utterly ignorant" about the mechanism whereby a cell
adapts itself to new tasks. Whatever advances have been
made in this respect, no real dent has been made on the
second fact specified by him as cause for apology: "The
study of the cell has on the whole seemed to widen rather
than to narrow the enormous gap that separates even the
lowest forms of life from the inorganic world." [53]

It should not be difficult to see what all this has to do with
the question of design, or rather with the designed character
of organic life. Biological studies provide a great many cases
which almost impose their characterization as being designed and for a purpose. Of course, when one says "designed" one no longer speaks as a biologist, but as a meta-
physician. At any rate, biological studies failed to reveal
data suggestive of long-stretch design. The steps from plant
to animal life, within animal life from one phyla through
classes to orders, are often too great to allow anything more
than surmises about the steps of transition.

Only below the level of families do the steps of transition appear less mysterious. It is only there that the steps
of transition can be guessed with "scientific" plausibility

which may qualify as a design though its purpose may amount to no more than to the instrumentality of one species in the production of another. As to the rise of the organism which is man, leading Darwinists are willing to admit that it is far from being an inevitable outcome.[54] Actually, increasing emphasis is being laid on the opposite view, namely, that man is a wholly unforeseeable product of chance factors.

This view has behind it a design aimed at promoting the celebration of the absence of any design. One wonders whether this pseudophilosophy should invade paleontology to the extent of letting Omar Khayyam appear there as a paragon of honesty with his often quoted quatrain:

> Into this Universe, and Why not knowing
> Nor whence, like Water willy-nilly flowing
>   And out of it, as Wind along the Waste
> I know not Whither, willy-nilly blowing.[55]

Some biologists still have to learn about the ability of *homo sapiens*, an ability stunningly demonstrated by the cosmology of the General Theory of Relativity, to form a reliable notion about the universe which is, of course, but a mere word in the foregoing quatrain. With the universe taken for a reality, far more appropriate will be the perception which haunted Thomas Hardy, so intent on basing his novels on a Darwinian perception of life. The mere view of a chrysanthemum, so much behind other flowers in blooming, evoked to him the presence of an overall design, however unspecified:

> Had it a reason for delay,
>   Dreaming in witlessness
> That for a bloom so delicate
>   Winter would stay its stress?

—I talk as if the thing were born
  With sense to work its mind;
Yet it is but one mask of many worn
  By the Great Face behind.[56]

As long as the universe remains a mere word, so remains
any design, let alone the possibility of a universe designed.
That a biologically most defenseless species can comprehend all the universe is not something for the method of
biology to ponder, although biologists can never ponder it
enough.

Even a philosophically better equipped biology than the
Darwinist has not yet established data suggestive of a design
that would, with a fair measure of consistency, stretch
across the entire realm of the living. Consequently, the use
of the term "biological design," which in itself is a markedly metaphysical construct, does not provide even in that
respect a safe pointer to what its purpose may be. To say that
the purpose of life is to propagate itself is to bog down in
sheer tautology.

The witness of environment

There is still a far more fundamental reason against seeing in
evolutionary biology a heuristics of purpose. The reason in
question was spelled out in the early years of this century by
the Harvard biochemist Lawrence J. Henderson. His studies
and reflections on the fitness of environment[57] are seen today
as a prophetic anticipation of investigations that have been
most actively pursued for the past decade or two under
the general label of the anthropic cosmological principle.
Henderson developed in great detail that carbon, hydrogen, oxygen, and the compounds, water and carbonic acid,
constitute a unique ensemble of fitness, while being independent of one another, that is, not due to a common mechanism.[58]

It was in that connection that Henderson's reflections became most instructive for the purposes of this chapter. On the one hand Henderson felt "obliged to regard this collocation of properties as in some intelligible sense a preparation for the process of planetary evolution . . . and therefore be regarded as teleological in character."[59] On the other hand he as an agnostic felt also obliged to dilute the meaning of the term teleology as much as possible. He refused to grant that term a status other than "the vaguest possible term from which all implication of design or purpose has been completely eliminated."[60] Insofar as the great majority of biologists and philosophers was concerned, Henderson was right in referring to their "common consent" to take the word teleology for the lack of *telos*, that is, of goal.

The word teleology could not be so readily exorcized of its very significance. This is shown by the regularly recurring efforts of biologists to replace teleology with teleonomy[61] as a word not yet tainted through usage with metaphysical ideas, such as purpose and design. But Henderson's principal instructiveness lies in his seeing and not seeing at the same time what was his crucial problem. Since he could see no "*mechanical* cause whatever" for the properties of those elements, he felt impelled to think of those three elements as a sort of non-evolutionary preparation, carefully designed, of course, for the purposes of a subsequent evolutionary process: "In truth this is the only explanation of the connection which is at present imaginable. For we have recognized a pattern in the properties of the elements and as a pattern this is only to be described in relation to the diversity of evolution." Had he reflected on what a pattern is for the purposes of a scientist, though not for those of a philosopher, he might not have found being put "face to face with the problem of Design [writ large]."[62]

Design certainly implies pattern. But the registering of patterns and of their interconnection need not necessarily be connected with a pondering on whether they were designed and for a purpose. Not seeing a mechanical cause, Henderson felt that he should repeat what proved to be the basic defect of Paley's argumentation. The latter took the absence of an ascertainable mechanical cause for a justification to invoke a divine designer. But just as Paley was mislead by his religious zeal, the no less religious zeal of agnosticism became Henderson's pitfall. Only the word teleology as a mere word should now be seen as a far less satisfactory resolution of a real problem than the word God even when He is unnecessarily invoked as an explanation.

The only mitigating circumstance in Henderson's case is the state of science around 1917 when he published his *The Order of Nature*, his last reflections on the subject. Although Bohr's theory of the hydrogen atom was by then four years old, the unfolding of its potentialities for chemistry was still in the future. In 1917 Einstein has just published the concluding memoir, dealing with cosmology, of his General Relativity. The finest implications of that memoir were not revealed until the discovery, in 1965, of the 3°K cosmic background radiation. The latter powerfully encouraged further work on the genesis of all elements and their compounds, inorganic and organic. The unexpected new turn which this gave to speculations about design and purpose will be taken up in the next chapter.

Chapter Four

ANTHROPIC ILLUSION

Some "Copernican" turns

Any first has an importance of its own and especially when it comes in a memorable setting. Such was the Congress of the International Astronomical Union in Cracow in 1973, the five-hundredth anniversary of Copernicus' birth. There astronomers heard for the first time of a topic that quickly drew much attention after Brandon Carter of Cambridge University had read his paper, "Large Number Coincidences and the Anthropic Principle in Cosmology."[1]

The first to use the expression, "anthropic principle,"[2] Carter was not the first to note that the universe must have shown from early on very special characteristics if life was to emerge eventually. Carter offered nothing essentially new as he argued that the age of the universe could not be less than the time needed for the production of carbon. The minimum age the universe must have on that basis had already been calculated by Robert H. Dicke of Princeton University. He did so in 1961 in a letter to *Nature* which contained the phrase: "It is well known that carbon is required to make physicists."[3]

The age in question has to be the sum of two time spans, both of the order of five to six billion years. Remarkably, this sum, or about twelve billion years, is of the same order of magnitude as the age of the universe calculated from its expansion. It takes five to six billion years for certain huge stars to become supernovae in whose interior alone can elements heavier than helium be "cooked." Again the same amount of time is needed for the next process which begins with the explosion of supernovae whereby the elements "cooked" in their interior are scattered into cosmic spaces. In the first phase the cosmic dust, rich in heavier elements (with carbon a chief among them), coalesces into second-generation stars, such as our sun, possibly with proto-planetary systems around them. In the second phase such systems may turn into planets with a biochemical evolution similar to the one exemplified by the latest stage of our earth.

The physical characteristics which the universe must have if man is to emerge will be taken up later. Then special attention will also be given to Dicke's tacit inference that if there is carbon, there would be human beings as well. For the moment let it be noted that the "carbon therefore man" principle can but discredit whatever special position man may appear to have in the universe. Supernovae, the source of carbon, are not restricted to any part of the universe, let alone to a nook-and-cranny of it, such as the "cosmic neighborhood" or our solar system.

This should lead us straight back to that Cracow Congress of 1973, or Copernicus Symposium II.[4] Copernicus was mentioned there only as the one who had originated the "Copernican principle," about which Carter stated right at the outset that his paper was a reaction against "exaggerated subservience" to it.[5] According to Carter's first comment on that principle "Copernicus taught us the very sound lesson that we must not assume gratuitously that we occupy a privileged *central* position in the Universe." While Copernicus' writings contain no such "teaching," it has been customarily attributed to him in various publications on the anthropic principle.[6] They contain ample justification of Carter's second comment: "Unfortunately there has been a strong (not always subconscious) tendency to extend this [alleged teaching of Copernicus] to a most questionable dogma to the effect that our situation cannot be privileged in any sense."

This sweeping denial of a privileged position for man in any sense has, as one may expect, been reached in more than one step. The steps were not so much some major feats of astronomy as the reflections on them by astronomers not too careful about their own philosophizing. Non-astronomer philosophers readily followed suit. Not that Copernicus had given them any encouragement. When through Copernicus the earth, and with is man, was demoted from the center of the Ptolemaic universe, man could still retain some sense of centrality and enjoy with it the sense of purpose which such a position could, rightly or wrongly, generate. The sun and the solar system were the very center of the universe of Copernicus who, as will be seen shortly, found that configuration most expressive of that supreme purpose which is grasped by intelligent creatures whenever they recognize the Creator's glory.

Quite similar was the perspective of Kepler, the greatest among pre-Galilean Copernicans. In fact Kepler found the finite Copernican universe a cozily purposeful arrangement. He defended its finitude with an ingenious argument against Bruno's view that our sun was just one of myriads and, indeed, of an infinite number of suns. As Kepler rightly noted, the universe, as imagined by Bruno, had to look essentially the same from any point. This, however, could not be the case as long as one reasoned on the basis of astronomical data available around 1600 or so. By taking

two bright stars, visually close to one another, in the belt of
Orion, Kepler could claim that the sky had to appear to an
observer located on either of them as a "continuous sea of
immense stars, touching on one another as far as the vision
[of that observer] was concerned."[7]

The argument had, for Kepler, a bearing far beyond the
refutation of the idea of an infinite homogeneous universe.
According to Kepler the "insanely philosophizing sect" led
by "the unfortunate Bruno" pushed "astronomy into immensity" while "disrupting all places and regions." Kepler
rightly sensed that Copernicus was good for Bruno only
inasmuch as the heliocentric system seemed to destroy the
Aristotelian doctrine of natural places as so many targets of
purposeful motion. To vindicate purpose "astronomy was
to be impelled to return into its very confines. For certainly
nothing good was to be gained by vagabonding through
that infinity."[8]

The argument of Kepler, who was not enough of a philosopher to realize that no quantitative considerations, however
scientific, can substantiate purpose, did not retain too long
its apparently powerful validity. Within a few years Galileo's
telescope revealed the existence of many times more stars in
the sky than the 2000 or so visible to the naked eye. Even if
the sphere of the fixed stars was not thereby necessarily
abolished, its width had to appear much larger than Kepler's
estimate of it, a few thousand miles, a rather thin ground to
support an argument cutting through an immense, even if
not yet a strictly infinite, universe.

Kepler might have scored far better against Bruno had he
focused on Bruno's work, *La cena de le ceneri* or *The Ash
Wednesday Supper*,[9] a rank exploitation of Copernicus' system on behalf of a pantheistic infinity. More than ten years
before Kepler worked out his astronomical argument on
behalf of purpose, Bruno's pretensions of expertise about
Copernicus had burned to mere ashes. This happened when

some Oxonian scholars exposed Bruno's failure to understand some technical points in Copernicus' book in the
course of a debate which Bruno set up on an Ash Wednesday
of all days. It may, of course, be true that had Copernicus
lived to read the first treatise on his system, Bruno's *Ash
Wednesday Supper*, he would have bought up all copies and
destroyed them.[10] Yet questions about purpose, individual
or cosmic, would still have demanded the answers of philosophy and not of astronomy.

Such markedly philosophical questions and all too often
hardly philosophical answers given to them did not fail to
appear in the astronomical literature as the Copernican principle found its next astronomical perspective. This came
with the discovery of the cause of the visual appearance of
the Milky Way. To be sure, the sun still could appear to be
safely in the center of the Milky Way galaxy, but it was
quickly guessed that nebulous stars may also be galaxies,
that is, lentil-shaped vast agglomerations of stars. The center of those agglomerations could be everywhere and their
circumference nowhere. Did this new order of things seem
to embody some purpose?

To the three discoverers of the cause of the visual appearance of the Milky Way the answer seemed to be positive
though in widely differing sense. Johann Heinrich Lambert, the only self-educated and the most scientific among
the three, found some broader purpose in the prospect of
interstellar travel that would turn all humans into astronomers.[11] Thomas Wright took each star in each galaxy for an
abode of eternal reward or punishment.[12] In his much over-
rated youthful cosmological work,[13] Immanuel Kant took
the view that an infinite number of galaxies, evolving,
dying and re-emerging through infinite space and time,
bespoke that purpose which was the self-revelation of God's
infinite perfection.

Those attentive to young Kant's implicit claim that the
Creator could but create the universe as imagined by Kant,

had to be suspicious. They were justified when there appeared the second edition of Kant's *Critique of Pure Reason*
with its famous preface. There Kant claimed nothing less
than that his philosophical system codified what the Copernican turn meant to convey in the parlance of science: Only
when man's mind dictates to the universe will the latter
yield its secrets. [14] One wonders how many present-day
astronomers realize the extent to which they have become a
mere echo of Kant as they give their explanation of the
anthropic principle. Here let it be merely recalled that as
Kant further unfolded the implications of the epistemology
of the *Critique*, he made no longer any secret of his chief
message that Man, writ large, was his very own purpose. [15]

That galaxies were indeed lentil-shaped congeries of very
large number of stars was first verified by Herschel whose
giant telescopes revealed nebulae by the tens of thousands.
Herschel had, however, no means of estimating the size of
those nebulae that appeared particularly numerous around
the galactic poles when celestial photography came into its
own in the closing decades of the 19th century. Partly because of this our Milky Way could be taken for a much larger
stellar system than the other nebulae. Thus by the end of the
19th century, our Milky Way stood for many as the main
body in the "visible" universe which was believed to be
surrounded by an invisible infinity. [16]

Such a dichotomist if not plainly schizophrenic view of
the universe should have by itself exposed the temptation to
see something purposeful in the earth's central position in
the visible part of the universe. The temptation proved to be
a hollow lure when in the early 1920s, largely through the
work of Harlow Shapley, it had to be recognized that the
sun was not in the center of the Milky Way galaxy but in one
of its outer arms. The thinking in which purpose and spatial
position were intimately connected received its final blow
when shortly afterwards the Andromeda nebula turned out
to be a stellar system similar in size to the Milky Way. Soon

the Milky Way was spoken of as merely one of milliards of similar galaxies.

This was not, however, the last phase of those so-called Copernican turns. The very same 1970s that heard Carter enunciate the anthropic principle, also saw developments that constituted two further phases. One consisted in the unfolding of the logical consequences of the inflationary theory. First proposed as a solution of questions connected with the early history of the universe, such as its high degree of homogeneity and its horizon problem, the statistical nature of the theory invited a statistical approach to the universe itself. This meant that instead of one universe one had to talk of a very large number of "universes." The same logic further demanded that instead of one set of physical laws and constants, valid over the entire physical realm, a very large number of such sets be assumed so that each "universe" might have its own set of laws and constants. So was our universe, until then the Universe itself, demoted to the rank of just one of innumerable universes.

The other phase consisted in new-fangled speculations about forms of life (and intelligence) based on elements other than carbon, silicon in particular. If, however, life (and in particular intelligent life) could in principle be tied to any of the chemical elements, it could make but little sense to speak of individual human purpose. Even the purpose of a carbon-based mankind could not be taken for more than a brief and isolated flash with no connection whatever to life forms elsewhere in cosmic immensities. So much for the logic of those "Copernican" turns as they ultimately lead to a demotion of man from centrality together with his consequent deprivation of a proper sense of purpose.

The principle of Copernicus
What Copernicus would have thought of such purposeless vistas unfolded from the initial Copernican turn can easily

be guessed by anyone attentive to his very words. Copernicus might indeed be tempted to make a huge pyre of all writings whose authors celebrate in his name those purposeless vistas. Were he to take a less activist stance, he would plead for philosophical resignation. He would point out that no more than a philosopher does a man of science have control over what is made of his ideas. If he suspected some rank distortions to be made eventually of his ideas, they related to matters other than purpose. In defending the rationality of the heliocentric system in the Introduction of *De Revolutionibus* he may have thought of Luther's fulminations against the "madness" of putting the earth in motion.[17]

Copernicus may have also thought of efforts to turn him into a revolutionary thinker either in the scientific or in the philosophical sense. In both respects he had the consciousness of being a conservative mindful of broader purposes.[18] As to science, he was steeped in the past, remote and recent. His geometrical formalism was largely identical with the one codified by Ptolemy. He heavily relied on the Parisian tradition of impetus theory, first proposed by Buridan and Oresme, two hundred years earlier, as he coped with the dynamical problems posed by the twofold motion of the earth.[19] As to philosophy, he was a conservative above all in looking with utmost calm and confidence on the new world picture. Its coherence meant for him, as he put it in the dedication of his immortal book to Pope Paul III, that the universe could really be taken for a whole, worthy of "the Best and Most Orderly Workman of all."[20]

If one is to find a principle in Copernicus' thinking, it is this cosmic wholeness. This principle, so germane to having a sense of purpose, came through strongly in his book's very first paragraph:

> For who, after applying himself to things which he
> sees established in the best order and directed by divine

ruling, would not through diligent contemplation of
them and through a certain habituation be awakened to
that which is best and would not wonder at the Artificer of all things, in Whom is all happiness and every
good? For the divine Psalmist surely did not say gratuitously that he took pleasure in the workings of God
and rejoiced in the works of His hands, unless by
means of these things as by some sort of vehicle we
are transported to the contemplation of the highest
Good.[21]

Clearly, Copernicus offered much more than a stylistic cli-
ché if Alexandre Koyré, hardly a friend of the supernatural,
felt it proper to describe him as a "bon catholique."[22]
At any rate, Copernicus did not see a mere coincidence in
the fact that the fiery sun was in the center. He took it for an
evidence of design. He did not take it for a mere coincidence
that the heliocentric "correlation binds together so closely
the order and magnitudes of all the planets and of their
spheres or orbital circles and the heavens themselves that
nothing can be shifted around in any part of them without disrupting the remaining parts and the universe as a
whole."[23]
　　Nor did Kepler see a mere coincidence in his own finding
that those distances could be reproduced by putting inside
one another the five perfect solids in a specific order.[24] What
he really felt about that order was best expressed in a letter
of his to Maestlin, his former teacher in Tubingen, who had
helped reading the proofs of the *Mysterium cosmographicum*:

> May God make it happen that my happy speculation
> should fully exert everywhere among reasonable men
> the effect which I tried to achieve by the publication,
> namely, that belief in the creation of the world be
> strengthened through this incidental aid, that the Cre-
> ator's thought be recognized in its very nature, and

that his inexhaustible wisdom may shine each day
more brightly.[25]

Had Copernicus and Kepler used the word coincidence,
they would have used it in the sense that two or several
factors coincided in a manner suggestive of a design imposed from outside.

Large-number coincidences
Coincidence taken in that sense was not the thrust of Carter's paper which begins with a discussion of large-number
coincidences. The paper's deeper significance, not noted so
far, lies elsewhere. The first appearance in it of the expression "anthropic principle" is tied to an evaluation of cosmic
design that can but make illusory any talk about purpose,
cosmic as well as individual. This inner connection and how
it became spelled out as further work was done on the
anthropic principle is the chief subject matter of this chapter.

The start of that process, or Eddington's speculations
about dimensionless combinations of basic constants of
physics,[26] may in itself appear but an innocent interest in
numerology. There was no harm in his looking in coat-
rooms for the peg 137.[27] Contrary to his hopes, the atomic
fine-structure constant did not turn out to be a fraction with
an integer (137) in its denominator. Eddington's fondness
for that number should appear very different when seen as a
part of his penchant to derive from a priori considerations
the major quantitative features of the universe.[28] Apriorism,
when cultivated consistently, never fails to invite solipsism,
a stance that excludes a purpose propelling the subject beyond itself. Man should indeed seem trapped in himself for
no purpose if Eddington was right about modern physics. It
achieved nothing more, so he claimed, than making man see
his own footprints in tracing out ever more intricate patterns
of physical reality.[29]

Idealism, let alone solipsism, was not in the forefront when, shortly after Eddington, Dirac focused attention on three additional dimensionless numbers, all expressible as functions of powers of 40. That the agreement with theory is but roughly approximate is, of course, characteristic of cosmological speculations in which a difference of one or two orders of magnitude may not necessarily create a major problem. Those four numbers, together with the one particularly dear to Eddington, were

1. α_G or the gravitational fine structure constant or $Gm_p{}^2/hc \approx 5 \times 10^{-39}$, where G is the constant of gravitation, m_p the mass of proton, c is the speed of light, and h is Planck's quantum of action divided by 2π

2. α or the atomic fine structure constant or $2\pi e^2/hc \approx 1/137 \approx 10^{-2}$ where e is the electron's charge

3. T or the Hubble-age of the universe as included in the ratio $Tm_p c/h \approx 10^{42}$

4. M/m_p or the ratio of the mass M of the universe to the mass m_p of the proton, or $\approx 10^{80} \approx (10^{40})^2$

Subsequently, Dirac built around these four numbers a cosmology whose essence is that all physical constants vary as -1, 0, 1, and 2 powers of time.[30]

More than twenty years later Dicke found fault with Dirac's theory on the ground that on its basis there is but a small a priori probability for the present choice of T, that is, the actual age or time scale of the universe. Dicke's purpose was to show exactly the opposite, namely, the very high a priori probability for the actual value of T. Idealism was not, of course, overtly present in Dicke's statement that "T is not permitted to take one of the enormous range of values, but is somewhat limited by the biological requirements to be met during the epoch of man."[31] Nor should his next statement, already quoted, about the need for carbon to make physicists, be readily taken for a declaration of idealism. The same is true of his further statement that "T is not a 'random choice' from a wide range of possible choices, but is limited by the criteria for the existence of physicists."[32]

Cosmic fine-tuning

The limitations as pointed out by Dicke do not need to mean more than that organic biological life is part and parcel of the complex which is the physical universe. Since life in turn is a very special physico-chemical construct, the evolutionary universe too had to be very specifically tuned from its start to give rise to living organisms. Strikingly instructive details have been worked out about that fine-tuning during the last two decades. They all have for their starting point those dimensionless numbers.

Taken in themselves those numbers are not particularly striking insofar as they relate to the present state of the universe. Thus the gravitational coupling constant indicates a mass density, one atom per cubic meter, that may appear trivial in itself. Quite different is the case when that density is traced back to the earliest stages of the universe where it had to have an enormously high value. Its dilution to its very low present-day value had to be controlled by most specific factors. Thus, if gravity had been stronger by one part in 10^{40}, the universe would have long ago undergone a catastrophic collapse instead of a systematic expansion. Again, if the strength of the initial explosion, or Big Bang, had been different by one part in 10^{60}, the universe would have taken on a very different evolutionary course.

All these inconceivably fine tunings represent the coordination of at least two factors, gravitational force and temperature. Similar tunings of other physical forces too have been noted. One of them relates to the ratio of the combined masses of proton and electron to the mass of neutron. If that ratio had been slightly less, hydrogen atoms would become unstable and the sun would have long ago faded. Again a slightly different ratio of the respective strengths of the electromagnetic and nuclear forces would prevent the formation in supernovae of that very element carbon, which is the mainstay of organic life as we know it. Further, a mere five percent decrease in the strength of nuclear force would prevent the formation of deuterium which has a key role in the nuclear chain reaction within the sun and makes it possible for the sun to become a stable, long-lived star. As to neutrinos, the lightest of all fundamental particles, if their mass had been ten times larger than their actual value, or 10^{-34}kg, they would have, because of their very large number, caused a gravitational collapse of the universe.

All these primordial fine-tunings have left sharp traces of which the ones relating to the production of carbon are particularly telling. Details of those tunings became an avidly pursued research topic following the discovery of the $3°K$ cosmic background radiation. Information about the latter was not necessary for spotting fine-tunings in nuclear interaction that make possible the production of carbon in sufficient quantities. The particular mechanism, or the almost simultaneous collision of 3 helium (He^4) nuclei, should seem in itself a most improbable and inefficient affair. Furthermore, the collision of two such nuclei, which is a far more probable event, results in a short-lived beryllium (Be^8). Clearly, the chances are very small that a third He^4 nucleus should hit that Be^8 in the exceedingly short appropriate time. Also, the incoming He^4 must have a very special energy if its collision with Be^8 should result in carbon (C^{12}).

Fortunately, the average internal temperature of a stable star, such as our sun, appears to be finely tuned for turning that most unlikely event into a most likely occurrence. Through that temperature the very same special energy (7.656 Mev) is conveyed to the third He^4 as it hits Be^8 which is also a strong resonance level in C^{12}. There is still a further aspect to that fine-tuning so important for the eventual production of living organisms, all of them carbon based. Many of them are heavily dependent on oxygen which is produced when a He^4 nucleus hits C^{12}. Luckily, a strong resonance level in O^{16} lies safely below the thermal energy of its constituents so that the production of O^{16} will not unduly deplete the carbon atoms already on hand.

Surprised, though not by joy

This very special form of fine-tuning of resonance levels with the surrounding stellar temperature is not without an element of surprise. Joy was not mixed with Fred Hoyle's surprise when he first noted that strange resonance level in the mid-1950s. A professed atheist, Hoyle could not deny that common sense made it almost impossible not to see some "put up job" behind that resonance. Or to quote his very words:

> If you wanted to produce carbon and oxygen in roughly equal quantities by stellar nucleosynthesis, these are the two levels you would have to fix, and your fixing would have to be just about where these levels are actually found to be. . . . A commonsense interpretation of the facts suggests that a superintellect has monkeyed with physics, as well as chemistry and biology, and that there are no blind forces worth speaking about in nature.[33]

The superintellect evoked by Hoyle has some resemblance to a "creator" often invoked by over-eager divines. They expect that "creator" to do what the known laws of physics, working "blindly," that is automatically, as must all laws of physics, are unable to achieve. Such a "creator" has periodically been dislodged from the gaps of knowledge that are quickly filled as science progresses. It is now clear that the specifics of the carbon-oxygen synthesis are a straight consequence of a primordial fine-tuning. There, of course, physicists still have to regard as independent about half a dozen factors, such as the gravitational constant, the charge of the electron, the mass of quarks, the value of Planck's quantum, the speed of light, and the strength and range of nuclear force.

It is most likely that through further research some of these factors would soon be reduced to another, more fundamental factor. But in that process the new factor will not cease to be sharply specific. Nor will any success along those lines weaken the very specific physico-chemical internal-external conditions that are necessary for the existence of higher forms of life. Again, the vastly increasing knowledge of the physical evolution of the universe will only make even more specific the connection between the earliest and very specific stages of the universe and the present stage, which includes man, the highest form of organic life. The physicist will never cease spotting in the universe very sharp specificities. They should prompt him to consider the possibility whether they are not due to a superintellect who, instead of continually "monkeying" with the universe, has designed it in the first place along most specific lines. Some physicists may even distinctly rejoice in that perspective that carries them from physics into metaphysics. Most of them prefer to get stuck in physics.

Before taking a look at the variety of responses given by physicists as they ponder the ultimate cause of cosmic fine-tuning, one more instance of it should be recalled. It relates to the 3°K cosmic radiation which has the characteristics of a black-body radiation and therefore is isotropic and homogeneous. It can easily be shown that if the early universe had been anisotropic, much excess heat would have been generated within it. Such heat, by exerting a strong radiation pressure, would have prevented the formation of galaxies and consequently the formation of stars that can evolve only within galaxies. This in turn would have forestalled the formation of planetary systems that can form only around stable and single stars such as our sun.

Yet even with an isotropic start, the process of expansion might have generated in the long run enough anisotropy to foreclose the formation of long-lived galaxies. There alone can evolve supernovae necessary for the subsequent formation of stable stars such as our sun. As C. B. Collins and S. W. Hawking showed in 1973,[34] the universe would have remained isotropic for a sufficiently long time if its rate of expansion had almost exactly matched the contrary pull of the force of gravitation. Therefore the difference of these two factors working in the opposite sense must have had from the very start a value very close to zero. Had that value been noticeably less than zero, a too vigorous expansion would have prevented gravitational clumping and the subsequent formation of galaxies. Had that difference been noticeably larger than zero, the expanding universe would have quickly collapsed upon itself.

In sum, once the very specific physical conditions, that are present in higher biological organisms, man in particular, are looked upon in the broad ensemble of the physical evolution of the universe, a most momentous possibility looms large. It consists in the perception that the universe may have been tailor-made for the emergence of man.

Stances and footworks

Faced with that possibility one can adopt three very different stances. One may invoke genuine theism according to which the specificity of the universe can only be explained

as the Creator's choice among an infinite number of possi-
bilities, all very specific. The physical specificities accumulated by research on the anthropic principle contribute
powerfully to the cosmological argument which rests on
two foundations, both strongly supported by the best in
20th-century scientific cosmology.[35] One of them is that
cosmologists must, by their research, if not by their dicta,
take the universe for an intellectually most respectable notion. In fact they must take the universe for that all-
encompassing reality which it must be by its very etymology. Kantians of whatever variety have no chance in the
court of modern scientific cosmology with their basic claim
that the universe, to quote Kant's very contention in the
Critique of Pure Reason, is a bastard product of the metaphysical cravings of the intellect.[36]

Yet those specificities, even when accumulated by scientific research on the anthropic principle, do not by themselves amount to the cosmological argument. They do not
even constitute what is often called the design argument.
They certainly do not provide the philosophical considerations underlying the theistic perspective about cosmic purpose. There God's choice is looked upon as determined by
His aim for creating a universe as an abode for man. Man's
purpose, in that perspective, is to recognize his Creator and
find thereby his fulfillment in that trust which a Creator,
worthy of that name, is bound to generate.

Such is, however, a viewpoint very alien to the thinking
of most of those who have done scientific work on the
anthropic principle. They for the most part take another
stance which occasionally manifests itself in sarcastic remarks, similar to the one uttered by Hoyle. The stance
allows at most the kind of philosophical reflection which is
on hand when one characterizes the anthropic principle as
"thought-provoking." It is not, however, meant to be the
kind of "provocation" that evokes the existence of that Being who is the Creator of the universe.

The third stance consists in claiming that it is the observer who makes the universe what it actually is. The anthropic principle turns thereby into a radically anthropocentric and, in fact, most anthropomorphic proposition. Taken in that sense, the anthropic principle is the very opposite of the so-called "Copernican" principle. But when a false principle is replaced by an even more misleading one, an intellectual disaster may be in the making. In fact, as will be seen shortly, the disaster is nothing less than a complete loss of purpose, individual and cosmic.

Purposelessness, as camouflaged in sheer anthropocentrism, may not seem to be implied in typical comments on the so-called weak form of the anthropic principle. The latter is a registration of startling numerical coincidences and of their connection with the minimum age of the universe as demanded by man's existence. One of those typical comments is the one offered by Carter: "What we can expect to observe [in the universe at large] must be restricted by the conditions necessary for our presence as observers."[37] No less purely scientific, when taken at face value, is the comment of J. D. Barrow and F. J. Tipler:

> The observed values of all physical and cosmological quantities are not equally probable but they take on values restricted by the requirement that there exist sites where carbon-based life can evolve and by the requirement that the Universe be old enough for it to have already done so.[38]

No treacherous philosophy raises overtly its ugly head in comments such as that "our existence puts strong limits on the ratio of photons to protons in the universe,"[39] or that "the possibility of life as we know it evolving in the Universe depends on the values of a few basic physical constants—and is in some respects remarkably sensitive to their numerical values."[40] Quite innocent in itself may be the answer, "because we exist," which Collins and Hawking gave to the question why the universe is so isotropic.[41]

Yet, if one looks carefully at the lines which in the paper of Collins and Hawking precede this answer of theirs, one can see a treacherous philosophy lurking in the background. According to Collins and Hawking, to the question about the isotropy of the universe "the most attractive answer would seem to come from . . . the idea that there is a very large number of universes, with all possible combinations of initial data and values of the fundamental constants."[42] Life then would arise only in that universe in which the constant of gravitation allows for a good measure of isotropy in an expanding universe.

Most readers (all well-trained physicists) of that paper did not need special information about the ultimate source of the idea of a very large number of universes. The source is the Copenhagen interpretation of quantum mechanics which is a mixture of brazen pragmatism and rank idealism. The former ingredient inspired the fallacious inference, "what cannot be measured exactly cannot take place exactly."[43] It is on the basis of that fallacy that countless adepts of the Copenhagen interpretation claim the overthrow of ontological causality in nature. Rank idealism is the basis of another major claim of the Copenhagen camp, namely, that the act of observation produces physical reality. This claim has forced its champions into performing devious mental foot-work. It is aimed at creating the illusion that a scientist does not throw consistency to the winds as he commits himself to some sort of idealist philosophizing.

Advocates of the strong form of the anthropic principle are careful not to let their readers suspect the sinistrous perspective which their philosophical footwork performed about it should evoke. Once more Carter's paper may serve as a good starting point. According to him "the Universe (and hence the fundamental parameters on which it depends) must be such as to admit the creation of observers within it at some stage."[44] Since he did not mean a true creation of human intellects, his phrase could only conjure up the creation of the universe by observers produced by it.

The same idealist inversion of reality and its observation lurks behind the strong anthropic principle as proposed by J. Silk. Its context is his discussion of the sequence from primordial gravitational instability to giant clusters of galaxies, from there to stars and planets, and finally to planets that are habitable. According to him, "this unbroken chain is essential in a cognizable universe, and may therefore provide the key to understanding the significance of the fundamental dimensionless numbers of astrophysics and cosmology."[45] Silk's emphasis on cognizability should, on closer reflection, seem to be a mine loaded with the explosives of idealism. When one comes to such an unabashed physicist-champion of idealism as J. A. Wheeler, the mines are ready to explode. There can be no doubt as to the sense in which to take his answer, "because only so man can be," to the question of why the universe is as big as it is.[46] The same holds true of the real gist of his question: "Here is man, so what must the universe be?"[47]

Anthropic principle or anthropocentrism?
Of course, no physicist can be a consistent idealist as long as he has to work with instruments, some of them truly gigantic. Only the theoretical part of his work gives the physicist an illusory excuse for marketing his idealist philosophy as if it were a legitimate corollary of the best of science. Some physicists working on the anthropic principle yield to that illusion deliberately. Others fall for it almost unwittingly. The latter case is illustrated by B. J. Carr's account of the weak and strong versions of the anthropic principle.[48] His starting point is Dicke's assertion that the age of the universe must be of the same order of magnitude as the combined ages of a supernova and a stable star produced from its ashes. Such a life-span can be expressed as the product of α_G^{-1} and

the nuclear time-unit, $h/2\pi m_p c^3$, or the time 10^{-23}s necessary for light to traverse a proton. The stellar life-span in question is also of the same order of magnitude as the size which the universe has reached through its expansion during that time. The ratio of that size to the size of the atom has to be of the order of α/α_G or 10^{36}. Further, from the fact that the age of the universe is α_G^{-1} times the nuclear time-unit, it is possible to infer that the number of nucleons in the universe has to be $\alpha_G^{-2} \sim 10^{78}$, a figure that can be inferred on other grounds as well.

The starting point of this argument is the minimum time needed for the development of a stable star around which there can develop a planetary system with an earthlike planet within it. Such a planet is a basic condition for the evolution of organic life that culminates in a society doing atomic physics. Hence the argument's starting point is anthropic but only weakly so, because it assumes the numerical values of basic constants without predicting them.

In its strong form the argument predicts those very numerical values. This is done in two steps. One relates to the fact that planetary systems are feasible only around convective stars. Their mass lies below the critical mass above which stars, such as blue giants, become radiating. This critical value lies in the range which is about $\alpha^{-3/2}$ times the proton mass. Consequently, α_G has to be of the order of α^{20}. While the connective condition gives only the ratio of α and α_G, their actual values can be inferred from a condition of consistent quantum field theory. The latter is possible only if α^{-1} is of the order of $\ln \alpha_G^{-1}$. From this follow the values $\alpha \sim 10^{-2}$ and $\alpha_G \sim 10^{-40}$ as actually observed or rather calculated on empirical grounds. Carr then concludes: "In view of the simple dependencies on α and α_G of the different time-scales of structure in the universe, this suggests that the appearance of our universe is determined, not merely in part, but to a very large degree by our existence."[49]

Carr's conclusion is not necessarily an endorsement of an idealist philosophy which leads to the proposition: I think therefore the universe exists and exists exactly in the form dictated by my thought processes. But as an expression of the strong anthropic principle, Carr's conclusion invites the suspicion that it shares in the idealism of customary formulations of the principle. The suspicion is further strengthened by what is usually implied by self-consistent quantum field theory. Such a theory has very close ties with the Copenhagen interpretation of quantum mechanics. Within that interpretation absolute primacy is given to subjective observation over objective things. Further, a random character is assigned to all physical events because the method of quantum mechanics whereby they are investigated is strictly statistical.

That statistical principle was made much of by J. A. Wheeler in his efforts to dissipate whatever might be objective in the anthropic principle. According to that objectivity the universe is tailor-made for that rational being which is man though not made such by his observations of it. As a rational being man can be but prompted by the physico-chemical specificity of his existence to raise questions about its very purpose. As will be seen later, those questions may have very pressing aspects.

It is precisely those aspects that are eliminated by Wheeler's theory according to which our universe is merely one of an infinite number of universes, all different in their physical characteristics. [50] They are successively realized when the actual laws of physics cease to be applicable. This happens whenever the universe, after having gone through its expansion, completes its contraction into a superdense state. In such a picture the actual universe, tailored to man, becomes, together with the human intellect, a momentary flash along an infinitely extended time parameter. The latter is an endless chain of infinitely numerous other universes none of which can be specifically known from the platform provided by this universe. Within this scientifically coated cavorting in ignorance, man's knowledge, however vast and creative, will amount to a teasing exercise void of any abiding purpose.

The other tenet of the Copenhagen interpretation of quantum mechanics, or the absolute primacy of the observer over things observed, was carried to its logical extreme in the so-called multiworld theory.[51] In it the present universe becomes a function of the quantum-mechanical theory of measurement in which the act of observation makes a particular wave-function "collapse" into reality. The observed universe is therefore one of a countless number of other universes, all owing their existence to their being observed. Clearly, the theory destroys the oneness of our own universe because from the earth alone it is observed by countless observers.

Apart from this brazenly solipsistic consequence of the theory, it is open to strictly scientific objections as well. For one, any act of measurement assumes that the measuring device and the one who measures with it are "outside" the ensemble to be measured. This objection should seem to have a particular force in reference to the universe of which the observer and his instruments necessarily form a part. Further, on purely statistical grounds it is far more probable for a single galaxy (sufficient for producing convective stars) to develop than for a large number of similar galaxies which is the actual case.

A telltale loss of purpose

There is another objection which relates to the question of purpose. Although essentially philosophical, the objection appears on occasion in the context of scientific presentations of the anthropic principle. This only shows that philosophical points can be very pressing, indeed well-nigh inescapable. The following version of the objection is from a book, tellingly entitled *The Accidental Universe*, by P. C. W. Davies, lecturer in mathematics, King's College, London. "Can we really believe," he asked, "in limitless number of universes, created but never observed, serving no purpose except to ensure that, somewhere among the vast array of wasted worlds, will be the occasional cognizable accident?" Explanation of the large-number coincidences "by invoking an infinity of useless universes" appeared to him nothing short of "carrying excess baggage to the extreme." Yet, however objectionable this "scientific" situation could appear to Davies, it was not so objectionable as to keep him from countering it with an unspecified agnosticism: "The alternatives—a universe deliberately created for habitation, or one in which the very special structure is simply regarded as a pure miracle—are also open to philosophical challenge."[52]

Such is, of course, the voice of modern scientific man's carefully cultivated uncertainty about matters philosophical. Careful as that voice may be, all too often it is not careful enough to admit the futility of defending that uncertainty, hardly distinguishable from superficial agnosticism. Its customary tactic is to throw the burden of proof on those who press the champions of the anthropic principle on an inescapable consequence of its unphilosophical presentations. That consequence is nothing less than the allegedly inevitable emergence of intelligent beings everywhere in the universe.

The issue is far more deeply philosophical than to be disposed of by calculations of the very high improbability that our earth should have long ago been contacted by extrasolar and perhaps extragalactic civilizations if these existed at all.[53] While physics can be very useful in helping one grasp the utter unfeasability of interstellar travel, it can never present its actual progress as the very last stage that can be achieved by it. More importantly, physics, however advanced, remains wholly impotent in tackling far more important questions about contact with extrasolar civilizations. Physics is not about civilizations but about what civilizations can achieve in mastering mere matter. Only by advocating sheer materialism can one assume that just because there arose on earth a scientific civilization, it must also arise wherever there are suitable material conditions for life.

But is that very intelligence, which issues in civilization, scientific or not, really a product of mere matter? Further, is not there an eerie hint of something supra-material in the surprisingly very late rise of science in human history? For if science is a mere skill with tools, a view so dear to materialists,[54] why should it not have arisen among the ancient Hindus, Chinese, Egyptians, and Babylonians, or even long before their time? They all were great civilizations famed for certain technological feats, though they all failed to come up with science. Materialists still may find a semblance of support if science were a mere handling of quantities. In this case science should easily have had for its birthplace that Greece which was the cradle of logic and geometry. Yet, the Greeks of old conspicuously failed when it came to dealing with the quantitative aspects of the motion of things which is the real subject matter of exact science in all its branches.

The prevailing accounts, so heavily steeped in materialism (be it called pragmatism, operationism, and sociologism), of the rise of science in the West, cannot include a serious appreciation of a most non-materialist factor in that rise. The great breakthrough, Buridan's and Oresme's substantial anticipation of Newton's first law of motion, was due to their firm conviction in the creation of the universe out of nothing and in time.[55] Moreover, they owed this conviction of theirs to their belief in the Incarnation of a truly Divine Logos. This belief gave them confidence in the full logicality of the universe[56] and protected them against the lure of pantheism which was the ultimate cause of the stillbirths of science in all ancient cultures.

The anthropic principle will invite a skirting around its most crucial scientific aspects as long as it does not include an honest discourse about belief in that *anthropos* which God himself deigned to become. That belief as an empirical fact of cultural history on earth cannot be ignored, without doing injustice to the empirical method, if one tries on its basis to evaluate the chances of the rise of science on our earth. Hostility to that belief still does not dispense one of the duty of being consistent when the same estimate is made on the basis of Darwinian evolutionary theory. In its terms one cannot expect a repetition in another planetary system of the course which life has taken on earth. One cannot even assume on that basis the existence of hominoids elsewhere in the universe. Much less may one assume on the same basis that higher forms of life, physically very different from man, would have a mental life similar to his. Yet it is this identity which is assumed, though with no justification, by advocates of SETI, or Search for Extra-Terrestrial Intelligence.[57]

The real issue about the credibility of SETI is not whether one is an optimist or a pessimist with respect to the ability of science to discover things far beyond anything one may dream of. The real issue is consistency in thinking. Here the believer in the Creator is in a far more advantageous position than the materialist. Equally true, of course, for both is the gist of a story told by the British physicist, Arthur Schuster, as President of the British Association at its meeting in Manchester in 1915:

> An American friend, who possessed a powerful telescope, one night received the visit of an ardent politician. It was the time of a Presidential election, Bryan and Taft being the opposing candidates, and feeling ran high. After looking at clusters of stars and other celestial objects, and having received answers to his various questions, the visitor turned to my friend:
> 'And all these stars I see,' he asked, 'what space in the heaven do they occupy?'
> 'About the area of the moon.'
> 'And you tell me that every one of them is a sun like our own?'

'Yes.'

'And that each of them may have a number of planets circulating round them like our sun?'

'Yes.'

'And that there may be life on each of those planets?'

'We cannot tell for certain, but it is quite possible that there may be life on many of them.'

After pondering for some time, the politician rose and said: 'It does not matter after all whether Taft or Bryan gets in.'[58]

The moral of this story rests on the presupposition of the identity or universality of the intellect, as we know it in one very specific form, throughout the universe. It is there that the customary formulations of the anthropic principle merely beg the question. And precisely because of this they offer no help with respect to the even more important question of what is the purpose of a universe that is tailor-made for producing an intellect embodied in man. While man's very sanity depends on an unambiguous answer to that question, much of the literature on the anthropic principle is expressive of an intellectual malaise. It plagues all those who expect from science answers to questions which it cannot even raise, provided it remains consistent with its method.

Continued preoccupation, if not infatuation, with the anthropic principle may indeed turn its illusions into the kind of disillusion that tormented one of Anatole France's scientist heroes: "I hate science for having loved it too much, after the manner of voluptuaries who reproach women with not having come up to the dream they formed of them."[59] This inner logic has not failed to take its toll on major 20th-century philosophers as they aimed at securing purpose by taking some scientific idea for their starting point. They all lacked, as the next chapter will show, the elementary insight well known to a very successful cricket captain that it is always the first move that decides the outcome of the contest.[60]

Chapter Five

HOLLOW METAPHORS

Purpose and some philosophies
Twenty years ago Herbert Feigl came to lecture at my University.[1] For his starting point he took a once famous address by Emil Du Bois Reymond on what man can never know with certainty.[2] As a logical positivist, Feigl identified certainty with its kind that can be obtained with the methods of exact science. When questions could be raised I asked him whether he could know for certain that he had come for a purpose and whether that purpose had a sense similar to the one in which Socrates took it in a memorable way.[3] No, was his unhesitating answer to the second part of my question. As to its first part, he was obviously taken aback. After some hesitation he candidly admitted that, in view of what he had argued in his lecture, he had no right to know for certain that he had a purpose in coming.

In the late 1960s logical positivists, in the United States at least, seemed certain of having achieved their purpose of banishing any and all reference to purpose from intellectually respectable discourse. They succeeded in giving widespread credence in American academia to their claim that only a subjective, that is, non-scientific status, could be accorded to kinds of knowledge similar to the one of knowing the purpose of one's actions. The relatively few logical positivists left on the scene still have to perceive that what they call "subjective" knowledge remains the very basis of that "objective" knowledge which they equate with science.

Ironically, it was through their "scientific" contempt for such fundamental realities as the sense of always acting for some purpose that logical positivists forged a boomerang with which one can deal a potentially destructive blow at science by aiming first at the sense of purpose. The proof of this is that the best accommodation which logical positivists could afford for science never amounted to something more purposeful than the Procrustean bed of physicalism.[4] Yet even those mindful of the inexorable working of logic could not easily foresee the eventual capitulation of Alfred J. Ayer, once the quasi-constitutional king of the British philosophical scene. To the question, posed to him in a BBC interview, as to what were the "real defects" of logical positivism, he answered: "Well, I suppose the most important of the defects was that nearly all of it was false."[5]

Existentialists have been just as unsuccessful in avoiding being trapped in a logical contradiction with respect to purpose. Clearly, if purpose is anything, it has to be a reality, even if purely subjective, that transcends momentary experiences, so many isolated individual or atomistic events that alone existed according to Sartre and other leading exitentialists. Still, they all persisted, not for hours but for years and decades, in their most purposive effort to prove that atomistic events were the sole reality. In so doing they merely showed the staggering extent to which intellectuals can be trapped in glaring inconsistencies, contrary to their very purpose.

The phenomenologists, still another major group among 20th-century philosophers, proved themselves to be in no more enviable a status concerning the question of purpose. As purpose is not a phenomenon, one's sense of acting for a purpose can ever become the object of phenomenological research. Whenever phenomenologists, or existentialists, or logical positivists talk about purpose, they contradict their very method. This is why they all have spoken of purpose in a furtive manner, or in dramatic metaphors. The latter, such as Camus' use of the story of Sisyphus,[6] can be very effective in distracting the reader from the fact that rhetoric, whatever its literary merits, becomes a hollow exercise when it tries to supplement plain logic.

No less informative with respect to the status of purpose should seem the sudden demise of Marxism, institutional and doctrinaire, which only two decades ago seemed to be the wave of the immediate and long-term future. From Lenin on, Marxist ideologues and political activists have not left a stone unturned in stirring up revolutionary zeal all over the globe. All that propaganda made, however, no sense if it was true that socio-economic conditions necessarily implied the advent of classless society. Hegelian logic, in which contradictions serve only the purpose of demonstrating the ease with which major conceptual roadblocks are being removed ("aufgehoben"), could alone assure confidence in the procedure.[7] Apart from its dubious foundations, Marxist revolutionary purpose should seem a particularly sorry affair in the late 1980s when institutionalized Marxism openly courts its major antagonist, Western capitalism. The latter, whatever its need for constraints which its principles cannot supply, has never failed to hold high the cultivation of purposes, however short-term and unenlightened.

Muslim revivalism is the only major revolutionary movement of the second half of the 20th century that shows no signs of losing its momentum. A reason for this may be that the Muslim creed underlying that revivalism implies a clear statement of purpose, a purpose transcending man. A proof of this is the conviction that self-sacrifice in Holy War automatically earns one eternal happiness in God's presence. It is not the purpose of this chapter to decide whether the Koran's emphasis on Allah's will and power leaves logical room for the only genuine human experience of purpose that includes a sense of true freedom. The sense of *kismet* or inexorable destiny, that pervades Muslim milieux, is giving chronic headache to progressive philosophers and writers with a Muslim background. They invariably see in a resolute parting with that sense the very key for bringing the Muslim world into the 20th century.[8]

Such a parting is an act in which free will and sense of purpose are intimately joined together. The union between the two has always been an essential part of the contribution which Christian philosophy can provide about purpose as a fundamental personal experience. That answer will be the topic of another chapter as well as the question of the extent to which that experience can be illusory or counterproductive. The remainder of this chapter would therefore be best devoted to a group of major 20th-century philosophers who put the reality of purpose in the center of their systems, though with a twist. They did so by taking their chief guidance and inspiration from science. They are also alike in relying heavily on key words that, on a closer inspection, should appear markedly metaphorical. Whether, as proofs or justification of purpose, those words have a solid sound or resonate with a hollow ring is the task of this chapter to show.

The purpose of élan vital

The first of those philosophers is Henri Bergson whose name will forever be associated with the term, *élan vital*. It is hardly a term germane to the exact sciences, or mathematics in particular, for which young Henri Bergson showed an outstanding talent. At the age of 17 he worked out an original solution to the problem of three circles, first posed by Pascal to Fermat. The result so impressed Adolphe Desboves, his mathematics teacher at the Lycée Condorcet, that he secured publication for it in the *Annales de mathématiques*. Desboves was crestfallen when young Bergson chose not to pursue mathematical studies after he had entered the Ecole Normale. "You might have become a mathematician," Desboves told his unusually gifted student, "now you become just a philosopher."[9]

At first Henri Bergson had no intention of turning into the kind of philosopher whom Desboves loathed, the philosopher who turns his back on science and delves in quasi-mystical speculations. Young Bergson eschewed Emile Boutroux who at the Ecole Normale taught a spiritualized form of Kantian rationalism. Rather he threw his lot with the mechanistic evolutionism of Herbert Spencer. Young Bergson soon became known among his classmates as a positivist in favor of materialism. A graphic proof of this was their reaction when the professor in charge of the library upbraided young Bergson, a student librarian, for leaving books scattered on the floor. "Monsieur Bergson, you see those books sweeping up the dirt; your librarian soul ought to be unable to endure it." Bergson's classmates howled: "Mais il n'a pas d'âme!"[10] Twenty-five years later Bergson startled the world with a book, *Evolution créatrice* and its claim that ultimately the evolving universe was nothing but a universal soul. There Bergson, a future Nobel-laureate in literature, offered a wealth of sparkling phrases about the striving of that cosmic soul, but remained very vague about the purpose of that striving and even more so about the individual's share in it.

The grand conclusion of the third chapter of that famous book shows this all too well. It contains in a condensed form all the glittering vacuity that Bergson could draw from his key philosophical doctrine, intuition, to illuminate purpose:

Such a doctrine does not only facilitate speculation; it gives us also more power to act and to live. For, with it, we feel ourselves no longer isolated in humanity, humanity no longer seems isolated in the nature that it dominates. As the smallest grain of dust is bound up with our entire solar system, drawn along with it in that undivided movement of descent which is materiality itself, so all organized beings, from the humblest to the highest, from the first origins of life to the time in which we are, and in all places as in all times, do but evidence a single impulsion, the inverse of the movement of matter, and in itself indivisible. All the living hold together, and all yield to the same tremendous push. The animal takes its stand on the plant, man bestrides animality, and the whole of humanity, in space and in time, is one immense army galloping beside and before and behind each of us in an overwhelming charge able to beat down every resistance and clear the most formidable obstacles, perhaps even death.[11]

Immortality for mankind did not mean for the author of *Creative Evolution* the kind of purpose which finds its fulfillment in the immortality of the individual. On individual immortality only some ambiguous phrases could be gleaned from Bergson's book. There Bergson spoke in the same breath both of the pre-existence of souls and also of their being continually created. Not, of course, through creation out of nothing, an idea which Bergson emphatically rejected as a pseudo-notion together with the idea of God who alone can create in the strict sense of that word. Consequently, souls in Bergson's perspective were "nothing else than the little rills into which the great river of life divides itself, flowing through the body of humanity."[12] Aristotle, Plotinus, and Spinoza, to say nothing of other far less respectable champions of pantheism, would have nodded.

That without personal immortality the purpose of mankind could be but a pleasing, though hollow, metaphor was
conveyed by Bergson as he brought to a close the second
chapter of his book. As in the case of the human soul, with
respect to mankind's emergence from the animal matrix too
he quickly took back what he had first seemed to offer. On
the one hand he extolled the leap from animal to man as
being so sudden and extraordinary "that, in the last analysis, man might be considered the reason for the existence
of the entire organization of life on our planet." But he
added in the same breath that "this would only be a manner
of speaking. There is, in reality, only a current of existence
and the opposing current; thence proceeds the whole evolution of life."[13]

That evolutionary life was for Bergson so full of possi-
bilities as to imply the emergence of life-forms based on
elements other than carbon. He conjured up anatomies totally different from those observable on earth. He did not
stop to ponder the problem of how sensory-motor mechanisms, very different from the terrestrial ones, could still
achieve an essentially similar result. Champions of the anthropic principle that implies infinite forms of life and
minds, offer but trite variations on Bergson's words: "It is
therefore probable that life goes on in other planets, in other
solar systems also, under forms of which we have no idea, in
physical conditions to which it seems to us, from the point
of view of our physiology, to be absolutely opposed."[14]

The problem implied in such vistas was both philosophical and scientific. Science offered no clues whatever about
those very different anatomies. As to philosophy, only a
rhetorical brand of it provided justification for speaking,
however charmingly, from both corners of one's mouth. In
both aspects Bergson's system could invite scathing and far
from unmerited criticisms. To the cutting rationalism of
Bertrand Russell, Bergson's praise of intuition amounted to

glib anti-intellectualism: "Intellect is the misfortune of man, while intuition is seen at its best in ants, bees, and Bergson."[15] As to the scientific merit of the *élan vital*, Julian Huxley put it tersely: "To say that biological progress is explained by the *élan vital* is to say that the movement of a train is 'explained' by an *élan locomotif* of the engine."[16]

Of course, neither Bertrand Russell nor Julian Huxley were the kind of thinkers who concern themselves much with ultimate evolutionary purpose. But compared with Bergson, both should seem sober realists in admitting the failure of naturalism when a more substantial purpose is to be found within a purely pragmatic and short-term perspective. Only four years before the publication of *Evolution créatrice* did Bertrand Russell come up with what has become his most often quoted utterance in which dismissal of Providence and of purpose went hand in hand:

> That man is the product of causes which had no prevision of the end they were achieving; that his origin, his growth, his hopes and fears, his loves and his beliefs, are but the accidental collocations of atoms; that no fire, no heroism, no intensity of thought and feeling, can preserve an individual life beyond the grave; that all the labours of the ages, all the devotion, all the inspiration, all the noonday brightness of human genius, are destined to extinction in the vast death of the solar system, and that the whole temple of Man's achievement must inevitably be buried beneath debris of a universe in ruins—all these things, if not quite beyond dispute, are yet so nearly certain that no philosophy which rejects them can hope to stand.[17]

The soaring prose of the author of *Creative Evolution* should seem most unrealistic when set against Julian Huxley's plain diction about the "blind and cruel blows of fate" that ultimately crush all personal lives. Nevertheless, the only real touch which Bergson could offer compares well, as will be seen, with the inanity of Julian Huxley's efforts to put those blows "in proper perspective."[18]

Compared with these blunt references to most serious and grim realities, their handling in *Creative Evolution* should seem sheer irresponsibility. In a book full of beautiful phrases, seriousness was absent when most needed. Bergson, who held physical immortality for a possibility, however remote, took up the topic of death only once and wrote it off with the remark that "it does not seem at all like a diminution of 'life in general,' or like a necessity which life submits to reluctantly."[19] Why should Bergson have worried about death, if "the universe was a machine for making gods,"[20] and if one was not to worry about the heat-death in store for the universe?

Such shallow optimism could find an enthusiastic reception only at a time when the promises of progress appeared unlimited, especially to the uninformed. A good portion of Bergson's overflowing audience consisted of gullible minds ready to fill the Opéra which once was proposed as the only large and decorous venue for his lectures. These, as if symbolically, came to an end in the early summer of 1914. A decade later Bergson's philosophy had for some time been one of the bloodless casualties of a War that claimed belief in progress as a chief of its cultural victims.

When Bergson came out in 1932 with *The Two Sources of Morality*, the reception was polite but unenthusiastic. Of course, it contained a very different Bergson. While religion, let alone Christianity, was invisible in *Creative Evolution*, Christianity now represented, especially with its doctrine and practice of love, the highest manifestation and purpose of life. Not that Bergson had given an unqualified vote to the idea of a transcendental God and of the immortality of the soul. How could he, as he held fast to the doctrine that all morality, including its highest or Christian mystical forms, was in essence biological.[21] Yet he was ready to admit that a "great part of this [mystical] activity is independent of the body." Moreover, he saw life beyond death as something "identical with that life into which, even here below, certain privileged souls insert themselves."[22]

While much of the philosophical world chose to ignore the new trend of Bergson's thought, leading Catholic thinkers, such as Maritain and Sertillanges, took a close look at it. Just as Maritain did not recoil from sharp criticism as he devoted his very first book to Bergson's philosophy as mainly embodied in the *Evolution créatrice*,[23] he could be most appreciative of the innermost aspirations animating the *The Two Sources*. They centered on soul and purpose:

> The fundamental theme of the *Two Sources* is the distinction and opposition between that which in moral life proceeds from *pressure* and that which proceeds from *attraction*. Pressure comes from social formations and from the law of fear . . . that seeks only to turn to the routine and ferocious automatism of matter. *Attraction* comes from . . . the propulsive force of the emotion which at once invading the soul, makes it free, because it awakens the soul to its most secret inner vitality.[24]

Bergson was not unreceptive either to Maritain's or to Sertillanges' appreciation of the new thrust of his thought. Bergson's most explicit request was honored when at his funeral the Père Sertillanges recited the Our Father, the prayer nowhere tainted with hollow rhetoric. Only his sympathies toward his fellow Jews prevented Bergson from formally attaching himself to Roman Catholicism. He died with firm belief in the existence of his soul, the sole pledge of lasting purpose.

A nisus with no target

No such metamorphosis of mind and soul took place in Samuel Alexander who readily acknowledged his debt to Bergson.[25] Bergsonian *élan vital* may be different only in name from that *nisus* with which Alexander's philosophy remains associated. Not that Alexander used the word *nisus* prominently in his major work, *Space, Time and Deity*, based on his Gifford Lectures delivered at the University of Glasgow in 1915. None of its many chapter-subdivisions is on *nisus*, a word which does not occur in the detailed index of that two-volume work. Only a year after its publication in 1920 did Alexander feel it necessary to explain himself on *nisus* in an article, "Spinoza and Time," which he considered an important appendage to his metaphysics.[26]

In *Space, Time and Deity* Alexander emphasized the grandiose though impersonal aspect of *nisus* while leaving undefined the ultimate conquest it was to bring about:

> There is a *nisus* in Space-Time which, as it has borne its creatures forward through matter and life to mind, will bear them forward to some higher level of existence. There is nothing in mind which requires us to stop and say this is the highest empirical quality which Time can produce from now throughout the infinite Time to come.[27]

In order to remain consistent, Alexander had to pour cold water on the warmth that would be generated by so grandiose a view. Mind, human mind, that is, he noted, "is only the last empirical quality which we who are minds happen to know." The sequel, "Time itself compels us to think of a later birth of Time," was at best a metaphor but not a firm handle on higher forms of life. Whatever the mind could conjure up beyond itself amounted to mere speculation. Certainly such was the case with the deity, which Alexander described as the supreme quality which "the universe is engaged in bringing forth." Only he could not say anything specific about it: "What that quality is we cannot know; for we can neither enjoy nor still less contemplate it. Our human altars still are raised to the unknown God."[28]

It would be futile to take Alexander to task for his agnosticism about God. Quite open to criticism should seem his continual reliance on the Universe writ large. As one who often referred to Kant and faulted him for setting Space over Time, Alexander should have come to grips with Kant's systematic slighting of the universe, the supreme product in Alexander's philosophical system. Had he confronted Kant's claim about the unreliability of the notion of the universe, the word universe might have entered the index of *Space, Time and Deity*. Authors of major monographs on Alexander's philosophy also ignored another strange, though revealing, feature in that book. There the universe is spoken of only in a roundabout way, such as in the form of the question, "How can a variable God be the whole universe?" Just as revealing was Alexander's next topic, the world-soul.[29] He assigned a soul to the world without offering any justification for his conviction that there was a world or universe.

While Alexander's neglect to provide that justification should seem reprehensible from the philosophical viewpoint, he should not be overly criticized for his failure to see the scientific side of the problem. If he had a modest concern about science, it turned around the use of space-time, though not without a cosmic twist. Alexander felt that his space-time was not different at least in spirit from the scientific doctrine into which Minkowski synthesized the teaching of Lorentz and Einstein. In Alexander's summation of Minkowski's views "Space and Time are described as being shadows of the Universe. Only the Universe has self-existence."[30]

These lines could hardly be reconciled with the priority

which Alexander asssigned to space-time over the universe
regardless of Minkowski's doubtful realism. Apart from
this momentous inconsistency on Alexander's part those
lines of his, written around 1915, were out of date already in
1920 when they saw print. Even more so when in 1927
Alexander took up the science of relativity in the preface to
the new impression of his magnum opus. By then ten years
had gone by since Einstein unfolded the cosmological consequences of his General Theory of Relativity. There the
universe was not a mathematical construct of space-time and
world lines, but a consistent whole of material bodies,[31]
which generated a four-dimensional net of permissible paths
of motion.

Such a net was a sheer mathematical construct, called
space for brevity's sake, although, space was the very word
that should have been avoided in order to prevent endless
misunderstandings. As so many other philosophers Alexander too failed to take note of this radically new meaning
given to space by physicists who, with Einstein in the van,
quickly resumed references to space as an entity. No wonder
that Alexander did not feel the need to come clean on the
question of how his Space-Time, allegedly so germane to
the spirit of Einstein's relativity, could emerge into tangible
realities. Nor was this confusion of meanings noted by that
student of Alexander's philosophy who felt particularly agitated by an emergence from a mere idea into something
tangible.[32]

Philosophers as well as physicists, although very keen at
that time on Kant's precepts, failed, again with Einstein in
the lead, to note a most un-Kantian implication of General
Relativity. Taken in its cosmological consequences, General
Relativity represented the greatest scientific discovery ever
achieved by making possible, for the first time in scientific
history, a contradiction-free account of the totality of consistently interacting things.[33] The result roundly contra-

dicted Kant's claim that science supported the first antin-
omy about the inherently unreliable status of the notion of
the universe.

Yet it was on such "scientific" grounds that Kant tried to
secure the "Copernican" turn in philosophy that turned the
real universe into a purely regulative idea.[34] It was to regu-
late nothing and nobody. But once man's mental categories
determined the form of all existence, the universe had to
degenerate into a subjective entity. No better status could be
claimed for Alexander's universe. On a cursory look it
seemed to assure special value to all things, and to human
strivings in particular. Yet the assurance amounted to mere
Spinozean naturalism on which Alexander was ready to
stake the truth of his philosophical system. Towards the end
of his life Alexander viewed with satisfaction the prospect
that his cinerary urn would carry the inscription: *Erravit cum
Spinoza.*[35]

Such was a silver cloud with a dark lining to it. Alexander
himself hinted, though he never dwelt on the point, that
individual things represented a facet disturbing to his system. Why was it that the supreme universal, the universe,
had to break up into infinitely numerous particular things?
That question had already been posed to Spinoza and
printed in the English translation of his works with which
Alexander had to be most familiar.[36] There Alexander could
have also read Spinoza's frank admission that his system
offered no explanation why there were individual concrete
things.

Of those individual things none was more individual than
the human mind as a locus of personal consciousness. Nothing could bring into sharper relief the depth of that individuality than its possible survival of death. The prospect
bothered Alexander a great deal. The concluding pages of
Space, Time and Deity contained Alexander's admission of
the destructive threat posed by such a survival to his system:

Should the extension of mind beyond the limits of the
bodily life be verified, so that a mind can either act
without a body or may shift its place to some other
body and yet retain its memory, the larger part of the
present speculation will have to be seriously modified
or abandoned.[37]

Of course, Alexander misconstrued the threat. The latter
did not come from an empirical verification of the survival
of the mind, but from rational inference, greatly cherished
by Alexander, that there had to be such a survival and with it
an abiding purpose.

Alexander's system was most impersonal as well as purposeless. Witness is the furtive appearance of such words as
individual, person, and purpose in his *Space, Time and Deity*.
That highest human expression of purpose which is prayer,
Alexander held it to be no more than the illusory extrapola-
tion of one's fondest wishes.[38] To his credit, in his last year
he faced up to the possibility that his antagonism to purpose
embodied in personal immortality might have been rooted
not so much in objective as in subjective factors:

I have always been content to think that our minds are
too closely identified with our bodies (being indeed
another aspect of them as Spinoza held) for any personal survival. To live on in the thoughts and memory
of our friends and descendants and whoever else we
have affected or may affect is of course impersonal. . . . And equally any way of absorption into the
great good is impersonal. I can't help thinking that it is
even more inspiring (I don't say consoling) that each of
us has his chance and his responsibility for making
good use of it while he can, that is, while he lives. That
is certain, all the rest is insecure. . . . I am only trying
to be candid. And so I'll add this. Many and perhaps
most would say I entertain a bleak prospect. The
thought of personal continuance does not appeal to

> me, and I am ready to think that a deficiency on my
> part. It is rather, I believe, resignation to the inevitable,
> but perhaps some want of human feeling.[39]

Coming as it does from a keen philosophical mind, the
reference to a bleak prospect should first be appraised in the
light of philosophy. Undoubtedly, the union of mind and
body is not only close but extremely close. This is what
poses the philosophical challenge and especially if one takes
that closeness to mean that mind and body are but two
aspects of the same thing. In this case one is faced with the
duty of answering the question: What is a "thing" with two
so different aspects, what is its true nature? To say that it is
matter or body is to make meaningless the observation that
it shows such non-material aspects as are mental phenomena. Nor can that "thing" be but pure mind as long as one
can discourse about it only in words or in writing, two
plainly physical realities. But if that "thing" is neither body
nor mind alone, what is it?

Clearly, the two-aspect-theory of the mind-body relation-
ship gives neither body nor mind or soul. It merely leaves one
with a pleasing metaphor, hardly a matter of logic. Logic also
demands the recognition that purposeful activity is but another aspect of personal consciousness and not of body or
matter. Logic alone can make one see that matter progres-
sively unfolds its potentialities. Progress degenerates into a
mere accumulation of quantitites unless its phases can be
related to a purposeful activity or the pursuit of goals. Goals,
unless they are mere termini, point beyond mere matter, a
matter far more serious than to be resolved by a mere word,
such as *nisus*, however glittering when first used.

Emergents and emergence

That the word *nisus* quickly lost its erstwhile luster tells
something about a curious feature of the history of philoso-

phy, and especially of its very modern phase. It is a story of memorable words, not equally successful, although all too often meant to convey much the same idea. One such word is "emergence." It was not expected that its variant, "emergent," would take philosophy by storm when first proposed by George H. Lewes. This might have been the case had Lewes been an influential academic, rather than a popularizer, however readable. Also, Comtean positivism had already been sufficiently discredited in England by J. S. Mill and T. H. Huxley when in the 1870s Lewes, a lifelong champion of Comte, came forward with his multivolume *Problems of Life and Mind*.[40]

To be sure, Lewes was not the first to be struck by the fact that the mixing of two elements, such as hydrogen and oxygen or nitrogen and oxygen, should result in a compound, water and nitric acid respectively, with properties which its constituents did not possess. Reason for this surprise did not diminish as the science of chemistry, with the help of atomic physics, has almost completely cleared up the role of constituents in countless compounds. The latter did not cease to display novel properties and at times astonishing ones as shown by some truly marvelous synthetic materials.

While Lewes seemed to be impressed by the contrast between constituents and compounds, he did not want to be led thereby into the realm of metaphysics or ontology as an explanation of novelties. He held that ultimately science would fully account for any and all of them. Until then he felt it was useful that a distinction be made between two processes. One he proposed to call the process of resultants, the other the process of emergents. In the former the relation beween components and compounds could be stated in a scientific or mathematical formula, while in the latter this could not yet be done. Lewes' distinction between resultants and emergents was therefore purely provisional. Compounds, such as water, were to be given a better scientific explanation than the one provided by Lavoisier. "Some day, perhaps, we shall be able to express the unseen process in a mathematical formula; till then we must regard the water as an emergent."[41]

One cannot help feeling a disparity betwen the need felt by Lewes to denote a wide class of processes, yet unknown scientifically, by a special word and his reductionist convictions. More than he might have suspected, he cared about issues that were clearly metaphysical. But whatever he might have perceived about the metaphysical realm, he wanted none of it. He certainly did not want to discuss the purpose served by emergent processes. Still his anti-metaphysical clarity should be preferred to the philosophical obfuscation cultivated by C. Lloyd Morgan, a founder of a new branch of psychology, animal behavior. By 1923, when Morgan prominently referred to Lewes' "emergents" in the first chapter of his Gifford Lectures, *Emergent Evolution*, he had for half a century been in the grip of the very same problem that Lewes tried to resolve with the use of the word "emergents." To the end of his distinguished career Morgan failed to throw genuine philosophical light on it.

The reason for this emerges very clearly from Morgan's recollection of a respectful debate he had as a 19-year-old student at the Royal School of Mines with none other than T. H. Huxley. By then young Morgan must have pondered a great deal the problem of novelty in chemical and biological processes. Otherwise he would not have been able to insist on the merits of those novelties with remarks that impressed Huxley, a board member of the School, to the point of extending an invitation to the young student to spend a year with him in his South Kensington laboratories. As a parting shot, Huxley urged young Morgan: "Keep that light burning. But remember that biology has supplied a new and powerful illuminant."[42]

Years later, when Morgan joined Huxley in South Kensington, he was even more convinced that enlightenment about the question of novelty had to come from philosophy. Huxley seemed to sense this, otherwise he would not have steered a conversation of theirs to a remark in Mivart's *On the Genesis of Species*: "If then such innate powers must be attributed to chemical atoms, to mineral species, to gemmules, and to physiological units, it is only reasonable to attribute such to each individual organism."[43] Huxley obviously tried to cure young Morgan of the danger of Mivart's Scholasticism, more apparent than real. But young Morgan stood his ground. Although the analogy between the development of a crystal and of an organism would be of very doubtful validity, a point still could be made: "Both invite us to distinguish between an internal factor and the incidence of external conditions."[44]

Against Huxley's objection that internal factors could, as innate powers, be but mere Scholastic forms, young Morgan still insisted on respect for facts: "The Schoolmen and their modern disciples were trying to explain what men of science must perhaps just accept on the evidence."[45] Further, young Morgan pressed Huxley on his insistence, so different from Darwin's denial of leaps in nature, on the reality of such leaps. Huxley had no choice then but to fall back on full continuity in all processes of nature and, in particular, on continuity between neuroses and psychoses. Only twenty years later did Huxley, in his Romanes Lecture, make the admission that such a psychic phenomenon as love was a novelty not only unexplainable by Darwinian evolution but worked in a sense diametrically opposite to it. Yet this and similar novelties could only be obfuscated within philosophical Spinozism on which young Morgan took his final ground in that for him so memorable debate with Huxley. He relied on that ground especially during the latter half of his distinguished career that saw him exchange in 1911 the chair of zoology in Bristol for a chair in psychology and ethics, especially created for him.

Already in 1876 Spinozism offered to Morgan no more
than a reduction of the problem to mere words. Within
Spinozism, mechanism and novelty, causality and freedom,
necessity and purpose were but two aspects of the same
thing or process, identical with one another ontologically.
Morgan never got beyond the mere verbalism on which
alone could one fall back as a resolution of the Spinozean
identity of all with all. A proof of this is his specious distinction, in the last chapter of his Gifford Lectures, *Emergent
Evolution*, between causation and causality.[46] It was but a
replay of the book's general theme, the difference between
"within the system" or organism and "within the mind."
Such a distinction, which allowed only for a representational
theory of reality, prevented the mind from being confident
about its most purposeful activity in knowing the real in its
broadest and deepest sense.

Reality, insofar as it meant a sense of purpose anchored in
God, eluded Morgan in his other series of Gifford Lectures,
Life, Mind and Spirit, where he was particularly eager to
secure it. He had to leave unspecified the true provenance of
that "divine gift" which came by nature and is

> manifested in others and revealed in oneself in the
> determinate advance of natural events. If I may put it
> so, emergent evolution is from first to last a revelation
> and a manifestation of that which I speak of as Divine
> Purpose.[47]

To be sure, in his last years he tried to do better justice to
purpose than could be done by science alone. To the end he
could not spot beyond science anything more than Alexander's philosophy. Morgan's last book, *The Emergence of
Novelty*, shows this all too well. Its Epilogue is an imaginary
dialogue between Morgan and an interviewer representing
the philosophy of Alexander, Morgan's philosophical idol,
and comes to a climax on the topic of purpose. In a valid
sense, Morgan stated, Alexander's expression of "his ideal

of beauty is the abiding purpose which dominates his day-by-day procedure in artistic creation."[48]

Since that ideal enveloped the cosmos itself, Morgan hastened to add that cosmic purpose was not to be taken for an evidence of an objectively set design. But if such was the case, not only philosophy but science too had to appear useless in making sense of any novelty, including that look at novelty which is implied in one's sense of purpose. To Morgan's credit, he spelled out the only remaining remedy, a highly refined use of metaphors: "The main avenue of approach towards cosmic Purpose is not through natural science, but through dramatic literature in which the Activity of man, and that of other spirit-agents, has always been the focal centre of interest."[49]

Morgan failed to see the danger lurking behind his falling back on literature as a tool of philosophy. In particular he neglected to probe into the answer to be given by a novelist-philosopher to "the crucial question" he raised in concluding his book "whether scientific inquiry adequately covers the whole of that reality which is the perennial quest of the philosopher."[50] Neither he, nor those after him who used as their chief weapon the word "emergence" to rescue man's sense of purpose from the clutches of reductionism,[51] considered a most important point: Unlike the philosopher, the novelist is free to engage in metaphors with no obligation to specify their precise meaning. The word "emergence," whether used by Morgan and by others who wanted to be remembered as philosophers, could at best be suggestive while begging the explanation it was meant to provide. No different was the case with the word "process" to which Alfred North Whitehead secured a niche in the pantheon of misplaced philosophical metaphors.

The tangled prose of process
This is not the place to attempt even a modest summary of Whitehead's *Process and Reality*. Authors of learned essays on

that book have so far failed to unravel its "idiosyncratic terminology and labored attempt at producing a system."[52] Such is a remark of Dorothy Emmett, a chief authority on Whitehead's philosophy, who had advice for those who find (and who do not?) *Process and Reality* a reading excessively forbidding. They should go, she suggested, to Whitehead's last books, *Adventures of Ideas* and *Modes of Thought*, for enlightenment. The *Modes of Thought* is certainly enlightening in that it contains Whitehead's cryptic admission of his debt to Alexander. There Whitehead refers to *Space, Time and Deity* as a book whose title puts in a nutshell the whole subject of philosophy: "Time refers to the transitions of process, Space refers to the static necessity of each form of interwoven existence, and Deity expresses the lure of the ideal which is the potentiality beyond immediate fact."[53]

Whitehead's change of the original order may have been a mere slip of the tongue, but no less revealing than a deliberate act. Time takes on with Whitehead an even more fundamental, nay, ontological role than with Bergson and Alexander. In fact, Whitehead's reliance on the word "process" strikes, under the cover of time, at the very root of ontology. It does so by radically subverting the possibility for anything to share the quality of being as a means of maintaining some measure of identity in the welter of change. Whitehead sidestepped this all-important point as he emphatically stated:

> The very essence of real actuality—that is, of the completely real—is *process*. Thus each actual thing is only to be understood in terms of its becoming and perishing. There is no halt in which the actuality is its static self, accidentally played upon by qualifications derived from the shift of circumstances. The converse is the truth.[54]

This dictum of Whitehead, so categorical and so central to his system, calls for more than one remark. The first may be a recall of Whitehead's own warning that "an admirable literary style is no security for logical consistency."[55] This warning of his is applicable to most of his non-mathematical writings. It also gives away the linguistic impossibility of Whitehead's process philosophy. One indeed should be grateful to him for speaking of the "very essence of real actuality" and not, say, of the "very gist of real actuality." Unlike the word gist, which has a certain stylistic, that is, metaphorical elusiveness, the word essence has behind it a long and formidable philosophical tradition.[56] The better part of that tradition is steeped in the recognition that it is not possible to speak with consistency of change, be it a process, unless something remains unchanged while the change or process goes on. Otherwise that very connectivity, by which Whitehead set so great a store, becomes a hollow metaphor. Most importantly, if there is no permanence, there can be no ultimate finality. Its absence in Whitehead's system is best stated in his very words:

> The immensity of the world negatives the belief that any state of order can be so established that beyond there can be no progress. This belief in a final order, popular in religious and philosophic thought, seems to be due to the prevalent fallacy that all types of seriality necessarily involve terminal instances. It follows that Tennyson's lines, 'that far off divine event to which the whole creation moves,' presents a fallacious conception of the universe.[57]

Whitehead's reference to Tennyson is a poetical red-herring. It serves the purpose of distracting attention from Whitehead's own idea of the universe. His use of the phrase, "the immensity of the world," is no less poetical than Tennyson's lines. It may seem unbelievable, but the author of *The Principle of Relativity* and *Science and the Modern World* remained silent on the cosmological consequences of Einstein's General Relativity. There the scientifically meaning-ful universe is strictly finite.

It is that definiteness of the finite which Whitehead tried to dilute at every turn into a vague process. A specific and central victim of his efforts was one's own personality and with it any meaningful talk about purpose. Indeed, in speaking about the 'I' as "my process of shaping this welter of material into a consistent pattern of feelings," Whitehead was careful not to suggest that the 'I' strictly transcended successive moments of that process. He rather presented the next moment of the 'I' as "a continuation of the antecedent world."[58] Yet he also declared that the validity of speaking of purpose depends on the permanence of individual per-sonal identity: "Any tendency to a high-grade multiple per-sonality would be self-destructive . . . of the very essence of life, which is conformation to purpose."[59]

Whitehead would not have remained faithful to his own philosophical purpose had he not insisted that the purpose of it all, the all-inclusive purpose, cannot include personal pur-pose. The ultimate goal of the Great Cosmic Adventure is Beauty "with self-forgetful transcendence."[60] Such tran-scendence should seem dubious, to say the least, and the same is true of Whitehead's definition of the "teleology of the Universe" as being "directed to the production of Beauty."[61] Only at the end of the *Adventures of Ideas* did Whitehead come down from the rarified heights of abstract beauty and touch, rather briefly, on matters of harsh, indeed tragic realities. "This is the secret of the union of Zest with Peace:—That the suffering attains its end in a Harmony of Harmonies. The immediate experience of this Final Fact, with its union of Youth and Tragedy, is the sense of Peace."[62]

In writing these lines in 1933 Whitehead might have thought of his youngest son, an aviator shot down in France in 1918. World War I, which has come up more than once in the preceding chapters, played a pivotal part in Whitehead's perception of purpose, cosmic and individual, anchored in a universe with no finality in it. According to his own account, reflections on that War's countless tragedies led, shortly after it was over, to the maturing of his doubts about Christian faith which he had imbibed in his father's parsonage. He concluded that "Christianity did not invent human worth." By worth Whitehead meant purpose as well. Otherwise he could not have stated, we are in 1944, the grimmest year of World War II, that for all their diverse convictions, all those young men were "dying for the worth of the world."[63]

A deluge of metaphors

In all likelihood Whitehead died without learning of one who as a stretcherbearer in World War I carried quite a few dying men and would have readily endorsed the foregoing phrase if taken out of its categorically anti-Christian context. Father Teilhard de Chardin could hardly be outdone in composing prose-hymns of an evolutionary universe. His war experiences inspired his singing the praises of suffering as the best means of bringing the heroic out of man as if by natural selection. His *Writings in Time of War*, a collection of essays published posthumously,[64] give a generous foretaste of his power with words. They aim at conveying the message that nature is bound to achieve its supreme purpose by turning, through its own dynamics, into a supra-nature about which Father Teilhard was all too ready to suggest that it reflected the supernatural itself.

Most of those words and expressions were markedly metaphorical. To the unwary they amounted to a conceptual deluge and Father Teilhard delighted in throwing its floodgates wide open. As long as one did not care for precise meaning, one could let oneself be carried with abandon on the crest of waves which had such labels as auto-evolution, cerebralisation, circumflexion, co-consciousness, eu-complex, excentration, humanity's in-folding, natural self-arrangement, noodynamics, pan-organisation, cosmic re-coiling, planetary in-folding, ultra-ego, ultra-personalization, ultra-human, the within and the without of things, radial and tangential energy, and withdrawal, as if some intoxication with words had to be counteracted. Those quasi-mystical words were crowned by such quasi-celestial neologisms as super-creativeness, super-centration, super-individual, super-nature, and super-soul.[65]

If a biologist was given the task to evaluate the scientific message, unabashed neo-Lamarckism hiding behind such big and vague words, he could but endorse Medawar's devastating strictures of Teilhard's science[66] as different from his strictly anthropological researches that were far from extraordinary. (Teilhard may indeed have been an unwitting co-conspirator in the Piltdown hoax.) A scientist did not have to be a materialist, such as Julian Huxley, to put in a disclaimer about Christ as the Omega point of evolution.[67] Only by stretching standard evolutionary thought beyond recognition was it possible to make evolution not only purposeful but fertile with a purpose that far transcended it.

Christian theology too seemed to burst at its seams once Christ was claimed with no reference to original sin, a dogma which Teilhard carefully skirted. Theologians aware of the utter gratuitousness of grace, could be but utterly puzzled by Teilhard's presentation of ultimate purpose in which nature seemed to generate automatically the supernatural:

> The exclusive task of the world is the physical incorporation of the faithful in the Christ who is of God. This cardinal task is being carried out *with the rigor and harmony of a natural evolution.*[68]

And what if that rigor and harmony had under its sway even that being, God, by standard orthodox theological definition the absolute unchangeability?[69]

Ambiguities, at times shocking, invariably arose whenever Teilhard turned his discourse to the primary locus of
purpose which is man's intelligent nature. He could hardly
ignore the close relatedness between entitative and ontological as he took up, in 1920, the question of the "entitative
progress" of the Universe:

> The question of whether the Universe is still develop-
> ing then becomes a matter of deciding whether the
> human spirit is still in process of evolution. To this I
> reply unhesitatingly, 'Yes, it is.' The nature of Man is
> in the full flood of entitative change.[70]

Toward the end of his career he was ready to risk a clash on
this point with eminent representatives of what he called the
"immobilist" position. The incident took place at the bicen-
tenary celebration of Columbia University in 1954 where
Teilhard was one of a seventy-strong panel convened for
clarifying the unity of human knowledge. "In my section,"
Teilhard wrote shortly afterwards to his brother in France,

> a deep and vital 'cleavage plane' became apparent be-
> tween the humanists and the scientists, which turned
> ultimately . . . on the new Galileo question: Is man
> still moving biologically upon himself? With [Julian]
> Huxley and the majority of scientists I, of course,
> vigorously attacked the immobilist position taken up,
> alas, by the more Christian-thinking members of the
> section, such as Gilson, Malik (Lebanese representa-
> tive at the League of Nations), Battaglia, lay rector of
> the University of Bologna, and even Van Dusen.[71]

Was this an unwitting acknowledgment on Teilhard's part
that his position was less Christian than it should have been?
Indeed his position on this and other points could seem to
pose a systematic threat to that sense of purpose which
Christian faith in the immortality of the soul gives to those
who live by that faith. Such was the most considered view

of none other than Etienne Gilson.[72] If those who defend Teilhard's orthodoxy as a Catholic priest are right,[73] his alleged advocacy of an evolving God may be a matter of verbal imprecision, though not easily excusable.

At any rate, it is true even of the philosophical pudding that its ultimate test is in the eating. And what if the "eating" consists in swallowing most bitter existential pills? All sweetness was Teilhard's vision of a cosmos ever more enveloped in the noosphere when a friend of mine, a prominent businessman, had his first taste of it. Nothing short of intoxicating was for him the prospect of a cosmic Christ ruling over a galactic and extragalactic brotherhood. His older son was nineteen when he stayed out an entire summer night and got home at the crack of dawn plainly intoxicated. Only months later did it begin to transpire that he had returned also cracked up. Things began to fall in place only after a most tragic event, the young man's committing suicide by blowing his head to pieces.

What could be the purpose of this tragedy? Suddenly Teilhard's vision of cosmic brotherhood failed to provide an answer. In the face of the harsh realities of life, cosmic purpose as propelled by *élan vital, nisus*, Emergence, Process, or even by an Omega point, could have but a hollow ring. It was precisely with an eye on much of mankind's miserable condition, that a sober student of Whitehead's philosophy raised the question of whether it was any good except in the comfort of prestigious academic chairs.[74] Clearly, not much can be gleaned about purpose, individual and cosmic, from philosophies that by their cultivation of mere metaphors dilute the significance of purpose as experienced through one's own unchangeable personal identity tested in the crucible of existence. It may therefore be worthwhile to interrogate that very individual experience of acting freely for a purpose about the lessons it may provide about the purpose of it all.

Chapter Six

HEURISTICS OF PURPOSE

Darwinian delusions

The most obvious context where one encounters the reality of purpose is one's immediate experience of pursuing a goal, trivial and short-term as it may be. Since experiences of this kind are very frequent, nothing should seem more reasonable than to make the most of them for a far from trivial purpose. It corresponds to a reasoned justification of the reality of purpose as a directive cause of actions and processes, whether conscious or not. A chief obstacle to such an enterprise is the fact that reason has now for centuries increasingly come under the sway of science and scientists. Hardly any claim can nowadays be made on rationality unless there is on hand some scientific endorsement, be it no more than a scientist's mere opinion, if not plain delusion.

Such endorsement, very positive as it may appear on a cursory look, may in fact leave one empty-handed. Asking from science more than it can deliver amounts in fact to giving away the game. At the risk of stating once more the obvious, science or rather its method, has its built-in limitations. A scientist only deludes himself whenever he becomes unmindful of a precept laid down by no less a scientist than James Clerk Maxwell: "One of the severest tests of a scientific mind is to discern the limits of the legitimate applications of scientific methods."[1] Almost a hundred years later the same test loomed with fearsome severity against the backdrop of atomic weapons-testing. It was then, in the mid-1960s, that a prominent American man of science, Vannevar Bush, raised his warning voice: "Much is spoken today about the power of science, and rightly. It is awesome. But little is said about the inherent limitations of science, and both sides of the coin need equal scrutiny."[2]

Indeed, whenever licence is requested from the so-called scientific method for dealing with realities beyond its validity, and their number is legion, one will end up with their mere shadows. In the process a sinister shadow may also be cast on the very purpose and purposefulness of science itself. Quite positive or enlightening may therefore be the outcome whenever an apparently negative approach is taken to science. It may consist, for instance, in recalling the haplessness and delusions of prominent scientists as they come face to face with immediate realities. One such reality is man's consciousness for acting for purpose, a commodity markedly non-scientific though indispensable for carrying on with the enterprise known as science.

The slighting of that consciousness on the part of Darwin and many Darwinists should seem telling for reasons particularly germane to a fully reasoned justification of purpose. After all, Darwinism has become widely perceived as the peremptory refutation of the belief that anything takes place for a purpose. This perception might not have gained wide acceptance had proper awareness been kept of Darwin's frankness about his own perplexities. He voiced them time and again, though mostly in private, with a directness that showed no trace of embarrassment about crude fumblings in matters philosophical.

Particularly instructive are Darwin's fumblings about the philosophical status of purpose in the letters he wrote in 1861 to Asa Gray, the famed paleontologist at Harvard. They were a follow-up to Gray's essay, "Natural Selection Is not Inconsistent with Natural Theology," in the July, August, and October 1860 issues of the *Atlantic Monthly*.[3] The essay might just as well have carried the title, "Natural Selection Is not Inconsistent with Design."

While Gray proposed a fairly nuanced notion of design, he did not see clearly as far as the point where one can catch a glimpse of the possibility of an unconscious process being the carrier of purpose. Compared with Gray, Darwin was crudely shortsighted. Such an idea of purpose could not arise at all in the context of Darwin's obsession with the alternative: production of each and every form of life by natural selection or a direct creation by God of each and every species. When two years later Darwin confronted Gray with that alternative, he did it rather naively. He assumed that the opinion of a fellow scientist could be decisive in a purely philosophical question:

> You speak of Lyell as a judge; now what I complain of is that he declines to be a judge. . . . I have sometimes wished that Lyell had pronounced against me. When I say 'me', I only mean change of species by descent. That seems to me the turning point. Personally, I care much about Natural Selection; but that seems to me utterly unimportant, compared to the question of Creation or Modification.[4]

Yet, this unphilosophical attitude had already showed through two years earlier when Darwin saw in a most purposeful action, animal breeding, a decisive evidence of the supreme rule of natural selection. With commendable candor he spoke of that rule as "my deity." The variations on which the animal breeder based his work were, Darwin wrote to Gray, far from "making my deity Natural Selection superfluous." Yet, it was one thing to consider those variations as a marvelous field for the working of natural selection and another to ignore the weight of the most purposeful action of the breeder.

Three months later, in September 1861, Darwin saw somewhat farther, namely, to the point where he caught a glimpse of the irony of his shortsightedness. The context was his reference, again in a letter to Gray, to the countless individual differences which domestic breeding can produce in the nasal bones of pigeons. He expressed his disbelief that those variations represented a stream directed by design, an idea supported by Gray and Lyell: "I must think that it is illogical to suppose that the variations, which natural selection preserves for the good of any being, have been designed." There was, of course, plenty of irony in Darwin's rejecting design while endorsing the working of natural selection "for the good of any being." Worse, Darwin found his thinking to be in a muddle right there where resided the ultimate source of confidence in design as well as purpose. He saw nothing of the relevance of free will to purpose as he offered, in his very next phrase, a philosophical confession: "But I know that I am in the same sort of muddle (as I have said before) as all the world seems to be in with respect to free will, yet with everything supposed to have been foreseen or preordained."[5]

The idea of free will, as will be seen in the next chapter, was more central to the topic than could have been suspected by Darwin and Darwinists. None of them pondered the obviously free nature of their biological researches aimed all too often at demonstrating that all processes of nature were strictly mechanical. Much less did they pause to reflect on the fact that those researches of theirs could be considered purposeful only insofar as they were a freely chosen course of action. Moreover, any free choice was not only an immediately experienced act but also done for a purpose.

Had Darwin and Darwinists taken seriously their own consciousness of acting freely, they would not have been caught in a philosophical muddle of their own making. It was the muddle of expecting too much from the scientific method. That such was the case is illustrated in the same letter of Darwin where he also replied to Gray's question as to what would convince him of the reality of Design, writ large:

> If I saw an angel come down to teach us good, and I was convinced from others seeing him that I was not mad, I should believe in design. If I could be convinced thoroughly that life and mind were in unknown way a function of other imponderable forces, I should be convinced. If man was made of brass or iron and no way connected with any other organism which had ever lived, I should perhaps be convinced.

The best comment on all this was given by Darwin himself and in the same breath: "But this is childish writing."[6]

Darwin could, of course, be more certain of seeing others than seeing an angel, but this could still not provide him with assurance about the reliability of the angel's teaching. More importantly, could any "scientific" reason be given about Darwin's certainty of seeing other scientists? Again, what was the scientific proof that life and mind were of the same nature? Was it not sheer reductionism to assume that unless an entity appeared to be utterly unconnected with anything else, it had to be of altogether the same nature with its surroundings? Clearly, Darwin's inability to see design was rooted in his resolve, a very conscious and purposeful and therefore non-mechanical resolve, to value nothing but mechanism.

His basic error was to espouse plain reductionism. According to it only such mental operations or experiences are reliable as can be stated in empirical or quantitative terms. It escaped him and countless others that there was nothing quantitative or empirical in that basic tenet of reductionism. As a result Darwin could have no trust in the very foundation of all rational conviction, one's inner consciousness of knowing and for a purpose at that. Those mindful of the inexorable force of logic will not be surprised on seeing Darwin, in his letter of December 11, 1861, to Asa Gray, burying the question of design under a heap of ludicrous remarks:

> With respect to Design, I feel more inclined to show a white flag than to fire my usual long-range shot. I like to try and ask you a puzzling question, but when you return the compliment I have great doubts whether it is a fair way of arguing. If anything is designed, certainly man must be: one's "inner consciousness" (though a false guide) tells one so; yet I cannot admit that man's rudimentary mammae . . . were designed. If I was to say I believed this, I should believe it in the same incredible manner as the orthodox believe the Trinity in Unity. You say that you are in a haze; I am in thick mud; the orthodox would say in fetid, abominable mud; yet I cannot keep out of the question. My dear Gray, I have written a great deal of nonsense.[7]

Most of the orthodox, if informed about Darwin's letter, would have probably jumped on Darwin's characterization of belief in Trinity as an incredible, that is, irrational belief. Of course, by 1870 or so Darwin may have already forgotten an elementary part of his erstwhile catechetical instruction. Christians under no circumstance were to take the Trinity for the illogicality of equating three with one. Nobody in Darwin's entourage cared, of course, to pay attention to the masterly account which no less a logician than

John Henry Newman had given in the 1830s about the
development of the dogma of the Trinity.[8] At any rate, the
orthodox should first take Darwin to task on straight thinking, the etymological meaning of orthodoxy, in matters
philosophical and scientific. Moreover, they would best do
this by leading up step by step to a thought which, when it
dawned rather late in life on none other than Herbert
Spencer, the first proponent of the struggle for survival, had
a paralyzing effect on him.

A paralyzing thought
First, the orthodox should note that it was plainly crooked,
from the viewpoint of logic, to state with no qualification,
as Darwin did, that inner consciousness was a false guide.
For if such was the case no conviction, which is an act of
inner consciousness, about any fact or proposition, including Darwin's consciousness of being the author of *The Origin*, could be reliable. Second, it was not inner consciousness
that proved that man's body was designed. Inner consciousness merely assured each and every sane human being of
acting for a purpose on countless occasions. Darwin never
came even remotely close to seeing that the merit of his
question, whether man's rudimentary mammae evinced or
refuted design, depended ultimately on his trusting his inner
consciousness.

Not that Darwin did not notice the self-defeating character of his subjecting in full the mind too to his laws, blind
and random, of biological evolution: "With me," he wrote
to W. Graham in 1881, "the horrid doubt always arises
whether the convictions of man's mind, which has been
developed from the mind of lower animals, are not of any
value or at all trustworthy." Clearly, he could answer but in
the negative his question: "Would any one trust in the convictions of a monkey's mind if there are any convictions in
such a mind?"[9] He could not, however, muster enough logic

to say the same about the human mind too, including his own. He could not, tellingly enough, because he was unable, in spite of all his science, to accept that "this wonderful universe, and especially the nature of man," was the product of brute forces, that is, of forces not designed by a Creator. And since no scientist revealed so much about the orderliness of the universe than Newton, Darwin had no choice but to say: "A dog might as well speculate on the mind of Newton."[10]

For all that the mind or consciousness did not cease to raise more than purely speculative questions. No less an evolutionist than Herbert Spencer served evidence of the perception that one's appraisal of one's own consciousness controlled the answer to the question whether there was purpose or design in the universe. Furthermore, he provided that evidence as he admitted his growing tolerance of religious beliefs he had for long opposed. He came to take the view that religious beliefs were invariably generated by the inability of science to answer the question of cosmic purpose. Science could at best register the great current of evolution, from mere matter to consciousness, but could not comprehend it because comprehension, as Spencer rightly saw, could not be had outside that consciousness which science merely presupposed.

The Spencerian scientist had therefore no choice but to face up to the agonizing question: "And along with this rises the paralyzing thought—what if, of all that is thus incomprehensible to us, there exists no comprehension anywhere?" This perplexity, engulfing everything man could ascertain about the cosmos and even the cosmos itself, had, however, a specific source. Its locus was the evolutionist's refusal to trust man's consciousness as a unique phenomenon in the universe. For, if it was true that human consciousness "evolved out of infantile vacuity" and that "in some rudimentary form" it was "omnipresent," it then had to be looked upon as "no less inscrutable" than the evolutionary process itself.[11]

   A generation later, another evolutionary materialist, J. B. S. Haldane, registered the same impasse and in a context worth considering. That something in him would survive bodily death appeared to him a view utterly unreasonable on the basis of traditional arguments. He found most unconvincing either the proofs offered by Christianity or the claim that morality makes no sense without eternal life. Still he admitted as "immensely unlikely" the prospect that his mind would be "a mere by-product of matter." For if such was the case no meaning could be given to science in general, and in particular to his field, biochemistry, in whose problems he was more interested than "in the question of what, if anything, will happen to me when I am dead." Science, after it had banished philosophy, found itself threatened with banishment from the domain of comprehension:

> If my mental processes are determined wholly by the motions of atoms in my brain, I have no reason to suppose that my beliefs are true. They may be sound chemically, but that does not make them sound logically. And hence I have no reason for supposing my brain to be composed of atoms.[12]

Haldane was ready to concede a non-personal survival of his mind insofar as its perceptions of truth tied it to some absolute. Still his portrayal of that paralyzing dilemma was but a replay of the shortsightedness that had already trapped Darwin and Spencer. They all prided themselves on knowing about atoms and brains, but took no special pride in their mind's ability to know anything at all. As a result they had to face up to possibly despairing of science itself. Darwinist evolutionists should seem to be a most appropriate target of this remark. A particular reason is that they have invariably tried to trace man as well as his science into such remote and vague origins where nothing specific could be seen of their respective originations.

As to man's gradual "emergence," it could appear a plausible tale when in Darwin's time even the great apes could be taken for man's direct ancestors. Since then much has been learned about the startlingly fast evolution of the human brain, a point that cannot be emphasized enough. In fact the speed appeared to T. Edinger, a foremost investigator of that evolution, to spend itself in a mere instant:

> If man passed through a phase pithecanthropus-sinanthropus, the evolution of his brain was unique not only in its result, but also in its tempo. An increase of 50 to 100 percent of the cerebral hemisphere is a phenomenon that occurred also in the Equides, between the stages represented by Merychippus, of medium size, and Equus, of large size. In the Equides this transformation took twenty-five million years, with the Hominides the same increase seems to have taken place, geologically speaking, in an instant without having been accompanied by a major increase of [body] size. [13]

The emergence of tools in the hands of man's ancestors proved to be no less sudden. But such suddenness will not impress one who finds nothing wrong with Darwin's incredibly shallow attitude toward that marvel which is thought: "Why is thought, being a secretion of brain, more wonderful than gravity, a property of matter?" [14] Darwin, like most of his followers, was not intrigued by the fact that material man could talk about a "material" property, such as gravity, although, being the product of his abstractive powers there was nothing material about it. Those powers also served man as his most effective tool in his purposeful conquest of the external world, a conquest which began with his fashioning very concrete tools millions of years earlier.

Tools, design, and purpose
The thirty or so years that separate Darwin's flippant statement about thought from the publication of his *Descent of Man* did not make him any better a reasoner. This is thoroughly proven by the fact that there he thought he could undercut in three scant pages the claim that tool-making was a distinctly human faculty. Darwin made much of reports that monkeys in the wild used stones to crack nuts, threw stones to defend themselves, started avalanches of rocks to frighten away their attackers, and clothed themselves with big leaves against the sun's heat.[15]

At the same time, Darwin was eager to belittle primitive man's inventiveness. He opined that the mere accident of splintering a flint stone turned man into a tool maker. The sparks produced in such an accident made, so Darwin reasoned, man a systematic user of fire, curiously the only living species to do so. Darwin failed to ponder why apes failed to follow up their "discoveries," although they would have thereby greatly increased their fitness for survival. Worse, as he took up the Duke of Argyle's view "that the fashioning of an implement is absolutely peculiar to man . . . and forms an immeasurable gulf between him and the brutes,"[16] he did not notice the revealing nature of his comment that "this is no doubt a very important distinction."[17]

By conceding that much he offered the rhetorical device of giving mere lip-service to a serious problem as its appropriate solution. For if he had been serious about the distinction as being "very important," he should have called for two sets of investigation. One would have had for its object primitive man's tool-making with at least a touch of philosophical analysis of the meaning of tools. The other would have consisted in a systematic observation of what apes were really doing with their tools, which, even according to the reports at Darwin's disposal, were never of the apes' making.

Undoubtedly, Darwin would have resorted to his usual verbal footwork, of which he was most consciously proud as an evidence of mental finesse (he called himself a "wriggler"[18]), had he been confronted with something similar to W. Köhler's classic studies of the psychology of apes. Darwin most likely would have seized on Köhler's qualifying as "remarkable insight" the fitting together by Sultan, a male chimpanzee, of two bamboo tubes as a means of seizing bananas dangling too high for his forelimbs' reach. Darwin would have played down Köhler's insistence on the visible reward as directly available for Sultan and on the absence of any indication that an imaginary future reward would have worked just as well. Darwin would have, of course, but reacted with his customary dislike for the philosophical touch that set the tone of Köhler's conclusion:

> The time in which the chimpanzee lives [mentally] is limited in past and future. Besides in the lack of speech, it is in the extremely narrow limits in this direction that the chief difference is to be found between anthropoids and the most primitive human beings. The lack of an invaluable technical aid (speech) and a great limitation of those very important components of thought, so-called 'images,' would thus constitute the causes that prevent the chimpanzee from attaining even the smallest beginnings of cultural development.[19]

In the mid-twenties, with modern linguistics still in its infancy, it might still have been perhaps possible to take the sting out of Köhler's conclusion with a reference to future development. Half a century later no less an expert on linguistics than N. Chomsky minced no words: "It's about as likely that an ape will prove to have a language ability as that there is an island somewhere with a species of flightless birds waiting for human beings to teach them to fly."[20] Chomsky's words were aimed at splashy reports about the "intelligent" responses of apes to human words, reports duly exposed for their lack of rigor in reporting and reasoning.[21]

The exclusively human ability of tool-making received a major endorsement from no less a neo-Darwinist than W. Le Gros Clark who made a special study of South-African Australopithecines. Pundits who take the minute chromosomal differences between ape and man for a proof of the absence of essential difference between the two, would be but displeased by his conclusion: "Probably the differentiation of man from ape will ultimately have to rest on a functional rather than on an anatomical basis, the criterion of humanity being the ability to speak and to make tools."[22] The same pundits are not the ones who would find in Le Gros Clark another case of the Darwinist who fails to see the portent of his very findings about this or that ability unique to man.

There is a slight but no less revealing inconsistency in the introduction of *Man the Tool-maker*[23] by Kenneth P. Oakley, a chief authority on primitive man's tool-making skill. To be sure, he begins with an emphatic declaration of the uniqueness of man as a "tool-making primate." He also concludes that "the real difference between what we choose to call an ape and what we call man is one of mental capacity," a capacity especially revealed in the making of tools. But then why should that capacity be called also man's "chief biological characteristic"? For if mental and biological are to be so readily interchanged, there remains little point in noting that while almost all animals have developed specialized body-equipment that resemble tools, man alone "avoided any such specialization." It then remains to contradict the portrayal of two very different kinds of evolution with the remark: "While it is evident that man may be distinguished as the tool-making primate, it is questionable whether this definition gets to the heart of the difference between man and the higher apes."[24]

If one is to look for the source of this strange ambivalence in evaluating the obvious, more than one such source would come into view. One of them, the broader Weltanschauung or ideology of the scientist, plays, of course, a decisive role. Because of its personal nature, it may be left aside if other sources, much more suitable for an "objective" analysis, can shed sufficient light on the problem. One such source is the idea which the scientist entertains about the method of science.

Science as a purposive tool
Most biologists who offered their views on the role of design in nature, had shared Darwin's view of science as an empirico-inductive procedure. Darwin emphatically characterized his doing science along "Baconian principles."[25] Although by his time the futility of Bacon's method had been repeatedly and notably exposed,[26] Darwin took no notice. Insofar as Bacon's method was empiricist or inductive, it stood for a sedulous collection of data, with no suggestion as to what was to be looked for. A reason for this was Bacon's dislike and miscomprehension of teleology.[27] Moreover, in the absence of guiding goals the same method, so shallow in itself, could turn into its very opposite, a no less shallow deductivism, equivalent to a priori rulings. Something of this was perceived in the remark of Harvey, the best British scientist among Bacon's younger contemporaries, that Bacon legislated about science as if he had been its Lord Chancellor.[28]

Contrary to the belief of Bacon and other 17th-century

empiricists, there was a heavily deductive strain in science ever since its rise as a fully conscious venture from the early 17th century on. The deductive approach involved the emphatic setting of a goal, however insufficiently proven, together with the belief that the facts of nature would be found in full conformity with it. This is why Descartes felt confident that a mathematical approach would readily turn man into "the master and possessor of nature."[29] Behind More's *Utopia*, Campanella's *City of the Sun*, Bacon's *New Atlantis* there lay a most purposeful aspiration. It animated the Charter of the Royal Society,[30] the establishment of scientific academies on the Continent, and the vision of the *philosophes* about a Heavenly City on earth.[31]

On the more factual scientific level, the same purposeful pursuit found itself translated both into precise steps and into moves evocative of groping. The former were instanced by Newton's work and the subsequent development of celestial dynamics by Euler, d'Alembert and others. So many gropings were the various 18th-century speculations about electrical fluids and the nature of heat. In chemistry Lavoisier's work marked the transition from vague groping to specific research programs.

Throughout the 19th century there was a steady increase in the number of specific scientific targets, all pursued with ever greater intensity. To speak of physics alone, the purpose of research on electricity and magnetism could claim increasingly well-defined targets that ultimately stood for momentous advances. It should be enough to think of the distance that separates Oersted's accidental discovery of the magnetic field produced by a current and the experimental work that began, as the century closed, on electromagnetic waves. Much the same is true of the advances in atomic theory from Prout's theory to the discovery of the nucleus by Rutherford and to Bohr's account of the spectral lines of hydrogen.

Today science has reached the stage where the vastest targets can be formulated in most definite forms. Illustrations of this are investigations of fundamental particles and of cosmology. At the same time the scientific aims are pursued with feverish intensity as well as on a grandiose scale, in clear evidence of most specific purposes at work. It should be enough to think of the project for a complete mapping of man's genetic constitution and of the building of gigantic accelerators. The latter certainly demand careful specifications of the goals to be achieved.

Curiously, that most purposeful exploitation of the potentialities of the scientific method has created an atmosphere in which it becomes increasingly difficult to do justice to man's own sense of purpose. Such a sense can appear but an illusion if nothing more is perceived in it than an intricate network of feedback mechanisms. No sense of purpose can be justified on the basis of the widely entertained claim, that ultimately all processes in nature are but chance occurrences. Again, the claim, widely shared by scientists, that all science is but a game,[32] allows only for a parody of purpose. Unfortunately, that game is not what games have always been, a purposeful attention to unforeseeable opportunities, but a lucky sharing in its thermodynamical mimicry. But can there be a purpose in being part of a game that cannot be won because one cannot get out of it?

Misplaced heuristics
There is more than a purely conceptual paradox to this touch of purposelesness produced within the framework of a most purposeful activity which is doing exact science. The paradox presented itself right at the moment when the Greeks of old thought hard and fast of a mechanistic account of nature. A book which Anaxagoras wrote on "Mind" was such an account, without mathematics of course.[33] It ex-

erted an overpowering lure on most of its readers, one of them being none other than young Socrates. Before long he had to find out that an intellect bent on considering mechanical interactions alone becomes deprived of understanding the purpose of any conscious action. When the action meant a decision about life and death, such as whether Socrates was to drink or not to drink the hemlock, the poverty of exact science proved to be unbearable.

Hence the Socratic reaction, a most fateful turn in the history of physics, a point still to be perceived by a great variety of Socrates' interpreters.[34] To save purpose in its eminently human sense, Socrates proposed a new physics in which all physical processes became personified, or at least animated. They were taken to act for a purpose, or for the best. This Socratic account of the workings of nature, intimated in *Phaedo*,[35] became fully developed in Aristotle's physics where motion was defined in terms of goal-seeking, or of a trend for all things to seek out their natural places. To heighten the irony, if not plain cultural tragedy, Aristotle, most careful not to get involved in quantitative considerations while speaking about the processes of nature, offered a blatantly erroneous quantitative detail as he discussed the goal-seeking of falling bodies.[36] Such was a misplaced search for purpose which nipped in the bud the fortunes of physics right at the moment when it could have effectively started, as did much later Newtonian physics, on a course with an unlimited future.[37]

Interestingly, Socrates was very much remembered when physics came into its own through Newton's science of mechanics. Of course, it took Leibniz's many-sided genius to be concerned about the possible threat which such a science could pose to man's sense of purpose. With an eye on *Phaedo* Leibniz proposed a recasting of the basic laws of physics. He thought that the sense of purpose would scientifically be vindicated if the laws of motion were to be expressed as paths along which bodies in motion would go in the shortest time from one place to another.[38] Somewhat later this idea inspired Maupertuis' working out the law of least action.[39]

Such efforts aimed at securing a heuristics of purpose proved to be futile. The law of least action and all subsequent findings about the lowest energy levels which all bodies are allegedly "seeking" failed to strengthen man's sense of purpose. Mechanistic physics had in fact a cultural impact in exactly the opposite sense. The widespread taking of mechanistic physics for the truth of a mechanistic philosophy proved to be, so warned no less a physicist than W. Heitler, "a superstition far more dangerous than the one about the existence of witches: It leads to a general spiritual and moral drying-up which can easily lead to physical destruction. When once we have got to the stage of seeing in man merely a complex machine, what does it matter if we destroy him?"[40] In another context Heitler praised Dostoevski for foreseeing a global destruction as a consequence of the mechanistic ideology spawned by misguided reflection on science throughout the 19th-century.[41]

A more helpful situation seemed to arise with the advent of relativity and quantum mechanics. Some took the four-dimensional space-time manifold for an idea germane to the concept of organism and, by implication, to that of purpose.[42] The same was done in connection with quantum mechanics by none other than W. Heisenberg, one of its chief architects. He invoked the Aristotelian notion of potency as a philosophical foundation to his view that there was a "purposeful" relation between the quantum mechanical wave-function and its collapse, through conscious observation, into reality.[43]

Such speculations did not provide more assurance about man's sense of purpose than the facetious remark which Dirac made in the opening years of quantum mechanics, or rather of its Copenhagen interpretation. In observing that the *psi* function allowed only a statistical prediction about the direction of ionization tracks in cloud chambers, Dirac suggested that the actual track might have been "selected" by some unknown teleological factor from among an infinite number of possible tracks.[44]

Unfortunately for quantum mechanics, it has become almost synonymous with its Copenhagen interpretation. This outcome amply revealed the futility of seeing in modern science a heuristics of purpose. The reason for this lies in the strange mixture of idealism and pragmatism that sets the tone of the Copenhagen interpretation as mainly worked out by Bohr. Since both imply an aversion to ontology and objectivity, solipsism quickly claimed itself as the logical unfolding of that interpretation. Solipsism is, of course, the very philosophy within which it makes little sense to talk about purpose as a goal distinct from the goal-seeker.

Relativity and quantum mechanics have, in little more than half a century, vastly extended the range of phenomena that could be handled by exact science. Quantum mechanics particularly contributed to the onrush of new technologies. While they promoted comfort, they also increased the sense of frustration which man, increasingly at the mercy of his technological gadgets, has about his inability to find satisfactory purpose for his efforts.

No wonder that late-20th-century man tries to satisfy his hunger for purpose in myths that science had reputedly discredited once and for all long ago. Those who preach salvation through science can but be greatly embarrassed by the potent lure which astrology has for so many among the well-educated. Scientific circles have a large share in the rising popularity in the West of Eastern mysticism. The claim that modern physics is apiece with the mentality of Tao[45] finds a graphic support in Bohr's coat of arms where the symbol of Yin and Yang occupies the center place.[46]

It well represents the pragmatist-subjectivist philosophy which Bohr grafted on quantum mechanics. In that philosophy any talk about a reliable lasting purpose is just as much an impossibility as it is in the doctrine of eternal recurrences of which the Yin and Yang is a classic reminder.[47] The status of purpose is no less insecure in the latest of scientific fads, the Gaia hypothesis.[48] For if the entire earth is a quasi-living entity, the only logical purpose man can pursue is to assimilate himself in a quasi-mystical way to the forces of nature.

Purpose and its analogies

If science and its method, to say nothing of the myths they help foster, cannot function as a heuristics of purpose, philosophy remains the only candidate for the role. Its candidacy may appear a hopeless proposition. As was noted in the preceding chapter, in various major trends of modern philosophy the topic of purpose can be broached only at the price of contradicting initial presuppositions or of renouncing programmatic declarations. There it was also shown that only hollow metaphors have been offered by noted philosophers of this century who took biological evolution for an evidence of a purpose propelling the development of the entire universe.

Biology poses a major challenge as well as provides powerful support to advocates of a realistic metaphysics who aim at establishing a heuristics of purpose that transcends purely subjective experience. They must, of course, take for their starting point purposive individual consciousness as a chief and primordial witness of the reality of purpose. They should make much of its communicability, through language and other symbolisms. They should further see it in its countless tangible concretizations, namely, in man's production of an immense variety of tools, ever more sophisticated. Finally, they should not follow Darwin in his rather transparent tactic of surrendering substance for a gloss. Intellectual modesty is a mere gloss in Darwin's disclaimer of competency in respect to the designed character of the laws of nature: "I have no practice in abstract reasoning, and I may be all astray."[49]

Responsibility in matters philosophical cannot, however, be disclaimed by disparaging philosophy as abstract reasoning. In fact there were eminent biologists even in Darwin's time who, without being keen on abstract reasoning, were able to register plain evidence, though an evidence not biological in spite of its most intimate connection with life-phenomena. Nor were those biologists crypto-Lamarckians. In fact no leading biologist of the second-half of the 19th century was more intent on pushing the mechanistic explanation of life to its utmost limits than was Claude Bernard. Yet he also emphasized that mechanistic explanation did not do justice to the existence of biological organisms: "The general agents of physical nature capable of causing the appearance of isolated vital phenomena do not explain the general ordering, the *consensus* and concatenation of it."[50]

The key word, and the potentially most misleading word, in that statement is, of course, "consensus," the very reason why it has been quoted with emphasis. It conveys much more forcefully than the words "ordering" and "concatenation" the biologist's inescapable impression that a living organism is more than a mere juxtaposition of molecules. In fact a biologist, who is reluctant to take that impression of his for a delusion, should avoid speaking of biological mechanism as the strict object of biological research. For insofar as the word "mechanism" derives from the word "machine," it refers to a tool-like structure. Machines are, however, so many complex tools designed and made for most specific purposes. The biologist runs therefore the risk of turning himself into a philosopher of purpose whenever he specifies, as did Claude Bernard, the object of biological research as the investigation of biological mechanisms.

Claude Bernard did not seem to perceive this risk as he distinguished life as an organism from its mechanistic conditions to be investigated by the biologist:

> Life resides exclusively in the organic elements of the body: all the rest is only *mechanism*. The organs are only apparatus, constructed *with a view* to the preservation of the elementary properties. . . . Those collections of organs, which are called anatomical systems, are indispensable to the play of the organism, but not to life itself. They only represent simple mechanisms of precision, rendered necessary by the complication of the mass of anatomical elements which constitute the life of an organism more or less superior.[51]

The distinction between organism and its mechanistic conditions was a pointer towards philosophy which Claude Bernard did not wish to follow up. Yet he implied the indispensability of philosophy as he turned the table on a radical empiricist with a hint of his untenable position. He did so as he replied, "I have never seen life," to the question whether life was observable.[52]

How could a biologist save himself from being trapped in a contradiction by giving an answer so stupefying at first sight? The saving grace was philosophy, and in fact metaphysics, though by invoking it Claude Bernard limited himself to a short though respectful reference:

> In saying that life is the directive idea or the evolutive force of being, we simply express the idea of a unity in the succession. . . . Our mind lays hold of this unity as a conception imposed upon it, and explains it by a force. The mistake would be to believe that that *metaphysical force* is active after the fashion of a physical force. This conception does not pass beyond the intellectual domain. We must here, then, separate the meta-

physical world from the physical phenomenal world,
which serves as its basis. [53]

The reference had some distinctly Kantian overtones, such
as the definition of life as an idea and the imposition of the
idea of unity on the phenomenal world. Worse, if not cor-
rected by a better philosophy, the invocation could turn into
an animistic rite. For if the metaphysical force could not act
after the fashion of physical forces in what sense did it act?
Claude Bernard may have been too much under the sway of
neo-Kantianism, very pervasive in France from the 1870s
on, to see the impotence of a mere idea to act. He would
have also been the last, for good as well as for bad reasons,
to see God's direct action in that metaphysical force taken
for life. But if God was not the metaphysical force, in what
sense could it be more than a mere word? Did not biological
organisms keep acting in a way that inescapably suggested a
pursuit of some goal or at least a structure evincing some
design? This inescapability was attested even a hundred
years after Claude Bernard and in the teeth of all the stunning advances of biochemistry when a noted biologist declared that "organic adaptation, in its entirety, still awaits its
exhaustive explanation."[54]

In spite of his philosophical sensitivity Jean Rostand, the
biologist in question, made no attempt at an explanation of
that inescapability. One should not therefore be surprised by
the lack of such attempts in writings that represent a new
field, comparative biomechanics, in the study of living
organisms. The reason for this is tied to the very word,
biomechanics. Mechanics has always meant a methodical
exclusion of questions about purposes and goals. Yet the
more successful is the mechanistic explanation about a
complex phenomenon, the more it reveals the presence of
some design. This is particularly true in biomechanics because there the basis of explanation is the analogy of nature's

performance with that of man-made machines. In fact it is found all too often that nature has already designed machines still to be invented by man.

Such a machine would be a turbine that does not rotate but has airfoils to make the air rotate around it—and for a most important purpose at that. Nature produced such a machine 200 million years ago in the form of a female pine cone. Until recently the pollen-catching ability of that cone was likened to the baseball players' mitt. The analogy was far from perfect because it assumed that the pine cone merely caught the pollen carried towards it by the breeze. Actually, the cone was found to set up spiral currents in the breeze and guide thereby the pollen between its scales where the fertilization is completed.

To evaluate this as the work of a "coniferous air-traffic controller deliberately bending the flight paths of the pollen grains to its aerodynamic will"[55] may sound sheer rhetoric. Yet the phrase reveals the inescapable impression that a design is at work however unconsciously. Clearly, there is more to it than a random matching of a most specific shape to a most specific surrounding. Again, no full justice is done to the scientifically most ingenuous landing of coquina shells on the beach when one remarks that no molluscan intelligence is involved.[56] For if this means that no intelligence at all is in evidence in the process, it becomes impossible to admit the obvious. The latter is the very conviction that reference to a scientific design is most helpful in understanding such and countless other contrivances in nature.

To be sure, the intelligence evident in the shape of coquina shells and of pine cones and of myriads of other devices produced by nature has to be different from conscious human intelligence or else nature would be reanimated. A nature animated throughout may offer "plain" though very misleading solutions to puzzles of all sorts precisely because it would show everything to be on the same plane. But much the same happens whenever the claim is made, and in the name of science, that in all the marvelous devices of nature no intelligence whatever is involved. Intellectual history is most instructive about the stupefying consequences to which such mechanistic leveling can readily lead. Mechanistic assumptions hit nature by undermining first the very possibility of machines, so many products of most purposeful procedures.

If, however, the method of leveling, or the vagaries of one-level thinking, cannot do justice to reality, one has to take a multilevel approach which is such more than in name. In other words, instead of relying on metaphors, whose thrust is blunted no sooner felt, one has to rely on the age-old perception about the different realizations of the same basic reality. The perception nowhere found a better basis than in the multifaceted nature of the most basic reality, which is being as such. The being of the mind, of living matter, of mere matter, to say nothing of the being of God, they all manifest existence though in ways that are not the same but merely analogous. In the same way design and purpose may be conceived in analogous ways.

Analogy, taken in that sense, states exactly the opposite to reductionism. The latter, however useful in science, is useless when it comes to dealing with reality rich in mutually irreducible aspects. The doctrine of analogy is stemming from respect for the riches of reality and owes its undying appeal to nature's unfailing ability to present man with a multilevel reality. Unlike those glittering metaphors, that prompt one to evade the ontological question about the cause of novelty, the doctrine of analogy is a recognition of the need to posit a cause. This is why that doctrine can also serve as a heuristics of a purpose that is evident, though in an analogous sense, in all reality whatever its mutually irreducible levels.

Blind watchers of the Watchmaker

Attention to the heuristics of analogy, a heuristics profoundly metaphysical, should seem to be much more than intellectual luxury. The true stakes are revealed by biologists who deliberately try to account for purpose on a programmatically antimetaphysical basis. In doing so they end up by failing to find even the reason for reality, living or not, let alone for any purpose in it. One such biologist is Jacques Monod who wrote his *Chance and Necessity* just before computer simulation of scientific solutions has become a vogue.

Monod's book begins, tellingly enough, with a declaration that assigns to science the task as its "ultimate purpose to clarify man's relation to the universe." Biology should, according to Monod, play a pivotal role if "human nature is to be framed in other than metaphysical terms."[57] No less significantly, Monod's first step in that momentous enterprise is to take the metaphysical sting out of the overwhelming impression that biological organisms represent the materialization of purpose in much the same sense as do man-made machines. Monod does this, as was done by many biologists who did not wish to appear rudely materialist, by endorsing and diluting in the same breath the purposive character of biological organisms. The breath, a rather malodorous one, is aimed at blowing away the "germs" of objectivity that may be carried by references to purpose:

> Rather than reject this idea (as certain biologists have tried to do) it is indispensable to recognize that it is essential to the very definition of living beings. We shall maintain that the latter are distinct from all other structures or systems present in the universe through this characteristic property, which we shall call *teleonomy*. But it must be borne in mind that, while necessary to the definition of living beings, this condition is not sufficient, since it does not propose any objective

criteria for distinguishing between living beings themselves and the artifacts issued from their activity.[58]

This is not the place to follow Monod's illogical recourses to chance and necessity of which the former he leaves undefined. That chance as imagined by Monod cannot be the ground of existence, let alone of purpose, becomes all too evident when he takes up the origin of life in the universe. The fact that its emergence by chance is "virtually zero" turns that emergence into a non-scientific problem because, as clearly seen by Monod, modern science, so heavily steeped in probabilistic methods, "can neither say nor do anything about a unique occurrence."[59] But then, by the same stroke, the universe becomes a non-scientific object: "Among all the occurrences possible in the universe the *a priori* probability of any particular one of them verges upon zero. Yet the universe exists,"[60] although, as being a single event, it should not exist at least for Monod's science.

Monod, apparently unaware of the scientific cosmology of General Relativity, is fully conscious of at least one consequence of his "scientific" approach. It does not entitle one to posit necessity as the cause of the universe. Yet his true reason for this admission, which deprives him of explanation of all material existence, may have lain with his suspicion that a cosmic necessity would bring back, however surreptitiously, the reality of purpose, cosmic and individual. Of course, Monod would not have written his book for no specific purpose. In view of what has recently taken place in the "socialist" part of the world, Monod's plea for a "socialist humanism" as mankind's only reasonable goal, may seem highly ironic. Even more so his last claim that his plea might not appear "an incoherent dream" in spite of his grand conclusion: "The ancient covenant is in pieces; man knows at last that he is alone in the universe's unfeeling immensity, out of which he emerged only by chance."[61] Emergence by chance (undefined) should seem in itself a most indefinite process and even more so if about its material substratum, the universe, science is supposedly in total blindness owing to its statistical methods.

As to computer simulation of scientific solutions, which is the ace-card in *The Blind Watchmaker* by Richard Dawkins, a recall of the remark, "garbage in, garbage out," may not be amiss. The garbage is not, of course, the set of initial programming which yields a sequence of figures evocative of the "evolution" of the full-bodied structure of insects from almost nondescript initial shapes.[62] The garbage is the inattention to two points: One is the inevitability of a specific sequence given one specific set of programs. The other is the studied vagueness about the data constituting the initial program. In terms of both inattentions the science of evolution is bound to look like conceptual garbage in which a conclusion becomes its unsavory kind which is a foregone conclusion, or perhaps even worse, a plain tautology.

A foregone conclusion cannot have that imperfection which is possible variability, an invariable postulate about evolution. No evolutionist would dare to postulate the exact repetition of evolution on earth were it to start again. Dawkins' hostility toward the idea of purpose leads him into performing further somersaults in logic such as his advocacy of "tamed chance." He means "slow, gradual, cumulative natural selection" as "the ultimate explanation for our existence."[63] A similar howler is Dawkins' refutation of God's existence on the basis that deity is an impossible idea because chance can only produce imperfect beings. He should have rather paid attention to what physics has revealed about the stunning measure of precision in the universe. There is far more reason than Paley would have ever imagined to see behind the cosmos a Watchmaker, and someone infinitely greater than a mere Watchmaker would be even if given a cosmic reach.

Dawkins' blindness to this point is at one with his logic, culminating in his hostility to purpose, already observed in Monod's case. It is revealed in Dawkins' claim that fundamental particles are so simple as to need no explanation.[64] What Dawkins tries to achieve by this claim is that there is no need to invoke a Creator. Actually he loses hold on the universe itself which is anything but "simple," that is, non-specific. Of course, fundamental particles, if any of those presently known are truly such, may appear simple from the safe distance usually occupied by amateurs. On a moderately close look each of them appears staggeringly specific with most sharply defined properties worthy of a cosmos that can rightly be compared to a clock for two reasons. One is its precision, the other is the fact that in all evidence it is destined to run down once it has been wound up and let go.

The system of those particles represented a most complex coordination that restricts to an extremely narrow track all their successive interactions, including the ones that represent the first stage in organic life on the cosmic timetable. There may be on hand one day a reduction of the uncounted forms, so many marvels of coordination, of unconscious life to a set of those particles. Yet such a success will not blunt the sharp characteristics of such a set. They will forever challenge the consciousness of man to see behind those complex coordinations a cause, not only mechanistic but also teleological, at work. The impression will remain inescapable that the primordial set of those particles is designed.

They are designed because they are specific. As I argued elsewhere, the overall specificity of the cosmos, insofar as it is a universe or a totality embracing all, can only have its cause in an "outside" factor, which only a Creator can be in respect to that totality.[65] As a supreme infinite intelligence, the Creator can only work for a purpose, although the clearly designed coordination of the physical components of the universe, can merely convey its general reality as embodied in analogous ways on the various levels of existence.

Cosmic purpose is indeed so generic as to fail to touch on those aspects of purpose that in the human context are of burning importance. They are such because of man's ability to burn himself whenever he misuses his freedom.

In a scientific age that has witnessed the misuses of freedom through crime and violence reach unprecedented proportions, little attention is paid any longer to an apparently harmless, though most sinistrous abuse of freedom. It consists in playing a dubious intellectual game with man's free will, mostly in the name of Darwinism. The game is aimed at denying free will and taking the denial back through transparent rhetoric. However, if we are, as Dawkins claims, but mere "survival machines for our genes," he cannot also claim that "we have the power to defy the selfish genes of our birth and, if necessary, the selfish memes of our indocrination."[66] Dawkins' second claim is disingenuous also in that he failed to include specifically among those memes the ones produced by Darwinist indocrination taught in the name of good evolutionary biology. Darwinism has, of course, man's sense of purpose as its chief and immediate target. That such a sense cannot be attacked without aiming a blow at free will as well is but one evidence that between the two there is a vast and profound interconnection that deserves a special discussion to which we must now turn.

Chapter Seven

PURPOSE AND FREEDOM

Communists and Capitalists

Once Lenin was asked about the measure of freedom in Marxist society. He answered with the question: "Freedom? Why?" Obviously he meant to ask: Freedom? For what purpose? Individual freedom should, of course, seem purposeless in a system which is based on the inevitability of the march of events towards a society where the absence of classes means pretty much the absence of choices. Projected into the future that march could appear as the assurance of all types of freedom, especially when the projector still had to reach real maturity. Karl Marx was only twenty-five when he compared what he called "the ordinary or natural" society with its future communist fulfilment in respect to the measure of freedom and of the wealth of choices they make respectively possible.

Natural or ordinary society, so Marx stated in his youthful work, *The German Ideology*, was based on the distribution of labor. Owing to that distribution "each man has a particular, exclusive sphere of activity, which is forced upon him and from which he cannot escape. He is a hunter, a fisherman, a shepherd, or a critical [literary] critic, and must remain so if he does not want to lose his livelihood." In other words, division of labor and the natural society based on it, meant the absence of freedom in that all-important respect which is to choose and change jobs.

Quite differently did Marx see man's situation in a communist framework. There "nobody has one exclusive sphere of activity but each man can become accomplished in any branch he wishes." The reason for this was a mere idea, namely, a society thought of independently of the individuals forming it. No wonder that the result (including productivity) has remained in Marxist regimes mostly an idea and a markedly utopian one:

> Society regulates the general production and thus makes it possible for me to do one thing today, another tomorrow, to hunt in the morning, fish in the afternoon, rear cattle in the evening, criticise after dinner, just as I intend to, without ever becoming a hunter, fisherman, shepherd or critic.[1]

Here too, as in all utopian utterances, there was a slip of the tongue. Very utopian must appear a society in which the raising of cattle can be left to the evening.

Apart from that, the record of communist states, now more than two tragic generations old, has given a resounding lie to Marx's expectations. Marxist states have always heavily interfered, especially on the professional level, with the individual's choice of career. As to freedom of movement, it usually existed only on paper if at all. The explosive yearning for freedom that today shakes Communist states to their very foundations shows the extent to which Marx misread the forces that truly shape history. His error was a misconception about human freedom which he could not envisage as a firm adherence to a free choice aimed at implementing a purpose. He saw mere social rigidity where commitment to a purpose was really at play: "This fixation of social activity, this consolidation of what we ourselves produce into an objective power above us, growing out of our control, thwarting our expectations, bringing to naught our calculations, is one of the chief factors in historical development up till now."[2]

The fact is that in modern times no political regime has put so much systematic restraint on freedom, including the free expression of thought, as has been the case with communist countries. Only communism could inspire such gripping literary accounts of the imprisonment of the mind as well as of action as Koestler's *Darkness at Noon*, Orwell's *Animal Farm*, and Solzhenytsin's *The Gulag Archipelago*. The ultimate reason for this is the exceedingly narrow range of purpose which is allowed for human existence within Marxist ideology. Its very logic was spelled out by Lenin when he dismissed purpose and freedom by the same stroke.

This is not to suggest that capitalism has an essentially better answer to the question of freedom insofar as it is stated in terms of its purpose. That such is the case received a dramatic illustration last June in a course of conferences given by a group of American scholars and men of public affairs in Moscow at the invitation of the Soviet Academy of Sciences.[3] The group included a Senator, a Congressman, and a professor of economics, all three well-known champions of a free-market economy. They alike hammered away at the incontestable ability of the capitalist system to produce many more goods than communist economies could ever dream of. Nobody contested, of course, the fact that a free-market economy largely depends on giving free rein to the individual to innovate.

The three Americans also were at one in another important respect: They showed no readiness to probe deep into the purpose of a free-market economy aside from its ability to produce a plethora of goods and provide thereby opportunities for a healthy and comfortable life, rich in cultural attainments. Such a prospect still did not provide a satisfactory answer to the question of whether the production of goods might turn into a self-defeating process in which production is for its own and not for man's sake. Even more intractable proved the question of how to specify those cultural attainments. Somehow the capitalist society seemed to be caught in a utopian predicament, not too dissimilar from the one which young Marx dreamt about. It is a sort of a capitalist dream that many, if not all, would hunt in the morning, go fishing in the afternoon, play the literary critic after dinner, and leave the raising of cattle to those, obviously very few, who find personal enrichment in day-long hard work.

The West is too familiar with the spells of emptiness which a "full" life can generate. The situation has worsened since 1966 when the American Psychiatric Association heard Erich Fromm's warning:

> Man sits in front of a bad television program and does not know that he is bored . . . he joins the rat race of commerce, where personal worth is measured in terms of market values, and is not aware of his anxiety. . . . Theologians and philosophers have been saying that God is dead, but what we confront now is the possibility that man is dead, transformed into a thing, a producer, a consumer, an idolator of things.[4]

Graphically accurate as such a diagnosis may be, it still falls far short of the frank incisiveness with which a Soviet scholar at that Moscow conference went to the heart of the matter. Growing increasingly impatient with the vagueness of references to the purposes of production, he asked for the floor and bluntly inquired: "What *is* the purpose of life?"

This question, easily the most important of all questions,

is hardly ever raised in contexts where it most properly belongs. Such a context is the subject of free will, the very factor that makes for human actions. Instead of contexts one may speak of broad cultural milieux. The rise of totalitarian systems in the 20th century was due not only to the consummate skill of revolutionaries, but also to the readiness of many to find escape from the burden of choices and initiatives in a system imposed from above.[5] The appeal of the welfare state, with its care from cradle to grave, is not without a touch of escapism.

On the intellectual level the radical existentialism of Sartre and Camus is a major illustration of the unease modern man feels when faced with the purpose of his freedom. Utmost reluctance to face up to that purpose lies at the bottom of the resolve of Sartre and others to acknowledge but strictly momentary acts, however freely chosen. Such acts can but foreclose questions about purpose which, if it is genuine, always projects the individual well beyond the moment. The existentialists' cavorting in momentary free actions suggests, as do all extremist positions, that it is chosen because the very opposite, a human existence with no free choices whatever, is unattainable. Such is the wellspring of Sartre's wistful remarks about a human condition unburdened with responsible decisions.[6] Questions about purpose cannot arise in that imaginary existence.

Free will at the mercy of science

Those questions are given but scant justice whenever considerations about free will are cast into a scientific mould. Of course, as long as the mechanistic view of the universe was held as an ultimate and universal truth, perplexity alone could be generated whenever the topic of free will arose. A case in point is Voltaire as a champion of Newtonianism taken for much more than physical science. For him not only the interactions among bodies stood in strict causal connection with one another but also all of man's thoughts and choices. It would be strange indeed, he wrote, that "all nature, all the planets, should obey eternal laws, and that there should be a little animal, five feet high, who in contempt of these laws, could act as he pleased, solely according to his caprice."[7]

In this mechanistic view man's freedom could not amount to more than to his implementing, in some undefined measure, one or another of those capricious wishes. The measure had to appear very meager, but Voltaire found comfort in the fact that stars, immensely larger bodies than man, did not have even that scant measure of freedom.[8] Whatever purpose man was left with in that perspective could only be the object of Voltaire's mockery. He let his "ignorant philosopher" claim that the concepts of what is just and unjust were grafted by God on human nature and that moral consciousness was the best proof of God's existence.[9]

Beneath this mockery there lay a bewilderment about the purpose of anything. The scientific heaven, which Diderot tried to bring about on earth with a splendid set of illustrations of all mechanical arts,[10] offered no logical room even for conscious human love. In that heaven even comets had to be thought of as influencing of necessity all human thoughts and sentiments. When asked by his mistress, Mme de Vaux, about a recent comet, Diderot confessed: "If I think that I love you of my own free will, I am mistaken. It is nothing of the sort. Oh, what a fine system for the ungrateful! It makes me wild to be entangled in a devil of a philosophy that my mind cannot deny and my heart gives lie to."[11]

A modern age that saw free will threatened by physical science could sigh with relief when the same science seemed to lift its opposition to it. This happened with the formulation of the principle of indeterminacy in the late 1920s. Eddington, who gave a memorable welcome to that principle in such a respect and even calculated the measure of freedom allowed by it, concluded on further reflection that the whole idea was sheer nonsense.[12]

At any rate, Eddington never took up that question of purpose, although he reflected along a broad range on the philosophical implications of modern physics. Had he been taken to task on that score, he might have referred to the limits of his studies, physics and its philosophy, though hardly to the basic perspective in which he considered them. The perspective was that of a philosophical idealism bordering on solipsism. He never parted with it after having made it the final note of his first major non-technical book, *Space, Time and Gravitation*. Its last chapter, "On the Nature of Things," came to a close with the words: "We have found a strange footprint on the shores of the unknown. We have devised profound theories, one after another, to account for its origin. At last, we have succeeded in reconstructing the creature that made the footprint. And Lo! it is our own."[13]

Particularly ironic should seem the context of such a parody of the purpose of science. The context is a book on Einstein's theory of General Relativity and by no less an expert on it than Eddington himself. The principal merit of that theory was the making possible, for the first time in scientific history, a contradiction-free treatment of that largest objective reality which is the universe.[14] Eddington's inattention to this fact certainly shows something of the pitfalls of a radical idealism verging on solipsism. As the latter claims objective reality as its primary victim, the freedom of the will and human purpose too become victimized by the same stroke.

Respect for objective reality, if predicated on science, can prove itself just as inept a safeguard of free will and purpose. Einstein is a classic illustration. He was the chief of those very few physicists who refused to see in the solipsistic Copenhagen interpretation of quantum mechanics the last word in physics. But he is also best remembered as the one who carried to its full logic a very mistaken assumption about physical reality. According to that assumption the predictability with perfect accuracy of future physical events is the condition of their being fully determined in a causal sense. The assumption shows the inordinate fondness of physicists for exact measurements, a fondness which makes them forgetful that such measurements are the function, though not a necessary one, of the causal, that is, ontological determinism of physical events. [15]

Oversight of this basic philosophical point played a part in Einstein's failure to see the distinctness of mental processes from purely physical ones. He praised Spinoza for seeing no merit in the question "of the interaction of soul and body, as well as the problem which of both be the 'primary'."[16] A logical consequence of this was Einstein's view of thought processes as being fully deterministic.[17] He never reconciled this view with his emphasis on the physicist's need for creativity if he wanted to make important discoveries.[18] Another consequence was Einstein's endorsement of Spinoza's argument against the notion of free will as being independent of causality. Einstein took that notion for "an illusion resulting from an ignorance of causes operative within us."[19]

Here the point of interest should, of course, relate to Einstein's views on purpose as a function of his dictum that "objectively, there is, after all, no free will."[20] Such a denial of free will can but land one in an indefensible stance about the more restricted problem of morality. Einstein proved to be no exception. In the context he referred to the responsibility of none other than Hitler, who could then hardly be charged with any misdeed. Indeed, Einstein was prompted to ask: "What need is there for a criterion of responsibility?" Clearly, if free will had no objective status, there could be no such criterion. But then there could be little point in Einstein's blaming "the mechanization and dehumanization of our lives" for "the horrifying deterioriation in the ethical conduct of people today."[21]

No wonder that Einstein felt lost about the purpose of life. In 1950 he thematically voiced his disbelief in that purpose in reply to the inquiry of a 19-year-old university student. The latter, who asked Einstein to pull no punches, began with the question, "What is the purpose of man on earth?" and concluded with the frank statement: "All I know is that I must die, but what I know least is this very death which I cannot escape." Einstein pulled no punches. In his reply he insisted that a reasonable answer to the purpose of life ought to mean no more than to specify the desirable and undesirable consequences of one's actions. Even the goal of human community should have to do "at least indirectly with fulfillment of desires of the individuals which constitute society." Einstein knew that the student's question about purpose implied much more. That crucial surplus Einstein could not grant:

> If you ask for the purpose or goal of society as a whole or of an individual taken as a whole the question loses its meaning. This is, of course, even more so if you ask the purpose or meaning of nature in general; for in those cases it seems quite arbitrary if not unreasonable to assume somebody whose desires are connected with the happenings.[22]

That somebody was, of course, a personal deity, a nonentity for Einstein though the only ground, as will be seen, for that broader purpose as well as for the reality of genuinely free human will.

In the absence of such a ground even the limited purpose of scientific life could become a questionable matter. While still in Germany, Einstein was asked by a correspondent in England for a reply to the question: "If, on your death bed, you looked back on your life, by what facts would you determine whether it was a success or failure?" Einstein's reply, sent on November 12, 1930, was straightforward: "Neither on my death bed nor before will I ask myself such a question. Nature is not an engineer or contractor, and I myself am a part of Nature."[23]

Undoubtedly, it made sense to claim that if, as Einstein repeatedly claimed, there was no personal God, Nature, writ large, too had to be impersonal. As such, Nature had to be indifferent to success and failure insofar as both had intrinsically personal connotations. It was another question why in such a Nature there could be beings capable of raising questions about success and failure in implementing some purpose. About that Nature, and about any part of it, what Einstein's philosophical idol, Spinoza, had stated had to be true: "Only that thing is free which exists by the necessities of its own nature, and is determined in its actions by itself alone."[25]

Free will taken in that sense amounted to a mere word which could make but hollow any claim about science as an objectively free enterprise. Very high indeed was the price to be paid for an exclusive commitment to a scientific world picture or to the exclusive validity of the scientific method. Such a commitment could but make the mind unapprecia-tive of elementary facts which, though not accessible by the scientific method, provided all the rationality and objec-tivity of science. Very objective, and most relevant for scien-tific thinking, should seem the fact that, as Chesterton, no scientist at all, put it, "No fatalists work fatalistically."[26] Recognition of this elementary truth may seem scientifically more credible when it comes from a first-rate scientist such as Henri Poincaré who coined the priceless phrase: "C'est librement qu'on est déterministe."[27]

More graphically was the same point made by the physi-cist, A. H. Compton, in his Terry Lectures of 1934 on human freedom:

It seems unfortunate that some modern philosopher has not forcibly called attention to the fact that one's ability to move his hand at will is much more directly and certainly known than are even the well-tested laws of Newton, and that if these laws deny one's ability to move his hand at will the preferable conclusion is that Newton's laws require modification.[28]

Compton's words were a just reflection on some sad aspects of modern philosophy. No less sad a reflection on not a few prominent physicists was what Compton added: "Yet I suppose such an argument would have been scorned by the physicist, who has found it necessary to show in his own way the inadequacy of Newton's laws."

Such a physicist was Compton himself. He found in the alleged indeterminacy of all physical events as "proved" by a better physics than that of Newton the proof that free will was not an illusion. To make matters worse, Compton prefaced his falling back on the indeterminacy principle with a Socratic analysis of those who invited him to lecture. They did not doubt that he would show up at the right place and right time, although in view of his many travels it was, as a physical event, of "fantastically small" probability. Was it not, Compton asked, because they looked at him in the perspective of Socrates and therefore "they knew my purpose, and my purpose determined that I should be there"?[29] At this juncture, so close to the heart of the matter where freedom and purpose form a seamless garment, Compton threw away the game. While he granted that purposes can be very effective, he did not consider them to be a proof that he had freely met his engagement.

For a proof he looked in a rarified form of physical reality which seemed to be implied in Bergson's claim that consciousness, as somehow being more than cerebral activity, "has a part in determining human actions, which thereby become free."[30] Still, Compton was haunted by "Socrates'

contention that the knowledge which comes to us intu-
itively through direct experience is of a more fundamental
kind than that based upon intricate arguments concerned
with delicate tests." Once more Compton stepped from
clear waters into a muddle. Whatever the value of Socratic
morality steeped in purpose, it lacked "true meaning if
consciousness is ineffective."[31] Clearly, Compton took consciousness for some mysterious physical force.

The Greek predicament

Compton's vacillations are indicative of the modern intellect's inability to ascribe real weight to kinds of knowledge
other than scientific or apparently scientific. Socrates was in
a reverse predicament, owing to his failure to appreciate
scientific knowledge. As a result, Socrates ascribed a quasi-
conscious purpose to every physical process in order to
secure recognition for human purpose. He might have
avoided this dubious strategy had he taken his primary
stand on man's free will. Here too Socrates proved to be
more effective in raising questions than answering them.

Undoubtedly, the justification Socrates gave for his decision to drink the hemlock would have been different had the
atomists not insisted on universal determinism. According
to his only surviving statement Leucippus was emphatic:
"Nothing occurs at random but everything for a reason and
necessity."[32] It was, however, one thing to obey freely the
"divine" voice of conscience, another to articulate that freedom conceptually. There Socrates and the Socratic tradition
failed to see the difference between two aspects of the free
will. One was its fact as evidenced in immediate experience,
the other its proverbial weakness to do the right thing.
Socrates was certainly bent on proving that the weakness
was not complete debility or else virtue would not have been
teachable. But overemphasis on the teachability of virtue
could entail the proposition, on which the dispute in *Pro-*

tagoras came to a head, that "everything was knowledge—justice, temperance, and courage alike."[33] In that perspective the full intellectualization of free will was an almost foregone conclusion.

Plato was all too ready to carry the teachability of virtue to its institutionalized extreme in the ideal state described in the *Laws*. The rigid regimentation prevailing there showed that the intellectualization of free will could easily deprive it of meaning. The concluding myth in the *Republic* amply revealed that Plato would not endorse free will as a metaphysically ontological reality. The outcome should seem all the more dispiriting as in the *Republic* Plato tried to show that compliance with morality constituted the soul's truly natural and therefore happiest condition. But was that compliance truly free?

In answering this all-important question Plato began by affirming free will in words which none other than Lachesis, the daughter of Necessity, addresses to souls ready to begin their life on earth:

> No divinity shall cast lots for you, but you shall choose your own deity. Let him to whom falls the first lot first select a life to which he shall cleave of necessity. But virtue has no master over her, and each shall have more or less of her as he honors her or does her despite. The blame is his who chooses. God is blameless.[34]

But shortly afterwards Necessity appears to have the upper hand as suggested by the messenger from the other world: "the [souls'] choice was determined for the most part by the habits of their former lives."[35] This, of course, should have appeared a foregone conclusion in view of Lachesis' introductory reference to a particular life as being just another phase in the "cycle of mortal generation where birth is a beacon of death." The soul, including its free will, was no

less subject to the inexorability of eternal cycles than anything else or in fact the universe itself. Embodying an inescapable treadmill, those cycles raised despairing questions
in the minds of those who considered them with the utmost
consistency. Surprisingly, they did not include Aristotle.

Less fond than Plato of myths as carriers of metaphysical
messages, Aristotle avoided giving graphic glimpses of his
true thinking about freedom and purpose. One can, however, surmise that the contradictory character, already observed in Plato, would have emerged had Aristotle probed
into the relation of a soul, enjoying some practical freedom
while in the body, to that universal soul to which it had to
return.[36] Much the same perplexity would have come into
focus had Aristotle pursued the question of individual purpose for a soul that ultimately could not retain its identity.
Consequently, no more than ennobled pragmatism can be
seen in Aristotle's most often quoted statement on free will:
"A man is somehow responsible for his moral state, he is
somehow responsible for what appears good to him; while
if he is not, virtue is no more voluntary than vice, each
man's end being determined for him not by choice but by
nature or in some other way."[37]

One may be surprised, perhaps even shocked, on seeing a
great mind like Aristotle wrap in a series of "somehows" the
plain fact of free will. His ambivalence about it did not fail to
evoke puzzled comments.[38] His pivotal terms, *hēkon* and
akōn, are not best translated as "voluntary" and "involun-
tary." They rather relate to the measure of psychological and
sociological conditionings of human actions. Aristotle feels
more at ease when, for instance, in the *Politics*, he gives his
reasons why tyranny rules the people of the North (Par-
thians) and of the East (Persians). The former have but
courage, the latter but intelligence, and only the Greeks
have both: "Therefore they live in freedom."[39] In saying this
Aristotle did no get deeper than the beautiful words, all too

often contradicted by a far from praiseworthy behavior,
which Thucydides put in the mouth of Pericles about freedom in Athenian democracy:

> Our constitution serves as a model to neighbouring
> cities. It is called a democracy because what it pro-
> fesses to seek is the interest of the whole people. Sub-
> ject only to the laws, we all enjoy equality; considera-
> tion is given to merit alone; the honours awarded by
> the State are to be obtained by virtue, not privilege.
> Even the poorest and most obscure are called to take
> their share in all public business. We are all of us free to
> give our opinions on affairs of State.[40]

These encomiums of democracy, hardly unknown to Aristotle, could but have a hollow ring in the ultimate Aristotelian perspective about which Aristotle never waxed
prolific. Yet he endorsed too explicitly the perennial recurrence of the same ideas and of the same political patterns to
let the Periclean ideal be an exception to the law of an eternal
treadmill. The cyclic processes in the physical world set,
according to Aristotle, a similar pattern for human events,
individual and social. He held this to be valid in both of his
"physical" treatises, the *Meteorologica* and *On the Heavens*.[41]
His attachment to the truth of that cyclic view of existence
can be gathered from its occurrence in the *Metaphysics*: "We
cannot help believing that the same ideas recur to men not
once or twice but over and over again."[42] Clearly, Aristotle
offered more than an aside when in the *Politics*, in connection
with the use of a common table in village communities, he
generalized: "It is true that these and many other things have
been invented several times over in the course of ages, or
rather times without number. . . . And we may infer that in
political institutions the same rule holds."[43]

Aristotle's reluctance to unfold the dispiriting perspective
of the perennial recurrence of the same sequence in all fields

of life, is apiece with his avoidance of facing up to the metaphysical status of free will. Had he done so he might have anticipated the efforts of Zeno the Stoic and especially his chief follower, Chrysippus. For ultimately the decisive question was how to fit purposeful and consciously free actions into a causally connected cosmic framework within which alone could man reason about his immediate and remote surroundings. The Stoic perspective was in fact so cosmic as to include even the lawfulness called *heimarmēnē* (fate) which previously had been taken for a mysterious divine factor.

But once Zeno had taken *heimarmēnē* for a topic accessible to philosophy, its threat to free will became immediately obvious. The analogies whereby Chrysippus tried to resolve the conflict could only aggravate it. In the analogy taken from medical lore the outside cause, say tepid water, had to find an inner factor, a weakened body, to cause sickness. The second analogy related to the rolling of a cylinder which could happen only when the external push was followed up by an inner factor, the cylindrical shape. Contrary to Chrysippus' intentions, both analogies reinforced the idea of the inevitability of the effect. Chrysippus himself, who did his very best to uphold the view that responsible purposefulness was indispensable for man's self-fulfillment,[44] obeyed the logic of his analogies. In almost all cases, he admitted, man's inner disposition, or rational nature, was too weak to resist the lure of external motivations.

This necessitarian thrust of Chrysippus' teaching on free will and causality found its radical expression in his book, now lost, "On the Cosmos" in which, according to the second-century Peripatetic, Alexander of Aphrodisias, he stated the numerical recurrence of all individuals: "Differences between the former and actual existences of the same people will be only extrinsic and accidental; such differences do not produce another man as contrasted with his counter-

part from a previous world-age."[45] Chrysippus' conviction
on this point readily translated itself into a graphic as well as
sweeping declaration:

> When all of the planets return with respect to both
> latitude and longitude exactly to the same point where
> they were located in the beginning when the World
> was formed for the first time, they all will become the
> cause of the extinction and destruction of all beings.
> Then as the planets retrace exactly the same route
> which they had already traversed, each being that had
> already been produced during the previous period will
> re-emerge once more in exactly the same manner. Soc-
> rates will exist again, and Plato as well, and also each
> man with his friends and fellow citizens; each of them
> will suffer the same trials, will manage the same af-
> fairs; each city, each village, each camp will be re-
> stored. This reconstitution of the Universe will occur
> not once, but in a great number of times; or rather the
> same things will reoccur indefinitely to no end.[46]

From this it followed that it was enough for the gods to look
over the events in one cosmic cycle or Great Year in order to
know everything before and after. While this long view
could delight the gods, it was another matter, not investigated by Chrysippus, whether a Plato would not have been
dismayed by it. As to Socrates, the prospect of his drinking
the hemlock in an infinite number of times could but make
him despair of the purpose of his heroic resolve.

No one understood this better than Epicurus who took
his chief inspiration from Socrates' example. No wonder
Epicurus' reaction to the Stoic "explanation" of cause and
free will became embodied in a book of his on Fate (*heimarmēnē*). Tellingly, Epicurus aimed at reinstating the earlier
meaning of *heimarmēnē* as a carrier of a strictly religious
mystery: the gods, so went Epicurus' famous dictum, must

be left in their eternal blessedness, that is, exempt of all necessity.[47] But the separation which Epicurus set up between the divine realm and human reason deprived him of the ground of doing philosophical justice to free will. His procedure has become a classic cause of amusement in his time and ever since. The chance swerving of atoms from their prescribed paths, that was supposed to vindicate man's free will, left man with no ground to discourse consistently about the external world either.

Such was a chief reason why the followers of Epicurus had been far outnumbered by the Stoics. In addition to the sweep of its cosmology[48] Stoic philosophy had a further appeal in its portrayal of the mastering of one's passions to the point of having no passions at all. This ideal of life free of the bondage of passions is set forth at great length in Marcus Aurelius' meditations, both moving and perplexing. A succinct portrayal of that ideal was given by Horace as he dealt with the servility of lascivious living:

> Who, then, is free? The wise man who is master of himself, whom poverty or death or bonds find unafraid, who bravely withstands his passions, and scorns unworthy ambition, who is at unity with himself and so completely unafraid that nothing from without can find a resting place on the polished surface of his life, and against whom the heaviest stroke of Fortune are futile.[49]

Occurring as it does in Horace's *Satires*, where the poet admits his own yielding to the lures of the flesh, the portrayal has an ironic touch to it. A far more serious irony than the one transpiring through foibles of character, however well rounded, touched on man's urge to construct a rapport with the divine. Two famous prayers, composed by Chrysippus' teacher, Cleanthes, illustrate this all too well. In one, man is a being who can freely turn for divine help:

> But thou, Zeus, the giver of good, in the dark cloud
> Lord of the lightning, rescue us children of men
> Out of the darkness of folly, O Father, and give us
> Part of that wisdom and virtue with which you your-
>   self rule the world. [50]

In the other, man's free choice of his own course turns out to
be a sheer necessity:

> Lead me, Zeus, and lead, Pepromene,
> Along my path which you have chosen.
> Unwavering I follow, To resist
> Is sin. And I must follow anyway. [51]

In view of all this, few utterances can appear so hollow as
the dictum, *Deo parere libertas est*, formulated by Seneca, the
foremost Roman Stoic. [52]

The perspective of Revelation

Seneca's dictum, wholly illogical within its pantheistic Stoic
context, was given a new life in the Christian perspective on
freedom and obedience. There alone developed about free
will a view within which its "mystery" could be put at its
conceivably most logical place in the chain of causation. The
process of reflection that made this ultimately possible had
begun, tellingly enough, with a new look at human purpose. The novelty is particularly striking when seen against
the massive presence of Babylonian and Egyptian cultural
lore in Old Testament writings that deal with the early
formation of the Jewish nation. For no trace of borrowing
appears when the future of that nation is predicated by
Moses on a free choice unique in more than one respect. The
choice has for its goal a prosperity which is valid through all
history. Moreover, if it is forfeited, the alternative is a doom
no less far-reaching and irrevocable.

Nor is that alternative set forth as a momentary proposition. Moses' final and lengthy instructions peak three times in his insistence on that alternative which becomes particularly pressing as the road opens into the Promised Land after the defeat of Og, King of Bashan. Prosperity or perishing in that land would depend on a choice between true and false worship (Dt 4:4ff). Later, the same alternative is held high in the form of a list of momentous blessings for obedience and of a list of curses no less momentous (Dt 28). In the third form, the very conclusion of Moses' last discourse, the alternative, "prosperity" on the one hand, "death and doom" on the other, underline the hallowed injunction, "therefore choose life!" With the heaven and earth, or the entire created realm, invoked as his witness, Moses gives his final warning:

> I have set before you life and death, the blessing and the curse. Choose life, then, that you and your descendants may live, by loving the Lord, your God, heeding his voice, and holding fast to him. For that will mean life for you, a long life for you to live on the land which the Lord swore he would give to your fathers Abraham, Isaac and Jacob.[53]

The extent to which these words shaped Old Testament consciousness over its entire stretch can be gathered from the Book of Sirach, postdating by well over a thousand years the first redaction of Mosaic ordinances. Much of the Book of Sirach is a series of instructions on various moral topics, interrupted here and there with reflections on the ultimate grounds of moral conduct. Such conduct is a series of free decisions. Their purpose is as ultimate and irrevocable as is the alternative between life and death. Once more the enormous dimensions of that choice are set in the perspective of genuine human responsibility, rooted in free human will. Although that freedom's origin is man's creation by God, God is in no way the author of man's sins:

Say not: "It was God's doing that I fell away";
  for what he hates he does not do.
Say not: "It was he who set me astray";
  for he has no need of wicked man.
Abominable wickedness the Lord hates,
  he does not let it befall those who fear him.
When God, in the beginning, created man,
  he made him subject to his own free choice.
If you choose you can keep the commandments;
  it is loyalty to do his will.
There are set before you fire and water,
  to whichever you choose, stretch forth your hand.
Before man are life and death,
  whichever he chooses shall be given him.
Immense is the wisdom of the Lord;
  he is mighty in power, and all-seeing.
The eyes of God see all he has made;
  he understands man's every deed.
No man does he command to sin,
  to none does he give strength for lies.[54]

The Mosaic inspiration of this passage is too unmistakable to write it off as an incursion of Greek thought. Undoubtedly, Greek philosophical and ethical lore had to be
very familiar to the author of the Book of Sirach, in all
likelihood a Jew from the large Jewish community in Alex-
andria. Yet he could not be exposed there or elsewhere to
what Greek thought did not contain, namely, a categorical
assertion of human free will together with its wide-ranging
ethical consequences.

At any rate, there can be no doubt about the purely
Hebraic or Palestinian provenance of Psalm 139, most likely
a post-exilic product. Moreover, there is something far
deeper in that Psalm than the appearance in it of God as a
sort of Heavenly Hound that cannot be shaken off by man
try as he might. The Psalm begins with the declaration of
God's full knowledge of all of man's actions including his

very purpose, however hidden. It is wholly vain for man to think that he can ever escape the searching eyes of divine knowledge. It is present in the highest heavens no less than at the seas' furthest end and readily penetrates the darkness as if it were broad daylight.

Furthermore a very specific reason is given for all this in three stanzas in which God is not merely credited with full foreknowledge of man's free actions but also portrayed as being the very author of them. To deepen that already very deep perspective, the nature of that divine knowledge is tied to the very depths of that foremost divine act which is creation. Creation out of nothing is not explicitly mentioned, but in view of the obvious immateriality of free human acts, it lurks between the lines as reference is made to the womb as the place of each man's creation:

> For it was you who created my being,
> knit me together in my mother's womb.
> I thank you for the wonder of my being,
> for the wonders of all your creation.
>
> Already you knew my soul,
> my body held no secret from you
> when I was being fashioned in secret
> and moulded in the depths of the earth.
>
> Your eyes saw all my actions,
> they were all of them written in your book;
> every one of my days was decreed
> before one of them came into being.

No less extraordinary depths are intimated by the same Psalm's conclusion about a need for infinity if the Infinite himself is to be fathomed:

> To me how mysterious your thoughts,
> the sum of them not to be numbered!

> If I count them, they are more than the sand;
> to finish, I must be eternal, like you.[55]

The portrayal in this Psalm of human free will and its purpose is most noteworthy for at least two reasons. One is their being intimately united as two aspects of one and the same reality. The other is a presentation of human free will in a perspective equivalent to its most philosophical aspect. As something really existent, free will (including all its exercise) has to be something created by God himself, while remaining genuinely free nevertheless. As such, free will can appear mysterious, a miracle indeed, though only in that general sense in which existence itself is a miracle, that is, something most intensively to be wondered at. Miracle taken in that sense means not so much a special intervention by God, as His general and fundamental operation of bringing things into existence. Only the modern mind caught in the syndrome of reductionism will take that basic wonder at existence itself for a sort of irrationality to be conveniently labeled as 'miracle'.

In all that philosophical touch, so unmistakable in Psalm 139, the novelty is more a matter of style than of substance. The same touch must be assumed to have been at work long before that Psalm was composed, or else a capricious inconsistency ought to be seen in two versions of the same metaphor. The metaphor in question, possibly the most fearsome among all biblical passages, is the hardening of the human heart as done by God himself. It looms large at the most crucial junction of salvation history, the very start of the Exodus from Egypt, which is triggered by the hardening by God himself of the heart of the Pharaoh (Ex 4:21). Yet the same event, fateful no less for the Jews than for the Pharaoh, is recalled in an equally early context (1 Sam 6:6) as something carried out by the Pharaoh himself as his own responsibility. Otherwise there remains little sense in the

exhortation given to the Israelites to live up, by not hardening their hearts as did the Pharaoh and the Egyptians, to
their task to recover the Ark of the Covenant from the
Philistines.

A similar duality is on hand in the use of another metaphor, the circumcision of the heart. In Moses' final instructions, assurance about the ultimate purpose is given with a
promise that "the Lord, your God, will circumcise your
hearts and the hearts of your descendents, that you may love
the Lord, your God with all your heart and all your soul,
and so may live" (Dt 30:6). Yet, as a rule, it is the people who
are called upon to circumcise their hearts, that is, to train
themselves in free acts about grave moral alternatives on
which hangs the implementation of a supreme purpose of
existence. Still another metaphor, which, as the two others,
recurs in the prophetic literature, is the blinding of one's
inner eyes, done at times by God himself (Is 6:9), although
usually taken for man's responsibility.

Ultimate purpose

In Moses' final instructions the purpose to be implemented
through free choices appears to be limited to the ordinary
course of human life and history. The latter, together with
the purpose connected with it, takes on an eschatological
perspective in the prophets. There the personal God, the
Maker of Heaven and Earth, appears even more powerful
through his ability to make a new Heaven and Earth. That
new set-up is a lasting reward for those who obeyed God's
commandments and a lasting punishment for those who
disobeyed them. The universal resurrection which Ezekiel
prophesied proclaims individual immortality beyond physical death.

Such immortality becomes an emphatic doctrine in the
New Testament. There the personal appearance of God in a
visible form puts in an even sharper eternal perspective the

purpose which free human acts are meant to implement. That purpose is a supernatural and eternal sharing in God's life. To that end every free human act is supposed to contribute. Final and universal judgment, subsequent to the end of history, forms the background of the rule laid down with dramatic solemnity: "Whatever you have done to the least of these brethren of mine, you have done it to me." The freedom of those acts is not lessened by God's mysterious help which Christ time and again speaks of as essential for recognizing the truth that alone can make man free.[56] Yet that help is described time and again in metaphors that may seem contradictory. Such a metaphor is Christ's declaration that no one can come to Him unless *drawn* by His Father (Jn 6:44). (The metaphor, as is well known, made theological history.) Yet Christ hardly discounted man's freedom as he urged (Mt 11:28) all those "who are weary and find life burdensome" or purposeless, to *come* to Him, and assured them of abiding purpose, in the image of refreshment for their souls.

When seen against this background, no innovation will appear in Paul's doctrine of grace. Not only does it safeguard the freedom and responsibility of believers to choose,[57] it also leaves intact the culpability of the Gentiles on two counts. One is their refusal to recognize the Creator from the evidence of visible things. As a result "they stultified themselves through speculating to no purpose." The phrase, tellingly enough, is from the first chapter of Paul's Letter to the Romans, that chief document of his on grace. The other count is also a culpability connected with purpose or rather with its sham which is on hand whenever man yields to disgraceful passions.

Paul's list of them could appear to a pagan of his time a most controversial document for its inclusion of homosexuality and lesbianism as plain perversions. Precisely because of this, it should appear a prophetically controversial document when set against the present-day glorification of the Pleasure Principle to be discussed in the next chapter. There attention will also be given to less "controversial" behavioral patterns which, whatever the moral label put on them, are most effective in vitiating progress. Not that Paul did not have in mind issues higher than "progress" as he painted the predicament of men as well as women:

> They are filled with every kind of wickedness: maliciousness, greed, ill will, envy, murder, bickering, deceit, craftiness. They are gossips and slanderers, they hate God, are insolent, haughty, boastful, ingenious in their wrongdoing and rebellious toward their parents. One sees in them men without conscience, without loyalty, without affection, without pity. [58]

Liberation from that predicament could only be effected through grace. Paul's doctrine about it would have hardly made its impact had it not been ultimately anchored in God's gracefulness. Whatever the abundance of sin, divine grace was superabundant. But if virtue was to win out over sin, a most positive, indeed eternal quality, had to be ascribed to all human acts as their ultimate purpose. Within the context of that eternal purposefulness, so different from and so superior to anything that had been said on that score by the best of pagans, belief in a progress that was more than a name, could but arise spontaneously.

Progress at last

Although freshly coined words often make history, political and intellectual, the word progress failed to do so when it made its first appearance in the modern sense. Lucretius, the author of De rerum natura, was certainly right in stating that repeated observations of the usefulness of this or that tool instructed man to "become progressive step by step." [59] Yet in the same breath he spoke of the actual state of crafts, arts, and learning as having reached its highest peak. That he could not conjure up a limitless future was due to two factors of which he was all too aware. One related to man's inability to be satisfied. Purple robes, Lucretius sighed, leave man just as dissatisfied as once was the case with animal skins. Far from enjoying an abiding sense of purpose

> mankind is perpetually the victim of a pointless and futile martyrdom, fretting life away in fruitless worries through failure to realize what limit is set to acquisition and to the growth of genuine pleasure. It is this discontent that has driven life steadily onward, out to the high seas, and has stirred up from the depths the surging tumultuous tides of war. [60]

Nothing could indeed be more tumultuous and more war-mongering than the depths of the human heart.

The other factor related to the inevitable collapse of the world as being subject to the inexorable sequence of birth, growth, decay—to be repeated to no end. Worse, Book Two of Lucretius' didactic poem came to a close with a warning that the actual state of the world was "far past its prime." [61] The evidence, Lucretius wrote, had to be obvious even to a plowman. The harvests of his day compared poorly with the harvests of yesteryear. Yet this proverbial praise of the "good old days" merely evidenced the state of mind of Lucretius. As an Epicurean, he had one purpose in sketching the "nature of things." Far from engaging in "progressive" pursuits, he felt that one did his best by cultivating indifference as a means of securing quiet resignation to the inevitable. A candid anticipation of what Voltaire's Candide was to say.

Lucretius would not have written differently had he lived to see the splendors of the Augustan age. Those splendors did not make less Stoical a Seneca who is often quoted as an early visionary of unlimited scientific progress:

> The day will come, when the progress of research
> through long ages will reveal to sight the mysteries of
> nature that are now concealed. A single lifetime,
> though it were wholly devoted to the study of the sky,
> does not suffice for the investigation of problems of
> such complexity, and then we never make a fair divi-
> sion of the few brief years of life as between study and
> vice. It must, therefore, require long successive ages to
> unfold all. The day will yet come when posterity will
> be amazed that we remained ignorant of things that
> will to them seem so plain.[62]

Seneca's vision represented not so much a long view as a
momentary flash even in its immediate context. There he
voiced despair about the human mind itself. In addition to
pointing at the mind's incertitudes, Seneca also held high
man's chronic irresolution. What was one to expect if it was
true, as Seneca put it, that "vice was still in its infancy"?[63]
As to the remote context, it consisted in Seneca's portrayal,
worthy of a genuine Stoic, of the inevitable disappearance
"of all distinctions. All will be mixed up which nature has
now arranged in its several parts."[64]

Not surprisingly, Seneca was eager to instruct his fellow
Romans about the Babylonian doctrine of the Great Year,[65]
the very doctrine in which that great champion of grace,
Augustine of Hippo, saw the quintessence of classical paganism. Conversely, the very gist of God's grace, as condi-
tioned on Christ's redeeming death and resurrection, could
but mean the "explosion" of the futility of endless repeti-
tions. The phrase, very logically comes from the first truly
progressive account of human history, Augustine's *De civi-
tate Dei*.[66] As one who emphatically specified the virtues and
skills of Romans as God-sanctioned reasons for their political success, Augustine in that same work also used a portrayal of cultural progress as a background of that progress
that has the Kingdom of God in heaven as its fulfillment:

Who can adequately describe, or even imagine, the work of the Almighty? There is, first, this . . . ability to attain eternal felicity, by those arts which are called virtues, which are solely given by the grace of God in Christ to the children of promise and of the kingdom. And besides this there are all the important arts discovered and developed by human genius, some for necessary uses, others simply for pleasure. . . . Think of the wonderful inventions of clothing and building, the astounding achievements of human industry! Think of man's progress in agriculture and navigation; of the variety, in conception and accomplishment, man has shown in pottery, in sculpture, in painting. . . . Then there are all the weapons against his fellow-man in the shape of prisons, arms, and engines of war; all the medical resources for preserving or restoring health. . . . Consider man's skill in geometry and arithmetic, his intelligence shown in plotting the positions and courses of the stars.[67]

As he listed those evidences of progress Augustine warned that "we are now speaking of the natural abilities of the human mind . . . without reference to the faith or to the way of truth, by which man attains to the life eternal." By not losing sight even for a moment of the ultimately important, Augustine did all-important service to pursuits less important. By resisting the Manicheans who denied freedom, and by opposing the Pelagians who belittled grace, Augustine did more for progress than any of its modern advocates. By serving a progress that was to last forever, Augustine gave purpose to temporal progress steeped in a freedom that meant much more than absence of constraint.

Above all, freedom, no less than grace, meant for Augustine a supreme gift of God. He alone could produce an entity, free will, which was to be genuinely free however fully created. Through that gift man could muster an abiding sense of purpose to be implemented by his efforts reborn in grace. Once one's sense of purpose was firmly rooted in belief in one's createdness to be perfected by grace, belief in progress could not fail to arise.

One did not have to be a believing Christian, it was enough to disavow Condorcet's hatred of Christianity, to see that free institutions, in which Condorcet saw the pledge of progress, were the offspring of the Christian principle of man's createdness. The connection was emphatically made by Fustel de Coulanges, and against the background of his penetrating investigations of what was best in classical Antiquity: "This new principle was the source of individual freedom. Once the soul was set at liberty, the most difficult task was accomplished and freedom became possible in the social order also."[68]

A half a century after Fustel de Coulanges even the origins of distinct consciousness about cultural progress were located in reflections that animated the medieval School of Chartres.[69] Whatever their fondness for Plato, the members of that School radiated an optimism far more tangible than its Platonic kind. Instead of being lost in mere ideas, that optimism had concrete targets, steeped as it was in belief in the Incarnate Logos. The concreteness of that belief could only gain by its being inseparable from a very concrete cult. Only when belief in progress cut itself loose from those moorings through systematic secularization did trust in cultural growth yield to disillusion. The rise of pseudocults of progress is a roundabout indication of the inseparable ties of progress with the sacred. It should seem already on that basis alone that the sacred, taken in its time-tested cultic form, can alone make progress part of a broad perspective about the purpose of it all, to be discussed in the next and last chapter.

Chapter Eight

THE CULTIVATION
OF PURPOSE

A cultic Pleasure Principle
From a very high point one may either gain an inspired look or expose oneself to a dizzying experience. Nothing can be more inspiring than seeing man's free will and his purpose endowed with an eternal relevance. Yet on that level, so much higher than the highest that can be reached by the senses or by a reasoning captive to them, a dangerous euphoria may blind one to harsh realities. To take them lightly would be all the more unjustified because they have been around since times immemorial. In the prehistoric caves of Altamira one can see depicted, and with stunning realism, not only bisons, stags, and boars pierced with arrows and darts, but also the imprints of human hands with fingers missing.

It is only natural to be baffled in the face of such cruelties. They can perhaps be explained as punishments for some hideous crime or as the vengeance of victors over the vanquished. An even greater problem is posed for scholarly speculations when one is confronted with human sacrifices, such as the ones performed on a large scale by the Maya and

especially by the Aztecs. The latter took most of their sacri-
ficial victims from captives from other tribes, but they also
victimized some of their own young men and women.
These could hardly take for an unmixed blessing the pleasures lavished on them for a few weeks prior to the moment
when their hearts would be torn from their chests.

Such and similar sufferings should pose a problem especially for those who tie the purpose of life to the Pleasure
Principle. It is endorsed in blatantly crude forms as well as
with sophisticated indirectness. The latter is present, for
instance, in idealized reconstructions of primitive and ancient cultures where, so it is claimed, pleasure reigned supreme until the advent of civilization, especially in its
Christian form. A recent report of Maya life in *National
Geographic* is a case in point.[1] There much is made of the
"pious rage" of the Spanish priest and future bishop, Diego
de Landa who, after his arrival in Yucatan in 1549, em-
barked on an "inquisitional" extirpation of Maya culture. To
draw attention away from the true nature of the "blood
sacrifice practiced by Maya priests," it is presented as a less
abstract counterpart of "Catholic ritual."[2] Pages later, a
picture of a jaguar sacrifice creates the dubious impression
that it had been a pleasurable barbecue for all concerned,
including the jaguar itself.

Advocacy of the Pleasure Principle also drew into dubious
tactics the Nobel-laureate physicist Dennis Gabor—and
partly in connection with the human sacrifices as practiced
among the Maya. In his book, *The Mature Society*, Gabor
tried to make it appear that those prehistoric victims whose
fingers were mutilated and the Maya maidens who were
bloodily sacrificed had both offered themselves voluntarily
"even if some forceful persuasion had to be exerted in the
last moment."[3] By predicating "voluntary" self-immolation
on last-minute "forceful persuasion" Gabor amply revealed
the weakness of his reasoning. He further weakened his case

by invoking a scene described in William Golding's novel, *The Inheritors*, a purely fictional account of what had taken place between the last of the Neanderthals and the first generation of homo sapiens. In view of this one can only be puzzled by Gabor's claim that the novel contains "a most convincing reconstruction of such a mutilation . . . which suggests that it was voluntary."[4]

Such reasoning only shows that scientists need not necessarily be expected to be mindful of the absence of real evidence whenever they venture outside their fields. At any rate, not only some very specific facts of unrecorded and recorded history, but myriads of ordinary facts of life are ignored when Gabor bemoans the breakdown of the Pleasure Principle with the remark:

> There was in homo sapiens from the beginning a deep feeling of guilt which has prevented him from enjoying the simple happiness of animals, and which, short of a mutation, will prevent him from following the Pleasure Principle along the straight path, except for short intervals.[5]

Better-grade novelists, among them Golding, best remembered as the author of *The Lord of the Flies*, come with a philosophical message. That there is in man an inborn bent on savagery was the message which Golding portrayed well. He articulated the same message rather poorly when it had to be translated into something akin to philosophy.[6] Much less can he be trusted as he theologized, such as when he ascribed to pre-humans a state of mind worthy of saints. That any of his reconstructions of primitive man's agonies can be taken for a factual portrayal, let alone for a trustworthy interpretation, is precisely the kind of statement that a scientist, whose principal duty is to respect facts, should especially avoid.

It would be tempting to focus on Gabor's gingerly handling of that guilt-feeling which homo sapiens had from the beginning. Gabor obviously did not mean a true beginning. As one ready to take novels about prehistoric man for true prehistory he merely endorsed the poetical side of Darwinism. There the origin of a startling novelty is sought in an artful smearing out of the steps leading to it into a chain of infinitesimally small and immensely numerous steps toward a goal of which nothing can be guessed in advance.

Whatever its evolutionary origin, guilt-feeling is one of those empirical facts that cannot be measured on a psychological Richter-scale although it can be more unsettling than the tremors of the earth. Its origin is the origin of man's higher than animal nature which deprives man of ever enjoying what Gabor calls the "simple happiness of animals." For whatever man may have in common with animals, the simplicity of animals is not a human characteristic. This is why man keeps defying the simple categories of science that have no room for such truly complex realities as consciousness, will, moral conscience, and their ultimate perspective which connects man with the divine.

Animal happiness itself is far from being a simple matter—though it may appear that way when viewed through the simplistic lenses of scientism, worn by Gabor and many unphilosophical scientists busy philosophizing. One wonders whether Gabor had ever read John Stuart Mill's statement, so factual in its grimness, that most animals should seem to be designed "to pass their existence in tormenting and devouring other animals." Most animals, Mill, continued, can be "divided into devourers and devoured, and a prey to a thousand ills from which they are denied the faculties necessary for protecting themselves."[7]

Whatever man's unhappiness since he has become homo sapiens, he must have been earlier a most unhappy animal. For millions of years he had to survive, and with enormous luck defying all probabilities, in the twilight zone of defenselessness. As his body gradually discarded its natural defenses—thick skin, fur, claws, sharp teeth and the like— he had to grope for primitive artificial means whereby to protect and feed himself. His environment—even apart from the threat of predatory animals—was very hostile to him, to say the least. One wonders whether homo pre-sapiens ever felt satiated to the point of enjoying with care-free abandon a colorful sunset.

Millions of years later, his science has made, compara-tively speaking, but little dent on that environment. If earthquakes no longer keep civilized consciousness in tremor for decades, as was the case with the earthquake that shattered Lisbon in 1755, it is because, owing to global communications, man is being informed about too many of them. Few references have been made to the almost one million who had perished in Tangshan on July 28, 1976, when word came about the earthquake that claimed, on December 7, 1988, thirty thousand in Armenia. The earth-quake that literally decimated Tokyo on September 1, 1923, and the one that caused almost a hundred thousand to die in Sicily on December 28, 1908, are far less remembered than the San Francisco earthquake of April 18, 1906, although the number of its victims, less than three thousand, should seem puny in comparison.

When the next major earthquake of San Francisco claimed, on October 17, 1989, a mere two hundred or so victims, no one agonized any longer over the ten thousand who perished in September 1985 in Mexico City or over the thirty thousand that drowned in the torrent of mud un-leashed by the volcano Nevado del Ruiz in Colombia the following October. Curiously, a good deal of the reactions about the recent San Francisco earthquake related to the amount of damage that might have been prevented had all the houses and highways been properly constructed. Those who moralized on an amoral basis offered shallow reflections similar to the one by the historian-educator, Kevin Starr:

> For cultures to be mature there has to be some inter-
> nalization of a tragic metaphor. This [latest earth-
> quake experience] gives a certain depth to a culture
> in San Francisco that was in terminal pursuit of the
> trivial. It was acting as if spending $100 million for a
> new baseball stadium was the greatest issue in his-
> tory, as if the next restaurant opening was akin to a
> new Shakespeare play at the Globe theater. San Fran-
> cisco has always had a temptation for frivolity. That's
> part of its charm, but this experience will give depth to
> the city again. [8]

The depth is not so much frivolous as it is tragic. The reason for this lies in the intense cult which for some time has been given to the Pleasure Principle in many places, among which San Francisco gained extra notoriety. At any rate, it should seem most unrealistic to think that technology would ever give protection against earthquakes that measure 8.5 or higher on the Richter scale. That such an earthquake is almost certain to hit Southern California within half a century reveals something of the fragility of the Earth's solid crust. Advocates of the Pleasure Principle and those, like Gabor, who make a cult of technology, would do well to recall a fact about that crust. Its thickness, relative to the Earth's radius, is far thinner than an eggshell is relative to its yoke. Almost literally mankind lives on thin ice. As to the even thinner atmosphere enveloping the earth, it is increasingly a cause for concern and not for pleasure. The magnitude of the problem can be gauged from the "ultimate" defense against the possible breakdown of the ozone layer: a metal dish of dozens of miles in diameter to be put in orbit around the Earth as a shield against cosmic rays and ultraviolet radiation. [9]

The cult of the Golden Age

The most pernicious threat to the Pleasure Principle lies not outside but inside man. A glimpse of this was given by Gabor as he admitted that the blessings of technology were not an effective road to the fulfillment of purpose equated with pleasure. In theory, technology would make it possible for a minority to keep running wondrous contraptions so that the majority may remain free for cavorting in pleasures. In practice, Gabor, noted, while "hedonistic minorities, the undeserving elites of the past, have existed for a few generations, a hedonistic majority would, in all probability, hardly survive one generation."[10]

Less than a generation was enough to let the Pleasure Principle reveal its ability to deprive its devotees of their sense of purpose. Once more faith in progress served as the background against which something of that fateful dénouement was perceived. Biological evolution taken in a broader sense, in which it is claimed to account for all aspects of man's psyche, served, not unexpectedly, as the interpretative framework, generating once more a stunning measure of shortsightedness.

Of course, in 1968, when Gunther Stent, a University of California biologist, completed his *The Coming of the Golden Age*, only the Vietnam War was a major concern for some American cultural pundits. Race-relations and poverty could seem to pose relatively minor problems once the war-machine had been dismantled. Stent saw no upheavals ahead as he brought to a close the first four chapters of his book which dealt with the progress of biology from Mendel through the double helix to genetic mapping. That genetic engineering may be a skill more explosive than the skill of making nuclear bombs was not noticed by Stent.

Equally unmindful was he of the explosiveness of some conceptual constructs, aimed at slighting rationality, although he held them high with unconcealed satisfaction. He

merrily echoed the view widely entertained in academia that
"there exist processes which, though they clearly obey the
laws of physics, can *never* be explained."[11] As an example of
such processes, Stent referred to man's free decisions. He
should have also referred to man's sense of purpose. After
all, the thrust of his book amounted to discounting any
other purpose than the one realized by the onset of a Golden
Age. It was to come about through the plethora of goods
made available by physics. Yet that very surfeit of commod-
ities, delivered by the rationality of science, was to render
meaningless the pursuit of further purposes and also any
cogitation about them.

Stent located the onset of the Golden Age in the sudden
appearance, in the early 1950s, of beatniks on the North
Beach district of San Francisco. With a touch of sarcasm he
recalled how the liberal-minded had first thought that those
aberrant young men and women would become responsible
citizens by the time they reached middle age. Others, no less
naively, even saw something healthy in the revolt against
parental authority and against all prevailing norms of civilized behavior. That by 1968 a huge following of the original
beatniks defied social respectability was taken by Stent for a
proof that his own reading of the sign of the times was on
target.

Actually Stent read his own mind into what was taking
place. A proof of this was his reading of the Report which a
Faculty Committee of the University of California presented in 1966 on the status of education on the Berkeley
campus. Under the heading, "Academically Oriented Students," the Report stated that "most of these students . . .
have fixed upon careers and are seizing the opportunities
offered by the University to educate themselves for a lifetime of work and advancement in their fields. They are the
self-disciplined, serious students who appear in every survey . . . Berkeley is fortunate in having a large number of

these students."[12] Only by not quoting the last phrase could
Stent make it appear credible his own evaluation of the
Report that according to it "an ever increasing number of
the better students no longer appeared to be 'academically
oriented, fixed upon careers . . . and advancement in their
fields'."[13]

Clearly, and contrary to Stent, there was not even the
slightest suggestion in the Report about a connection between an allegedly rising number of better students, dis-
trustful of academic orientation, and the coming to the fore
of noncomformist students. The Report discussed these students under a separate heading and only after discussing
"drop-out and rebel students." Moreover, the Report offered much more about them than their rejection of all
accepted norms of behavior, reasoning, and valuation as
quoted by Stent: "These students believed that Americans
'who claim to be moral are really immoral, and those who
claim to be sane are truly insane'."[14] While the Report
admitted that "too many highly-intelligent and sincere
young people are among the non-conformists for their pro-
tests to be dismissed out of hand,"[15] it also contained about
them some pointed observations. They should have cast a
pallor on anyone seeing in those non-conformists the heralds of a Golden Age first proclaimed from around the
Golden Gate.

To be sure, the Report characterized those noncomformist behavioral patterns as "outgrowths of the patterns of the earlier 'beat' or non-committed generation," a
point seized upon by Stent.[16] He was all too eager not to
take note of observations in the Report that, however unin-
tentionally, conjured up an ominous specter. From the vantage point of the late 1980s quite sinistrous in portent should
seem the Report's observations, so many roundabout warn-
ings, about the futility of trying to find purpose in contradictory, self-defeating ways. Those observations touch on

reason, will, and love, all equally indispensable ingredients
of a solid sense of purpose:

> Admitting their admiration for anarchism . . . they
> form groups to organize acts of protest-petitions,
> marches, vigils, and civil-disobedience. . . . Besides
> giving strength to their voices, organizations with a
> high purpose can serve to compensate for a lack of
> rewarding relationships in their private lives. To join a
> cause is part of the anxious search for a new 'sense of
> viable community' that makes this generation seem
> hardly less-other directed than its elders. . . . At times
> they seem to believe that a solution to society's ills is at
> hand if only their demands are met. . . . Except in
> moments of exhilaration . . . this confident appearance
> masks an underlying pessimism. They are not very
> hopeful of achieving instant freedom and instant re-
> form. Their acts of defiance are often acts of de-
> spair. . . . Some attempt pathetically to simulate love at
> first sight. Through the exchange of intense confi-
> dences, they seek to 'communicate' completely and 'to
> build meaningful relationships.' To little avail. Instant
> love proves exhausting and empty.[17]

Without quoting any of these observations, Stent, in a manner which is hardly a credit to an academic, took antira-
tionalism for a most creditable basis of Bohemianism.
While the Golden Age as a supreme flowering of Bohemianism needed such a basis, it was rationally baseless to praise
and damn, as Stent did, science and technology in the same
breath. After all, only science and technology could provide
everyone with the opportunity and the means for such complete self-enjoyment that would make unnecessary any purposeful pursuit of it. Yet in that Golden Age science itself
would not offer any really new objective worth pursuing.
Even the scientific understanding of the entire universe
could not, so Stent claimed, be considered meaningful.[18] As
to the arts, Stent took some present-day trends in painting,

sculpture, and music for so many proofs that, owing to their total freedom of expression, nothing really new can any longer be offered that would be perceived as really new. In a Golden Age cast in Bohemian terms only the fool's gold remained to be explored.

Long before beatniks, hippies, and their fellow travelers had to face the ultimate boredom, always a total lack of purpose, of not having anything new to pursue, a rude awakening was in store for many of them. Gayness was to turn into grimness, and especially around the Golden Gate. Early this summer, when a reporter noted the political inactivity of previously vocal gay sectors in San Fransciso, a saddened gay spokesperson was quoted as having said: "To organize and demonstrate? Not enough among us are left with sufficient strength to care for our sick."[19] None of them have indeed the strength to give some invigorating purpose to it all. The most they can boast of is their power to prepare for suicide—a denial of all purpose.

Only the jeer of a purposeless parody is conveyed when an avowedly homosexual AIDS patient schedules and attends his own wake. The sense of "wonderful," to say nothing of the "spiritual," seems to be turned inside out when with an eye on the proper amount of Seconal, a strong sleeping pill, another declares:

> It's incredible. Once you do this small preparation, you have such a sense of power. You've taken power away from the medical profession. You've taken power away from the disease. I'm in control now. It's quite wonderful and quite easy, isn't it? I rejoice in the fact that when the going gets rough, I don't have to put up with it. Spiritually I'm in a wonderful calm place.[20]

No victim of AIDS, that has taken a particularly heavy toll among Bohemians, and especially on the shores of the Pacific Ocean, is known to be in the grip of what Freud once described as the oceanic feeling. He held it high as the supreme reward for coming to terms with and giving free rein to one's subsconcious urges, with the libido ruling over all of them.[21] Freud was not always sure on that all-important reward. Take, for instance, his work, *The Ego and the Id*, where buried in a footnote runs a revealing remark of his: "Analysis does not set out to abolish the possibility of morbid reactions, but to give the patient's ego *freedom* to choose one way or the other."[22] With an eye on that remark one student of Freud claimed nothing less than that Freud "did not propagate the illusion that complete freedom is ever realistically in men's grasp."[23] As a further proof he recalled Freud's agreement with Moebius that "we are all to some extent hysterics."[24] Freudian psychoanalysis could not claim liberation from one's past, and much less could it offer a tie with the future in the form of a free commitment to an abiding purpose.

It should not therefore be any surprise that for Freud religion, which ties one above all to a Purpose writ large, appeared to be a psychological sickness. It took an arch-critic of Freud, Jung, to see deeper into matters of religion from the viewpoint of psychoanalysis. One should not, however, read too much into Jung's famous admission that in ultimate analysis all his patients required a religious solution to their inner conflicts.[25] The "solution" allowed within Jung's pantheism[26] cannot include the sense of purpose which belief in a personal Creator, let alone a Christian belief in Him, ought to generate. The most Jung and like-minded psychoanalysts could do with that sense of purpose was to respect it as a purely personal commodity with no objective content.

A rational Cult
The respect, which that sense of purpose deserves, rests on many more facts than could be accommodated within the

confines of psychoanalysis. Those facts now span over almost two thousand years as they pose a unique background to that sense of purpose, so unique in itself. Intellectually and morally that sense of purpose posed to human nature challenges markedly greater than did any other religion. It has in turn been subject to challenges unique by their relentlessness. Its response to them took, time and again, the incomparable form displayed by Thomas More. Belief in transubstantiation was, of course, a pivotal part of his commitment to that sense of purpose as embodied in Jesus Christ, but it did not play the immediate role assigned to it in a memorable passage of Macaulay. It was another, though just as concrete, aspect of that sense of purpose that made Thomas More refuse allegiance to Henry VIII as Head of the Church.

Belief in the primacy of Peter's successors as the Rock upon which Christ built the Church is the basis for their infallibility. It has been taken among "enlightened Christians" as well as within the militantly anti-Christian Enlightenment for as much an affrontery to the intellect as the dogma of transubstantiation. By reading "the primacy of Peter's successors" instead of "transubstantiation," factual justice can be restored to Thomas More's witness as reported in Macaulay's puzzled homage to it:

> No progress that science has made, or will make, can add to what seems to us the overwhelming force of the argument against the real presence. We are, therefore, unable to understand why what Sir Thomas More believed respecting transubstantiation may not be believed to the end of time by men equal in abilities and honesty to Sir Thomas More. But Sir Thomas More is one of the choice specimens of human wisdom and virtue; and the doctrine of transubstantiation is a kind of proof of charge. A faith which stands that test will stand any test.[27]

Sir, or rather Saint, Thomas More merely imitated, and was followed by, a host of others whose witness to that sense of purpose, as concretely and tangibly planted in the middle of history, echoed Paul's proof of charge:

> Who shall bring a charge against God's chosen ones? Who will separate us from the love of Christ? Trial, or distress, or persecution, or hunger, or nakedness, or danger, or the sword? As Scripture says: 'For your sake we are being slain all day long'; we are looked upon as sheep to be slaughtered. Yet in all this we are more than conquerors because of him who has loved us. For I am certain that neither death nor life, neither angels nor principalities, neither the present nor the future, nor powers, neither height nor depth nor any other creature, will be able to separate us from the love of God that comes to us in Christ Jesus, our Lord.[28]

Unlike the secularist media, for which anti-Catholicism has remained the only respectable form of anti-semitism,[29] Paul would not be forgetful today of what happened to Catholics in Hitler's Germany and Poland, in Stalin's Poland, Hungary, and Lithuania, in Mao's China, in Ho Chi Minh's Vietnam, in Kim Il Sung's North Korea, in Ceaucescu's Rumania, in Pol Pot's Cambodia, in Idi Amin Dada's Uganda, and elsewhere. Paul would also note that Catholics were the first choice for the role of sheep to be slaughtered.[30] He would, however, add to those bloody trials the lures of modern comfort created by science and technology. His pointing a finger at the purposelessness of those lures would find an echo in most unexpected quarters. Nobody expected a Bertrand Russell, who had defiantly listed his reasons of why he would not be a Christian,[31] to drop an intellectual and moral "atomic bomb" as he surveyed, with an eye on the making of the hydrogen bomb, the impact of science on society. He did so in a series of

lectures given at Columbia University as the twentieth century stood at its mid-point:

> The root of the matter is a very simple and old-
> fashioned thing, a thing so simple that I am almost
> ashamed to mention it, for fear of the derisive smile
> with which wise cynics will greet my words. The
> thing I mean—please forgive me for mentioning it—is
> love, Christian love, or compassion. If you feel this,
> you have a motive for existence, a guide in action, a
> reason for courage, an imperative necessity for intel-
> lectual honesty. If you feel this, you have all that any-
> body should need in the way of religion. Although you
> may not find happiness, you will never know the deep
> despair of those whose life is aimless and void of
> purpose; for there is always something that you can do
> to diminish the awful sum of human misery. [32]

Bertrand Russell was certainly right in saying that it was
enough to have *that* love in order to retain the sense of
purpose in the midst of human misery. What he overlooked,
and perhaps most intentionally, was the inseparable connection between *Christian* love and the love of Christ. He could
have easily studied that connection in vastly documented
lives of those saints, some of them canonized—who did
most to alleviate those miseries at their own expense and
not, as most social activists do, at the expense of others. As
an intellectual, who defiantly severed intellectual pursuits
from ethics, he should have at least looked into the ultimate
logical foundation set by Paul for that purpose as experienced through Christian love. The foundation stood for the
utmost intellectual effort, a resolve of logic, to go to the
bottom of things. No topic has indeed exercized human
logic in a more existential way than the topic of predestination in which Paul anchored God's providence that can make
all things work together and for a purpose:

> We know that God makes all things work together for
> the good of those who have been called according to
> his decree. Those whom he foreknew he predestined
> to share the image of his Son, that the Son might be the
> first-born of many brothers. Those he predestined he
> likewise called; those he called he also justified; and
> those he justified he in turn glorified. What shall we
> say after that? If God is for us who is against us? Is it
> possible that he who did not spare his own son but
> handed him over for the sake of us all will not grant us
> all things beside?[33]

The word predestination, burdened with ominous asso-
ciations, has more than one saving grace to it. The first and
foremost is that Paul in the same Letter to the Romans, the
Magna Charta of Christian faith in predestination, defined
that faith as a *logikē latreia* or reasoned worship (Rom 12:1).
Its rationality has always rested on the idea of the createdness of all. The very same idea, insofar as it means creation
out of nothing, sets apart Christian rationality from all other
kinds of rationalities. In the latter, the word creation, if it
appears at all, is invariably turned into a convenient metaphor to cover up more or less overt endorsements of pantheism. Tellingly, in the same Letter to the Romans, Paul
anchored Abraham's being destined to be the father of many
through faith in the power of God "who restores the dead to
life and calls into being those things which had not been"
(Rom 4:17).

The second saving grace about the Christian doctrine on
predestination is that neither Paul nor genuine and authoritative Christian theological tradition took that word in the
sense of positive condemnation.[34] The saving grace is similar to the one that makes tolerable the Christian doctrine
about hell, which certainly implies the ultimate and irrevocable throttling of human purpose. The dogma about the
existence of hell, or eternal damnation, has never included

knowledge about damned individuals. There is no such knowledge even about Judas Iscariot. As to Dante's gripping recount of those residing in hell, it is poetry not dogma. The same is true of some saints' vision of souls falling into hell as a thick shower of snowflakes.

Still another saving grace about predestination is its being but an aspect of a consideration which, tied as it is to the doctrine about creation out of nothing, makes it logical to speak about man's free will and about a providential governance in the universe, including a purposeful design in nature. The truth of creation out of nothing is the sole explanation of the fact that there is such a thing as a human free will acting for a purpose. To speak of human free will as a thing can, of course, be justified only if by thing a true reality is meant. Being a non-physical reality, free will enjoys an exemption from that physical causality that ties all material things into a tight-locking chain, the Copenhagen pseudophilosophy of quantum mechanics notwithstanding.[35] Inasmuch as freedom is reality, it can exist only insofar as it is created, like any other reality, material or nonmaterial, that on account of its limitation might have been otherwise and is therefore contingent.[36]

To see the human act both genuinely free as well as fully created even in its very free nature is merely to follow a twofold line of reasoning up to its full logic. The end result will appear a contradiction in terms only to those caught in the trap of reductionism. Once within that trap one will admit only one-track reasonings no matter what violence is done to reality. Illustrations of this are all the mistaken efforts to evaluate freedom in scientific terms, be they taken from classical mechanics or from quantum mechanics. All such efforts contradict their aim by the very fact that presumably they are freely pursued and therefore assume what is to be proved and in a way in which it cannot be proved.

222 THE PURPOSE OF IT ALL

Herein lies the fourth saving grace as a logical aspect of the very structure of human understanding which invariably has to cope with several classes of conceptual irreducibilities. Among them the deepest is the conceptual irreducibility of freedom to its createdness. The existence of free will is as "miraculous" an irreducibility as what is implied in creation out of nothing. Those who do not wish to look into such depths, still have to face up to other irreducibilities as long as they won't barter common sense for some uncommonly empty sophistication. Acceptance of conceptual irreducibilities makes possible the appreciation of the fact that one and the same reality, say a biological organism, or even a mere organ within an organism, can be seen as operating for a purpose while all its operations can also be described in purely mechanical terms. Another class of irreducibilities is on hand in the esthetic experience as distinct from the mechanism whereby a piece of art is being produced. Still another is the recognition that human acts can be value-loaded in the highest ethical sense while classifiable at the same time as mere patterns subject to purely statistical evaluations.

All such acts of appreciation are intrinsically dynamical cognitive and valuational processes. As such they are the very opposite to mental acts whereby sensory perceptions are merely registered and conveniently reduced to one another in ever more encompassing scientific systems. It is the easy sweep of this scientific approach that constitutes the chief lure of reductionism as if all human experiences could be done justice by it. Yet a great many and indeed the most important human experiences demand much more than mere registerings and convenient juxtapositions, a procedure more akin to statics than to dynamics. Reductionism may indeed be an option for an ultimate static order which is sheer inertia.

To overcome reductionism as a cultural malaise, more is

needed than brave slogans about the difference between facts and values.[37] In the foregoing appreciations one is rather faced with the kind of dynamical process which is on hand when one is to play simultaneously with two, let alone with several balls. Such an act, if it is to be carried out on a regular basis, presupposes a skill which will not be on hand unless it is continually practiced or cultivated. The practice demands all the more conscious application and discipline, the more intangible is its objective. Just as the skill needed in various crafts and arts should turn into a quasi-automatic habit, so should the skill in intellectual, moral, and spiritual matters become virtues. Such a virtue is the sense of purpose which, precisely because it is a virtue, has to be cultivated. No wonder that its most convincing manifestations come from distinctly cultic contexts.

The cult of Providence

In a Christian as well as English context there is no timelier illustration of this than the life and thought of John Henry Newman. The centenary of his death has drawn renewed attention to the monumental record of his relentless pursuit of truth and holiness. He saw that pursuit in the framework of a perspective in which Fate and Providence represented the fundamental alternatives. A classic instance of this is a memorandum of his, dated September 13, 1861, in reference to the writings of Charles Darwin, who had just put biological evolution into a mechanistic straitjacket, and to the writings of Henry Thomas Buckle, who had done the same with human history. Needless to say, Newman used the word wonderful in the sense of curious:

> To my mind it is wonderful that able men should take for granted that the notion of fixed laws is a new idea of modern times which is superseding, and to supersede the old idea of a Providence. . . . Why, it is the old idea

of Fate or Destiny which we find in Homer. It is no new and untried idea, but is the old antagonist of the idea of Providence. Between the philosophies of Providence and Fate there has been a contest from the beginning. Fate may have new and better arguments now, but Providence has been able to stand against it for 3000 years, and there is no reason why it should not keep its ground still, though the philosophy of Fate may still have followers.[38]

During the next ten years, or through the 1860s, Newman's mind was ever more in the grip of formulating a thoroughgoing argument against Fate. The essence of that argument, as set forth in his finest philosophical work, the *Grammar of Assent*, is that truth, natural and supernatural, can only be grasped through a dynamical approach to it, the very opposite to the reductionist or "scientific" approach.

In this age when philosophers are eager to barter their subject in order to appear "scientific," the *Grammar of Assent* should appear particularly relevant. Newman conceived it and wrote it over many years with an eye on an engineer friend of his who wanted mathematical, that is, reductionist certitude about basic facts of religion, all of which call for precisely a non-reductionist mental attitude.[39] In particular Newman wanted to show that assent, properly so called, cannot be given to mathematical, that is, reductionist propositions, but only to realities that, because of their multifaceted characteristics, remain so many elusive fish to the reductionist method. Assent to such realities had to be renewed, protected, and cultivated day in and day out, whatever its irrevocable nature as different from mere certitude.[40]

The connection of all this with the subject of purpose, or rather with the sense of purpose relating to the entire human and cosmic existence, should be easy to guess. Such a sense demands much more than facile games in logic if it is to be grasped with firm assent. The connection is also very Newmanian. Few saintly souls in modern times wrote more impressively than he did on the purpose of life taken as a most concrete individual reality. His most thematic utterance is a meditation he jotted down on March 7, 1848. In a genuinely cultic manner, it begins with God's purpose which is the world's serving God's glory: "God was all-complete, all-blessed in Himself; but it was His will to create a world for His glory." The meditation's second main assertion is the specific role given to each individual in God's plan:

> God has created me to do Him some definite service; He has committed some work to me which He has not committed to another. I have my mission—I never may know it in this life, but I shall be told it in the next. Somehow I am necessary for His purposes, as necessary in my place as an Archangel in his—if, indeed, I fail, He can raise another, as He could make the stones children of Abraham. Yet I have a part in this great work: I am a link in a chain, a bond of connexion between persons. He has not created me for naught. I shall do good, I shall do His work; I shall be an angel of peace, a preacher of truth in my own place, while not intending it, if I do but keep His commandments and serve Him in my calling.

The third point was, of course, the unconditional trust to be put in divine Providence, whatever the adversities of life: "Let me be thy blind instrument. I ask not to see—I ask not to know—I ask simply to be used."[41] These words, in proof of the stunning measure of consistency in Newman's life, echoed the lines he had penned fifteen years earlier: "I do not ask to see the distant scene—one step is enough for me."[42] What Newman said to himself in the privacy of meditation, he also said to the faithful at large. In his sermon,

"God's Will the End of Life," preached in 1848, he presented individual purpose as the further implementation of the greatest fulfillment of God's purpose which is Christ and the foremost cult performed in God's honor:

> If He, the Creator, came into His own world, not for His own pleasure, but to do His Father's will, we too have most surely some work to do, and have seriously to bethink ourselves what that work is. Yes, so it is, realise it, my brethren;—every one who breathes, high and low, educated and ignorant, young and old, man and woman, has a mission, has a work. We are not sent into this world for nothing; we are not born at random; we are not here, that we may go to bed at night, and get up in the morning, toil for our bread, eat and drink, laugh and joke, sin when we have a mind, and reform when we are tired of sinning, rear a family and die. God sees every one of us; He creates every soul, He lodges it in the body, one by one, for a purpose. He needs, He deigns to need, every one of us. He has an end for each of us.[43]

The passage has a searing timeliness in its simple explication of the purpose set by the eternal verities of Revelation, as well as by the challenges posed to it day in and day out. "The end of a thing is the test," was Newman's introduction to his recall of Christ's rising to the challenge of His final hours and of Paul's fighting the good fight to the end. With those words Newman raised to philosophical heights the commonsense truth about the proof of the pudding. The very same truth justified Newman's utter candidness as he bemoaned Christians, lost in worldly pursuits and unmindful of an inevitable change of perspective:

> Alas! Alas! how different will be our view of things when we come to die, or when we have passed into

eternity, from the dreams and pretences with which
we beguile ourselves now! What will Babel do for us
then? . . . Alas! alas! for those who die without fulfill-
ing their mission! who were called to be holy, and lived
in sin; who were called to worship Christ, and who
plunged into this giddy and unbelieving world; who
were called to be Catholics, and who did but remain in
the religion of their birth! Alas for those who have had
gifts and talent, and have not used, or have misused, or
abused them; who have had wealth, and have spent it
on themselves; who have had abilities, and have advo-
cated what was sinful, or ridiculed what was true, or
scattered doubts against what was sacred; who have
had leisure, and have wasted it on wicked companions,
or evil books, or foolish amusements! Alas! for those,
of whom the best that can be said is, that they are
harmless and naturally blameless, while they never
attempted to cleanse their hearts or to live in God's
sight![44]

Newman would not be surprised on finding that many of
his phrases accurately diagnose the spiritual physiognomy
of these affluent decades of ours. It is up to us to be surprised, or rather to be shocked, by man's chronic failure to
see a perennial pattern: Unless he cultivates the very purpose
for which he was created, all his other purposes become the
prey of ever volatile cultural fads. The failure stands out
with particular sharpness when set against answers which
science and philosophies based on it can give to the question
of what is the purpose of puny man in a vast universe.

The scientific witness

Instead of science one should rather consider the answer
given by scientists. They are, after all, the ones who claim
the authority to speak in the name of science even when their
discourse is much more philosophy than science. Quite a
few scientists are all too ready to pontificate on man's pur-

pose in terms of progress, evolution, patterns, emergence, and the like—so many artful ways of subverting the very sense of purpose. Only a few scientists are ready to note the incompetence of the scientific method to relate to man's supreme purpose, or to any purpose for that matter. Painfully small is the number of those men of science who not only perceive that ultimate purpose but also voice it without flinching.

One such man of science was E. T. Whittaker, professor of mathematical physics at the University of Edinburgh.[45] He is best remembered as the author of *History of the Theories of Ether and Electricity*, a still unsurpassed example of the scholarship which is required when full competence in physics is to be united with thorough historical studies.[46] Far less remembered are his lectures given at the University of Durham in 1942 and published as *The Beginning and End of the World*. There he faced an audience which contained relatively few of those who would have taken offense at his pointing at the futility of a world-process which, as far as physics can say anything on the subject, is slated for a complete coming to a halt. He did not aim at satisfying those who expected firm philosophical reasons for his claiming for man a purpose that does not perish with the universe. Clearly, more was needed than Whittaker's slightly agonizing question: "Can any man who reflects on the beginning and end of the universe believe . . . the grand sum total of existence to be so utterly futile as that?"[47]

The inexorable heath-death in store for the universe, a point well attested by physics, could be presented as a rebuttal "fatal to many widely held conceptions of the meaning and purpose of the universe, particularly those whose central idea is progress, and which place their hope in the ascent of man."[48] Physics, of course, was incompetent to adjudicate the contest between pantheism and creation out of nothing by a personal Creator, a contest crucial to the kind of conclusion one may reach about the purpose of it all.

Nor was it a real argument, but merely a signal in its direction, to call attention, as Whittaker did, to the importance which personal individuality holds within the human race and in distinction from all other biological races.

In sum, Whittaker merely stated his belief, without demonstrating it as a rationally most respectable position, that "the goal of the entire process of evolution, the justification of creation, is the existence of human personality: of all that is in the universe, this alone is final and has abiding significance." He did not elaborate on the immense support that such a view of human personality has gained from a supernatural context. Within the latter alone could one state with Whittaker that a special significance to man "has been granted, in the eternal purpose of God, in order that individual man, born into the new creation of the Church, shall know, serve, and love Him forever."[49]

Undoubtedly, it was courageous to say that much in front of an audience but partially hostile or largely indifferent to such a perspective about ultimate purposes. More courage is needed to say more when a scientist animated by that purpose happens to be among such peers of his who have only ill-concealed contempt for it. A classic case in this respect is the blue-ribbon panel on "Man and His Future," sponsored by the Ciba Foundation in London, in 1963.[50] The panel included Sir Julian Huxley, Albert Szentgyörgyi, Herman Muller, Joshua Lederberg, J. B. S. Haldane, Jacob Bronowski, James Crick—all well known for their materialist ideologies. In such a gathering, that witnessed more than one barb at Catholic beliefs[51] (in proof that anti-Catholicism is the "respectable" outlet for the antisemitism of some liberals[52]), it took more than usual courage for Colin Clark, the world famous expert on population studies, to state:

> Several people have raised the question of what is the purpose of man on earth. I feel a bit hesitant at entering this field and would have preferred a professional

[theologian] to have tackled it—but the main purpose of man on earth is to love God and obey his commandments. I know that poses a difficulty for people who deny God's existence but I think they ought to take a look at this view, and consider how other conclusions follow from it. Cultural fulfilment and enjoyment are secondary purposes in man's existence, not his primary purpose. [53]

About those secondary purposes it has become all too evident in this very scientific 20th century that they are bound to produce a malaise, if not something far worse, whenever cultivated apart from that ultimate purpose. Our century, to quote a phrase from Macbeth, has increasingly become "infirm of purpose." [54] Its great declarations of purpose, including the one about the "four freedoms," have not amounted to much. They fizzle all too readily and at times end in plain mockery of all purpose.

When those "four freedoms" were enshrined in the charter of the United Nations, many expected that the Nazi genocides would never recur. Clearly, they could appear not only most painful but also most senseless acts void of any purpose. This had already transpired when a young rabbinical scholar in Auschwitz asked his torturer why he behaved in the way he did. To the reply, "I don't know, I am just obeying orders," the young Jew replied with a question about the purpose of those who had given the orders. The reply was that "they don't know themselves." [55] Still to come was the colossal genocide instigated by Mao for the insane purpose of a "cultural" Revolution that was not worth a single life, let alone the lives of some 20 million Chinese. Little and much belated publicity was given in the West to "smaller" genocides, such as the one perpetrated in Cambodia that took "only" three million or so victims.

Compared with these colossally painful farces on purpose, quite amusing may appear statements of purpose in relation to some constructive projects, especially when the wisdom of hindsight is on hand. One wonders whether that wisdom is necessary to see the irony lurking behind President Hoover's endorsement of the Eighteenth Amendment imposing Prohibition: "Our country has deliberately undertaken a great social and economic experiment, noble in motive and far-reaching in purpose."[56] The experiment could not retain legal status for more than a few years. In practice it was from the start mostly honored in the breach.

A skillful engineer and a fine humanitarian Herbert Hoover certainly was, but as a statesman he helped engineer some notably failed purposes. The list of much vaunted purposes that failed in our century is rather long. Lasting peace, disarmament, the welfare state, eugenics, equal rights, the thirty-hour work-week, universal literacy, the gold standard, clean air, and child protection may come to mind. The mind may reel on weighing the true prospects of the anti-drug crusade. This and similar crusades would achieve more were they not being used, consciously or subconsciously, as substitutes for man's ultimate purpose. Something of this was perceived by Heisenberg as he pondered the question of values in his last major reminiscences on physics and what was beyond physics:

> If we ask Western man what is good, what is worth striving for and what has to be rejected, we shall find time and again, that his answers reflect the ethical norms of Christianity even when he has long since lost all touch with Christian images and parables. If the magnetic force which has guided this particular compass—and what else was its source but the central order?—should ever become extinguished, terrible things may happen to mankind, far more terrible even than concentration camps and atom bombs.[57]

Most "scientific" should seem the turning of order into anarchy as envisioned by Yeats. His vision of anarchical terror, as given in his poem, "The Second Coming," already quoted as used by the art historian Kenneth Clark, peaks in its last four lines, strangely omitted by Clark. There Yeats conjured up nothing less than a "rough beast" who, "vexed to nightmare by a rocking cradle and . . . its hour come round at last, slouches towards Bethlehem to be born."[58] Against such a backdrop Heisenberg's statement should seem an anemic cultivation of amorphously noble purposes. For he had in mind a Christianity without Christ about which the best one can say is that it has been often tried and found wanting. This is, of course, but the reverse of Chesterton's dictum: "The Christian ideal has not been tried and found wanting. It has been found difficult; and left untried."[59]

The Faithful Witness

The ultimate reason for this revealing pattern is the centrality of Christ in the Christian ideal. One need not be a believing Christian, though some broad Christian cultural background may be helpful, in order to perceive something of Christ's unique grandeur. G. Stanley Hall, who entered the history of psychology by making Freud, Jung, Ferenczi, and other pioneering psychoanalysts appear in the United States in 1909, is a case in point. In his long and involved work, *Jesus the Christ in the Light of Psychology*, Hall comes very close to seeing in Christ the anchor of all human purpose:

> Jesus incorporates all the good tendencies in man. He is the embodiment of all his resistances to evil through the ages. In the contemplation of his character, achievements, and teachings man remembers his better, unfallen self, and by seeing the true ideal of his race

incarnated even the most formal recognition of this
enfleshed ideal does something to evoke power to resist evil within and without, and gives some incentive
to reapproximate his unfallen self, and indeed may
start subliminal agencies that will issue in a regenerate
life, bring a new sense of duty, a new passion of service, and give man self-reverence, self-knowledge and
self-control.[60]

But if Christ represents the kind of mental sanity which is a
psychological miracle, then the pressing force of logic becomes even more overwhelming in the alternative as C. S.
Lewis set it forth:

> A man who was merely a man and said the sort of
> things Jesus said wouldn't be a great moral teacher.
> He'd either be a lunatic—on a level with the man who
> says he's a poached egg—or else he'd be the Devil of
> Hell. You must make your choice. Either this man
> was, and is, the Son of God: or else a madman or
> something worse. You can shut Him up for a fool, you
> can spit at Him and kill Him as a demon; or you can
> fall at His feet and call Him Lord and God. But don't
> let us come with any patronising nonsense about His
> being a great human teacher. He hasn't left that open
> to us. He didn't intend to.[61]

It is by leading up to this gripping alternative, whether
Christ was a lunatic or God himself, that C. S. Lewis asked:
"And now, what was *the purpose of it all?*" (Italics added). All
too eager to settle for a "mere Christianity,"[62] C. S. Lewis
could not make his readers face up to the ultimate theological perspective which is the holiness of God and which is
also the only solid purpose of it all. Severed from an emphasis on that holiness, reflections on the redemptive work
of Christ can easily turn into mere dicta on moral therapy
and human wholeness.

This is not to suggest that such dicta cannot tell an awful lot about the purpose of it all. This is especially true when one sees those dicta phrased by those who tried to keep Christ at more than arm's length in a world that appears to have come to the end of its tether. Sometime before H. G. Wells gave that quaint phrase a memorable role in connection with the eventual collapse of civilization,[63] he had already given an ample glimpse of his own inner life as being in a state of collapse. At a party given on his 71st birthday in 1937, he told the guests: "Gentlemen, I am 71 years old, and I've never found peace. The trouble with the likes of me is that the man from Galilee, Jesus of Nazareth, was too big for my small heart."[64]

That heart could indeed be so small as to lower to its own miserable level Almighty God himself. Such is the gist of H. G. Wells' explanation, to his mistress, Rebecca West, of why he was not a theist: "God has no thighs and no life. When one calls to him in the silence of the night, he doesn't turn over and say, 'What is the trouble, dear'?"[65]

The worth of these words, however shocking in their shallowness, is their utterly candid character. They should be preferred to T. H. Huxley's secretiveness as he admitted that he had "motives for not wanting the world to have a meaning."[66] He ignored that during his lifetime frankness for its own sake began to be taken for the highest criterion of merit, literary, artistic, societal, philosophical, and political. At the time when belief in progress reached its zenith, just when the Great Exhibition opened, ardent believers in progress kept claiming that ultimately all that such a belief called for was utter sincerity with oneself. Thomas Carlyle, T. H. Huxley, and some lesser figures, who branded hypocrisy as the supreme evil, proved to be on occasion every bit as hypocritical by their lack of candor.

The cultivation of sincerity, though for no other purpose than being sincere, received a memorable formulation half a century ago by B. Dobrée, a British literary critic:

> In our present confusion our only hope is to be scru-
> pulously honest with ourselves, so honest as to doubt
> our own minds and the conclusions they arrive at.
> Most of us have ceased to believe, except provisionally,
> in truths, and we feel that what is important is not
> so much truth as the way our minds move towards
> truths.[67]

Since then an increasingly large number of much applauded literary works have revealed the inexorable working of the inner logic that unfolds the purposeless character of this new version of *l'art pour l'art*.

Some notable literary figures that have passed away in recent years illustrate this all too well, as did their efforts to give to their despondency a touch of purpose. In 1984, five years before her death, Mary McCarthy declared in a speech given at the MacDowell Colony: "We all live our lives more or less in vain. The fact of having a small *name* should not make us hope to be exceptions, to count for something or other." Clearly, it could not matter that she counted in the eyes of some.[68]

It is the futility of any more than ephemeral purpose that comes through in the nine reasons which Primo Levi, who died in 1987, offers for the act of writing, in his book, *Other People's Trade*.[69] Levi's being frank about his own reasons did not even justify his castigating others for the pur-poselessness of writing obscurely. At any rate, it simply was not true that there was "little sense of hopelessness" in Levi's book, as claimed by one of its reviewers.[70]

Following Samuel Beckett's death in 1989, his defiant pessimism received much accolade for no other purpose than for giving accolades. No other conclusion is possible as long as it remains true that the two tramps in *Godot*, and with them all other human tramps, must wait, while pass-ing their lives on earth, for a salvation that never comes.[71] For if that play illustrates anything it is T. S. Eliot's observation about the ultimate level of hopelessness: "You do not know what it is to have hope taken from you."[72]

Mere literary bravura about despair and about hope is of no avail when tragedy strikes. A graphic illustration of this is a mother, author of children's books, who lost her only child, a Syracuse University student, when Pan Am Flight 103 exploded over Lockerbie on December 21, 1988. Instead of courageous pessimism, there was but the pessimism of a total lack of hope, making courage meaningless:

> I haven't recovered. I never will. I cry much of the time. I who never before took anything stronger than an aspirin now take anti-depressants and anti-anxiety drugs every day, shored up by therapists. The loss of a loved child is the worst loss in the world. Theo was my future, and now I have no future. Theo's youth kept me young. Now I am old.[73]

The phrase that followed, "I've got a lot of questions," did not suggest any search for purpose. It rather introduced the most purposeless inquiry of why the American government had failed to take more effective preventive measures against terrorism.

Undoubtedly no help, in that foremost form of it which is the sense of purpose, could come from therapists, notoriously impotent in this regard. Rudolf Ekstein, a psychoanalyst friend of Bruno Bettelheim, volunteered, following Bettelheim's suicide on March 14, 1990, the information that "the blows that took the biggest toll were the death of his wife, Gertrud, in 1984; a stroke in 1987 that left him unable to write as he wanted; and a recent estrangement from his daughter Ruth Bettelheim, a clinical psychologist."[74] It sounds like a proof of the answer given to Dennis Gabor to a question, "Have you ever known a healthy and happy psychoanalyst?" He addressed this question to one of the doyens of psychoanalysts who had known just about all of them from Freud onwards. Gabor never got the cable promised to him that a happy psychoanalyst had been found.[75]

The world of psychoanalysis, a world more of beliefs than of facts, replicates the fashionable belief that the physical universe is chaotic and random. The claim that love can introduce meaning into such a world can be dressed in glittering literary paraphernalia, but for all that it will have a hollow ring to it. For if the universe is random, the purposelessness of help offered in the form of love, remains where it stood in Iris Murdoch's latest novel, *The Message to the Planet*. There, whatever the author's intentions to the contrary, the most prominent character, a Jew berating a fellow Jew, represents the bottom line with his claim: "Nothing is more important than that there is no God, and no purpose in history, and no punishments, and no Jewish or any other destiny. We just live in bottomless chaos and have to help each other, that's all."[76]

No help will come to that helplessness from sweetening up with "scientific" philosophizing man's physical loneliness in space and time. A renewed impetus to this dubious art was given by the tremendous technological success of Voyager 2. The close-up images transmitted of Neptune and the other large planets, so went an editorial in *The Independent*, "should for those with religious faith and for non-believers alike . . . inspire humility."[77]

Giving the same advice to believers, who should cultivate humility, and to non-believers, who can have no justification for it, is less than a piece of sound reasoning. No more sound is the reason brought forth in the same editorial, namely, that "beyond the earth, lies the void, neither friendly nor hostile, but simply indifferent."[78] As Eddington long ago remarked, it is not the physical puniness of man that forms the true ground for man's humility.[79] Nor are wisdom and resolve going to spring forth from remembering with the same editorial that "we are alone: no one is going to come and help us, and there is nowhere else for us to go, if we get it wrong."

The infinite empty spaces, to recall Pascal's famous remark, frightened not the believer but the libertine.[80] The latter, be he called a libertarian, is the modern man who is frightened because he finds in that fright a weak shield against a far more serious kind of it, the fear of the Lord. If that fear is also the beginning of wisdom, it is only so because wisdom means the spotting of purpose and the keeping of one's eyes focused on it. This is why philosophy should be a love of wisdom, with all the tenacity of love, and not merely an exercise in logic. This is also why philosophy has become a love of wisdom only in circles where God's wisdom, as given in Christ, the faithful witness,[81] has been cultivated. And since it is the wisdom of the living God, its acceptance by man means, in a memorable argument set forth by Christ himself,[82] a life with no end in the presence of that Holiness which is God. This was His message to Planet Earth, the only message ever worth listening to from that outer or tragically estranged space which is man's very interior.

The wisdom of that message cannot be possessed without courageously facing reality in its full range. It calls for something similar to that attitude which the legendary French pilot of World War I, George Guynemer, summed up in his motto, *faire face*. In facing up to the search for the purpose of it all one can behave either cowardly or with courage. Procrastination is not a third option. It should therefore seem most logical to join the ranks of those who are convinced with Paul that "the Spirit God has given us is not a cowardly spirit but rather one that makes us strong, loving and wise" (2 Tim 1:7). In communing with that Spirit resides the ultimate living assurance that there is indeed a purpose for that all which is the Universe, with man being its very purpose given to him from above.

NOTES

CHAPTER ONE

1. The letter, which appeared on p. 9, was written by Mr. John M. Taylor, MP for Solihull.

2. A one-volume reprinting of the original two-volume edition (1763) was published, with introduction and notes by C. C. Gillispie, in 1959 (New York: Dover). There is no reference in that introduction to the medieval provenance of much of 18th-century technology, although by the late 1950s medieval technological creativity had been put in convincing light through the researches of Lynn White Jr. Undue admiration for the Encyclopedists' ideology also prevents proper appreciation of Pierre Duhem's epoch-making findings, now almost a century old, about the medieval origins of some basic concepts of Newtonian science. For details, see my paper, "Medieval Christianity: Its Inventiveness in Technology and Science," read on January 10, 1990, at Michigan State University as part of its 1989-1990 Symposium on "Science, Reason and Modern Democracy," to be published in its Proceedings.

3. A.-N. de Condorcet, *Sketch for a Historical Picture of the Progress of the Human Mind*, tr. J. Barraclough, with an Introduction by S. Hampshire (New York: The Noonday Press, 1955), pp. 201-2.

4. H. Heine, *Concerning the History of Religion and Philosophy in Germany*, in *Heinrich Heine. Selected Works*, tr. and ed. H. M. Mustard (New York: Vintage Books, 1973), p. 281.

5. W. M. Thackeray, "De Juventute" (1860), published in the *Roundabout Papers*; see *The Works of William Makepeace Thackeray* (New York: Harper and Brothers, 1898-1921), vol. 21, p. 232.

6. W. Churchill, "Fifty Years Hence" (1931), in *Amid These Storms* (New York: Charles Scribner's Sons, 1932), p. 271.

7. Quoted in T. Roszak, *The Cult of Information* (New York: Pantheon Books, 1986), p. 45.

8. This and the following quotations are from the Saturday, May 3, 1851, issue, Vol. XVIII, Nr. 481, pp. 343-4.

9. *Charles Kingsley: His Letters and Memories*, edited by his wife (12th ed.; London: Kegan Paul, 1878), vol. 1, pp. 280-1.

10. H. Power, *Experimental Philosophy* (London: John Martin and James Allestry, 1964), p. 191.

11. J. Priestley, *An Essay on the First Principles of Government and on the Nature of Political, Civil, and Religious Liberty* (2nd ed.; London, printed for J. Johnson, 1771), pp. 45.

12. Exhibition Supplement, Nr. 484, pp. 391-2.

13. H. Spencer, *Social Statics, or the Conditions Essential to Human Happiness Specified and the First of them Developed* (London: Chapman, 1851), pp. 64-5.

14. Nr. 497, pp. 59-60.

15. W. R. Greg, *Literary and Social Judgments* (London: Trubner, 1877), vol. 2, p. 272.

16. F. Harrison, *Autobiographic Memoirs* (London: Macmillan, 1911), vol. 1, pp. 12-18.

17. For a typical account of the role of that cult among "progressive" Victorians, see Beatrice (Potter) Webb's autobiographical work, *My Apprenticeship* (New York: Longmans, Green and Co., 1926), pp. 112-23.

18. C. Kingsley, *Yeast: A Problem* (1851; reprinted with corrections and additions, New York: Harper, 1859), p. 82.

19. This was the last of 80 succinct propositions that had been set forth in detail in various contexts by the Pontif who urged a study of each of those contexts as the framework for proper interpretation of the errors condemned.

20. Quoted in Dr. Zeno, *John Henry Newman: His Inner Life* (San Francisco: Ignatius Press, 1978), pp. 227-8.

21. Especially in the lecture he read on "Christianity and Physical Science" in the School of Medicine of the newly founded Catholic University of Dublin, November 1855, printed as ch. vii in the second part, dealing with "University Subjects" in his *The Idea of a University*.

22. Macaulay did so in his review (1840) of Ranke's *History of the Popes* where he quoted with approval Voltaire's snide remarks on the meagerness of what natural theology offers in the way of eternal verities. See T. B. Macaulay, *Critical and Historical Essays* (London: J. M. Dent, 1907), vol. 2, pp. 4041.

23. See Macaulay's review (1830) of R. Southey's *Sir Thomas More; or Colloquies on the Progress and Prospects of Society*, ibid., pp. 187-224.

24. The series of seven short essays, which Newman signed as "Catholicus," were published together in a brochure under the title, *The Tamworth Reading Room*, because the occasion was the dedication by Sir Robert Peel of a science-oriented public library in Tamworth, his constituency. The brochure was reprinted in Newman's *Discussions and Arguments on Various Subjects* (1872; London: Longmans, Green and Co., 1897), pp. 254-305.

25. For details, see my essay, "A Hundred Years of Two Cultures" (1975), reprinted in my *Chance or Reality and Other Essays* (Lanham Md.: University Press of America, 1986), pp. 93-118.

26. T. H. Huxley, "The Progress of Science, 1837-1887," in *Method and Results* (London: Macmillan, 1894), pp. 42-129. There at the very start Huxley held high "the remarkable development of old and new means of locomotion and intercommunication."

27. The address was an elaboration on Harrison's "A Few Words about the Nineteenth Century" (1882). See his *A Choice of Books and Other Literary Pieces* (London and New York: 1896), pp. 417-47.

28. First published in 1898, New York: Dodd, Mead and Company.

29. F. Nietzsche, *The Genealogy of Morals*, tr. W. A. Haussmann in *The Works of Friedrich Nietzsche* vol. X (New York: Macmillan, 1907), pp. 95-6.

30. Quoted by Prof. O. Stern, of Columbia University, in his guest editorial, "In Europe, a Time for Humility," *The New York Times*, Jan. 14, p. E20, col. 2.

31. W. B. Yeats, "The Second Coming," in *The Collected Poems of W. B. Yeats* (2nd ed.; London: Macmillan, 1950), p. 211.

32. The case is fully documented in P. Forman's study, "Weimar Culture, Causality and Quantum Theory 1918-1927. Adaptation by German Physicists and Mathematicians to a Hostile Intellectual Environment," *Historical Studies in Physical Science* 3 (1971), pp. 1-115. Unfortunately, Forman justifies those scientists as he dismisses ontological causality as a sort of mysticism. On the role of ontology in a realist interpretation of causality, see my essay, "Determinism and Reality," in *Great Ideas Today 1990* (Chicago: Encyclopedia Britannica, 1990), pp. 276-302.

33. J. B. Bury, "The Science of History" (1903), in *Selected Essays of J. B. Bury*, ed. H. Temperley (Cambridge: University Press, 1930), p. 22.

34. J. B. Bury, *The Idea of Progress: an Inquiry into Its Origin and Growth* (London: Macmillan, 1920), pp. 351-2.

35. Ibid., p. ix. This statement is part of Bury's own introduction which was regrettably omitted in the American edition (1932) of his work, reprinted by Dover in 1955.

36. Ibid., p. 346.

37. Ibid., p. 347.

38. Ibid.

39. P. J. Bowler, *The Eclipse of Darwinism: Anti-Darwinian Evolution Theories in the Decades around 1900* (Baltimore: The Johns Hopkins University Press, 1983).

40. G. B. Shaw, *Heartbreak House* (1919; Penguin Books, 1964), p. 13.

41. W. R. Inge, *Outspoken Essays* (*Second Series*) (London: Long-mans, Green and Co., 1923), p. 175.

42. Ibid., p. 173.

43. G. Murray made this statement in his Presidential Address to the Classical Association, January 8, 1918, published as *Religio grammatici: The Religion of a Man of Letters* (Boston: Houghton Mifflin, 1918), pp. 26 and 22. His perplexity derived from his realization that spiritual and esthetic achievements seemed to be neither progressive nor cumulative in the sense in which technological progress is.

44. December 1, 1936, p. 17.

45. December 2, 1936, p. 26.

46. H. G. Wells, *The Mind at the End of Its Tether and a Happy Ending: A Dream of Life* (New York: Didier Publishers, 1946), p. 17.

47. F. Hayek, *The Constitution of Liberty* (Chicago: University of Chicago Press, 1960), p. 39.

48. Ibid. For some penetrating comments, see R. Nisbet, *History of the Idea of Progress* (New York: Basic Books, 1980), p. 299.

49. See the opening pages of his *Science and Human Values* (New York: Harper Torchbooks, 1956).

50. Medawar offered those strictures in his Presidential Address, "On 'The Effecting of All Things Possible'," delivered before the British Association for the Advancement of Science, September 3, 1969. See his *The Hope of Progress* (London: Methuen, 1972), pp. 110-27, especially pp. 126-7.

51. They are surveyed in Nisbet's *History of the Idea of Progress*, pp. 352-7.

52. A. D. Sakharov, *Progress, Coexistence and Intellectual Freedom*, edited with Introduction, Afterword, and Notes by H. E. Salisbury (New York: W. W. Norton, 1968).

53. Ibid., p. 82.

54. That very month of November witnessed the beginning of the collapse of the Wall separating the two Germanies, with

pressing consequences that some Western leaders tried to ignore or underplay. At a time when President Mitterand spoke of a reunification of Germany "within ten years," a German scholar visiting at Corpus Christi College, Oxford, found wholly unrealistic my view that German unity might be a pressing problem for the West within ten months and possibly in a mere ten weeks.

55. Sakharov, *Progress, Coexistence and Intellectual Freedom*, p. 82.

56. Ibid., p. 83.

57. Ibid., p. 84.

58. See *The New York Times*, June 14, 1989, p. A6, col. 1.

59. F. Fukuyama, "The End of History?" *The National Interest*, Summer 1989, pp. 3-18.

60. J. Z. Muller's remark in his essay, "Capitalism: The Wave of the Future," *Commentary*, December 1988, p. 23. It was used as the punchline by J. Atlas in *The Guardian* (Manchester), Nov. 4, 1989, p. 25, in his survey of a wide spectrum of opinions on the true merits of Fukuyama's thesis.

61. Thus, for instance, D. Gabor, whose views will be discussed in ch. viii.

62. Thus, in Britain crimes of violence, that remained almost at the same level between 1930 and 1940, doubled between 1950 and 1960 and again between 1960 and 1970, amounting to a total rise from 2,123 to 32,654. In New York City, the year 1988 was marked by 1,691 murders and 78,890 robberies, a sober rebuttal of Herbert Spencer's forecasting the inevitable disappearance of evil as a consequence of progress. The latter hardly appears in a favorable light through frequent news about the overcrowding of prisons.

CHAPTER TWO

1. M. Planck, *The Philosophy of Physics*, tr. W. H. Johnston (New York: W. W. Norton, 1936), p. 99.

2. R. S. Lull, *Organic Evolution* (1917; New York: Macmillan, 1926), p. 604.

3. P. J. Bowler, *The Eclipse of Darwinism: Anti-Darwinian Evolution Theories in the Decades around 1900* (Baltimore: Johns Hopkins University Press, 1983). Contrary to its title, the book's last chapter is dedicated to the contention that dissent from Darwinism has been negligible in recent decades. See my review in *The Tablet*, Feb. 11, 1984, pp. 135-36.

4. See *Report of the Eighty-Fourth Meeting of the British Association for the Advancement of Science. Australia, July 28-Aug. 31, 1914* (London: John Murray, 1915), p. 10.

5. T. Dwight, *Thoughts of a Catholic Anatomist* (1911; Longmans, Green and Co., 1927), p. 44. Elsewhere Dwight spoke of the "remarkable spectacle that just when many scientific men are all agreed that there is no part of the Darwinian system that is of any great influence, and that, as a whole, the theory is not only unproved, but impossible, the ignorant, halfeducated masses have acquired the idea that it is to be accepted as a fundamental fact."

6. F. Le Dantec, *La crise du transformisme* (Paris: F. Alcan, 1910).

7. L. Cuénot, *La génèse des espéces animales* (2nd ed.; Paris: F. Alcan, 1921), p. 453.

8. This remark of Driesch, quoted in A. Lunn, *The Flight from Reason* (New York: Longmans, Green and Co.: 1931), p. 88, well reflects Driesch's strictures on Darwinism in his Gifford Lectures, *The Science and Philosophy of the Organism* (London: A. & C. Black, 1908), vol. 1, pp. 260-2, 283-4, and 293-5.

9. V. L. Kellogg, *Darwinism To-day: A Discussion of Present-day Scientific Criticism of the Darwinian Selection Theories, together with a Brief Account of the Principal Other Proposed Auxiliary and Alternative Theories of Species-Forming* (New York: Henry Holt and Company, 1908), p. 26.

10. Ibid., p. 233.

11. G. Romanes, "Notes for a Work on a Candid Examination of Religion by Metaphysicus," in *Thoughts on Religion*, ed. C. Gore (London: Longmans Green and Co., 1895), pp. 97-183. The essay was Romanes' disavowal of an earlier work of his,

A Candid Examination of Theism, heavily influenced by Mill's criticism of natural theology, which he had published under the pseudonym, "Physicus."

12.   T. H. Morgan, *Evolution and Adaptation* (New York: Macmillan, 1903), pp. viii-ix. In the Preface of his *A Critique of the Theory of Evolution* (Princeton: Princeton University Press, 1916), the text of his Vanuxem Lectures delivered in March 1916 at Princeton University, Prof. Morgan stated: "Occasionally one hears today the statement that we have come to realize that we know nothing about evolution. This point of view is a healthy reaction to the over-confident belief that we knew everything about evolution" (p. v).

13.   T. Dwight, *Thoughts of a Catholic Anatomist*, p. 42. Earlier in that book he compared that tyranny to the "Terror" of the French Revolution and added: "How very few of the leaders of science dare tell the truth concerning their own state of mind!" (p. 20).

14.   E. Chain, *Responsibility and the Scientist in Modern Western Society* (London: Council of Christians and Jews, 1970), p. 14.

15.   *Nature* 174 (1954), p. 279.

16.   *Nature* 173 (1954), p. 227.

17.   *Evolution* 10 (1956), p. 333.

18.   *Supplement to Royal Society News*, Nov. 12, 1981, p. v.

19.   J. S. Gould, "Is a New and General Theory of Evolution Emerging?" *Paleobiology* 6 (1980), p. 120.

20.   S. M. Stanley, "A Theory of Evolution above the Species Level," *Proceedings of the National Academy of Sciences*, 72 (1975), p. 650.

21.   E. Mayr, "The Evolution of Darwin's Thought," *The Guardian*, July 22, 1980, p. 18.

22.   From the one by H. Drummond (1894) to the one by J. Bronowski (1973). A variation on that theme is *The Ascent of Life* (Toronto: University of Toronto Press, 1961) by T. A. Goudge.

23. *The New York Times*, Jan. 22, 1978, p. E6.

24. F. Darwin, *The Life and Letters of Charles Darwin* (London: John Murray, 1887), vol. 2, p. 234.

25. See note 23 above.

26. Lull, *Organic Evolution*, p. 604.

27. G. Hardin, *Nature and Man's Fate* (New York: Mentor, 1961), pp. 225-6.

28. See note 23 above.

29. Darwin expressed this sentiment of his in his letter of March 29, 1863, to J. D. Hooker; see *The Life and Letters of Charles Darwin*, vol. 2, p. 18.

30. On a television program in 1959.

31. See *Darwin's Early and Unpublished Notebooks*, transcribed and annotated by P. H. Barrett (New York: E. P. Dutton, 1974), p. 446 (B Notebook).

32. Ibid., p. 289 (M Notebook).

33. Ibid., p. 451 (C Notebook).

34. Ibid., p. 33 (N Notebook).

35. Ibid., p. 256 (M Notebook).

36. Ibid., p. 450 (C Notebook).

37. For this and other trenchant observations of Chesterton on Darwin and Darwinism, see ch. 3, "Critic of Evolutionism," in my *Chesterton, a Seer of Science* (Urbana, Il.: University of Illinois Press, 1986).

38. "Everybody is talking about it without being shocked," were Darwin's comments, reported in *The Life and Letters of Charles Darwin*, vol. 3, p. 133.

39. C. Darwin, *The Descent of Man* (1871; new ed.; London: John Murray, 1901), p. 935.

40. A. Huxley, *Ends and Means: An Inquiry into the Nature of Ideals and into the Methods Employed for their Realization* (London: Chatto and Windus, 1937), p. 273.

41. Ibid., p. 274.

42. T. H. Huxley, *Evolution and Ethics and Other Essays* (New York: D. Appleton, 1914), p. 37.

43. Ibid., p. 83.

44. Ibid.

45. Ibid., p. 80.

46. G. G. Simpson, *The Meaning of Evolution* (New Haven: Yale University Press, 1949), p. 344.

47. J. Dewey, *The Influence of Darwin on Philosophy* (New York: Henry Holt, 1910), p. 13.

48. J. Huxley, *Evolution in Action* (New York: Harper and Brothers, 1953), p. 7.

49. See W. I. B. Beveridge, *The Art of Scientific Investigation* (1950; rev. ed.; New York: W. W. Norton, 1957), p. 83.

50. Or the substitution of teleological by teleonomic.

51. A. Gray, "Charles Darwin," *Nature*, June 4, 1874, p. 81.

52. *The Life and Letters of Charles Darwin*, vol. 3, p. 189.

53. Ibid., vol. 2, p. 201.

54. "But perhaps the most remarkable service to the philosophy of Biology rendered by Mr. Darwin is the reconciliation of Teleology and Morphology, and the explanation of the facts of both which his views offer." T. H. Huxley, "The Genealogy of Animals" (1869) in *Darwiniana: Essays* (New York: D. Appleton, 1894), p. 110.

55. T. H. Huxley, "On the Reception of the 'Origin of Species'" in *The Life and Letters of Charles Darwin*, vol. 2, p. 201. See also his *Lay Sermons: Addresses and Reviews* (New York: D. Appleton, 1871), p. 301.

56. *The Autobiography of Charles Darwin and Selected Letters*, ed. F. Darwin (New York: D. Appleton, 1881), p. 316.

57. T. H. Huxley, "On the Reception of the 'Origin of Species'," p. 202.

58. *More Letters of Charles Darwin*, ed. F. Darwin and A. C. Seward (New York: D. Appleton, 1903), vol. 1, p. 321.

59. C. Darwin, *The Origin of Species* (6th ed.; London: John Murray, 1876), p. 428.

60. Ibid., p. 67.

61. *The Descent of Man*, p. 219.

62. A. R. Wallace, quoted in R. Nisbet, *History of the Idea of Progress* (New York: Basic Books, 1980), p. 176.

63. H. G. Wells, *The Mind at the End of its Tether* (New York: Didier, 1946), p. 4.

64. Ibid., p. 40.

65. Darwin did so in a letter which is catalogued in the British Museum as A DD Ms37725 f6. Its photocopy faces the title page of *L'évolution du monde vivant* (Paris: Plon, 1950) by M. P. Vernet.

66. J. Martineau, "Nature and God" (1860), in *Essays, Reviews and Addresses* (London: Longmans, Green and Co., 1891), vol. 3, p. 160.

67. For details, see my *The Relevance of Physics* (Chicago: University of Chicago Press, 1966), pp. 307-8.

68. Quoted in R. Gore, "What Caused Earth's Great Dyings?" *National Geographic*, June 1989, p. 672.

69. Ibid., p. 673.

70. First pointed out by D. M. Raup and J. J. Sepkoski Jr., "Periodicity of Extinctions in the Geologic Past," *Proceedings of the National Academy of Sciences* 81 (1984), pp. 801-5. In their paper's concluding paragraph they characterize the periodic mass extinctions ("with kill rates for species estimated to have been as high as 77% and 96%") as regularly recurring "bottlenecking" effects that have on evolution an impact "more profound than the local and regional environmental changes normally considered" (p. 805).

71. See note 68 above.

72. D. M. Raup, "Conflicts between Darwin and Paleontology," *Bulletin*, Field Museum of Natural History, 50 (Jan. 1979), p. 45.

73. S. J. Gould, "The Chance that Shapes Our End," *The New Scientist*, Feb. 5, 1981, p. 349.

74. S. J. Gould, "The Terrifying Normalcy of Aids," *New York Times Magazine*, April 19, 1987, p. 32. See also my critique, "Normalcy as Terror: The Naturalization of AIDS," in *Crisis*, June 1987, pp. 21-23, reprinted in my *The Only Chaos and Other Essays* (Lanham Md.: University Press of America, 1990), pp. 144-50.

75. A. N. Whitehead, *The Function of Reason* (Princeton: Princeton University Press, 1929), p. 12.

76. S. J. Gould, *Wonderful Life: The Burgess Shale and the Nature of History* (New York: W. W. Norton, 1989), p. 291.

77. Ibid.

CHAPTER THREE

1. This and subsequent quotations from Paley's *Natural Theology* are taken from its text in *The Works of William Paley* (Edinburgh: Thomas Nelson, 1846), pp. 435-554. The problem discussed in this chapter is not treated in the best modern study on Paley, *The Mind of William Paley: A Philosopher and His Age* (Lincoln: University of Nebraska Press, 1976), by D. L. LeMahieu.

2. I. Kant, *Critique of Pure Reason*, tr. N. K. Smith (New York: Macmillan, 1929), pp. 518-24.

3. Ibid., p. 520.

4. For an unsparing and authoritative exposure of the fallacies in Kant's antinomies, see N. K. Smith, *A Commentary to Kant's Critique of Pure Reason* (2nd ed.; London: The Macmillan Press, 1923), p. 519.

5. Kant, *Critique of Pure Reason*, p. 521.

6. F. R. Tennant, *Philosophical Theology* (Cambridge University Press, 1928-30), vol. 2, p. 79.

7. Paley, *Works*, p. 437.

8. The series "On the Power, Wisdom, and Goodness of God

as manifested in Creation," the general subtitle of the Bridgewater Treatises, comprised by March 1833 eight volumes, among them *The Adaptation of External Nature to the Physical Condition of Man* by J. Kidd, *Astronomy and General Physics, Considered with References to Natural Theology* by W. Whewell, and *The Hand: Its Mechanism and Vital Endowments as Evincing Design* by Sir Charles Bell, the discoverer of the difference between the motor and sensory nervous systems.

9. Paley, *Works*, pp. 437-8.

10. Ibid., p. 517.

11. In fact, in his paper, "On the Ring of Saturn, and the Rotation of the Fifth Satellite upon Its Axis," read before the Royal Society on December 15, 1791, Herschel not only stated that his observations provided incontrovertible evidence about the composite nature of Saturn's ring, but also that it served some purpose: "This opening in the ring must be of considerable service to the planet, in reducing the space that is eclipsed by the shadow of the ring to a much smaller compass." See *The Scientific Papers of Sir William Herschel*, ed. J. L. E. Dreyer (London: The Royal Society and the Royal Astronomical Society, 1912), vol. 1, p. 428.

12. Paley, *Works*, p. 518.

13. Ibid., p. 551.

14. See "General Scholium" in F. Cajori's translation of the *Principia* (Berkeley: University of California Press, 1962), pp. 543-47.

15. As recorded by Herschel himself. See *The Herschel Chronicle*, ed. C. A. Lubbock (New York: Macmillan, 1933), p. 310.

16. For details, see ch. 8 in my *Planets and Planetarians: A History of Theories of the Origin of Planetary Systems* (Edinburgh: Scottish Academic Press, 1978). As to the earth-moon system in particular, see ch. 7 in my *God and the Cosmologists* (Edinburgh: Scottish Academic Press; Washington, D.C.: Regnery Gateway, 1989).

17. For interesting details, see S. Vogel, *Life's Devices: The Physi-*

cal World of Animals and Plants (Princeton: Princeton University Press, 1988).

18. Paley, *Works*, p. 534.

19. See *The Autobiography of Charles Darwin, 1809-1882*, with original omissions restored, edited with appendix and notes by his grand-daughter Nora Barlow (1958; New York: W. W. Norton, 1969), p. 90.

20. *More Letters of Charles Darwin: A Record of His Work in Hitherto Unpublished Letters*, ed. F. Darwin and A. C. Seward (New York: D. Appleton and Co., 1903), vol. 1, p. 321.

21. J. W. von Goethe, *Poetry and Truth from My Own Life*, tr, M. S. Smith (London: G. Bell and Sons, 1930), vol. 1, p. 19.

22. In the concluding or 30th chapter of *Candide* the despondent remark that "attention should be given to the vegetable garden," is repeated in addition to the observation that "to work mindlessly is the sole means of making life bearable." See edition, with introduction and notes, by J. H. Brumfitte (London: Oxford University Press, 1968), pp. 149-50. The same edition also contains Voltaire's poem, "Poème sur le désastre de Lisbonne ou examen de cet axiome: tout est bien," (pp. 153-60), a poem aimed at Alexander Pope's optimism stated in the *Essay on Man*.

23. See Paley, *Works*, pp. 251-97. The 41 sermons reprinted on pp. 575-712 are a selection out of some hundred.

24. *The Letters and Diaries of John Henry Newman*, vol. XXV (Oxford: Clarendon Press, 1973), p. 97.

25. Newman's reply was sent on April 13, 1870. His reference was to the concluding sections of ch. IV of Part I. See Doubleday Anchor Books edition, pp. 70-73.

26. Ibid. p. 71.

27. See E. Gilson *Reason and Revelation in the Middle Ages* (New York: Charles Scribner's Sons, 1938).

28. *The Letters and Diaries*, vol. XXV, p. 97. The context of Cardinal Manning's statement ("I took in the whole argument, and I thank God that nothing has ever shaken it") in

his Journal from 1878-82, which relates to his school-days at Harrow 1822-26, suggests that he referred to Paley's *Evidences of Christianity* and not to his *Natural Theology*. See E. S. Purcell, *Life of Cardinal Manning* (New York: Macmillan, 1895), vol. 1, p. 18. The opposite is suggested by LeMahieu (who does not give the context of Manning's remark).

29. *The Autobiography of Charles Darwin*, p. 59.

30. *Shelley's Prometheus Unbound: A Variorum Edition*, ed. L. J. Zillman (Seattle: University of Washington Press, 1959), p. 126.

31. C. Darwin, *The Origin of Species* (6th ed.; London: John Murray, 1876), p. 143.

32. Letter of April 3, 1860, to A. Gray, in *The Life and Letters of Charles Darwin*, vol 2, p. 296.

33. L. Cuénot, *Invention et finalité en biologie* (Paris: Flammarion, 1941), pp. 57-8.

34. Ibid., pp. 192-3.

35. G. Hardin, *Nature and Man's Fate* (New York: Rinehart and Co., 1959), p. 74.

36. In a personal communication to F. J. Tipler, quoted in J. D. Barrow and F. J. Tipler, *The Anthropic Cosmological Principle* (Oxford: Clarendon Press, 1986), p. 133.

37. A. D. Ritchie, *Civilization, Science, and Religion* (Harmondsworth: Penguin, 1945), p. 140. It is precisely its "negative" character that should suggest the distinctly postulational, and indeed, metaphysical character of natural selection. Not that one could expect A. Weismann to specify, at the celebrations of the 50th anniversary of the publication of Darwin's *Origin*, as metaphysical the "quite other grounds" than those "of demonstrative evidence" that "we rely on when we champion the doctrine of selection as a scientific truth." See *Darwin and Modern Science*, ed. A. C. Seward (Cambridge: University Press, 1909), p. 25. Again, J. Grey could rightly characterize as the Waterloo of natural selection Julian Huxley's admission that "the human species today is burdened

with many more deleterious mutant genes than can possibly exist in any species of wild creatures," *Nature* 173 (1954), p. 227. As to the rhetorical hypostatizing of natural selection, so ubiquitous in the writings of Darwinists, it calls for the scathing remark which C. Sherrington handed down on the creation of the word *protoplasm* to "explain" the material of the cell: "It might perhaps better have been called an unknown quantity. But that would have been less attractive and intriguing. . . . To call it protoplasm helped to substantialize it." *Man on His Nature* (Cambridge: University Press, 1940), p. 77. It is no exaggeration to state, as P. G. Fothergill did, that had Darwin not given natural selection an exclusive role in the first edition of the *Origin*, the history of modern biology could not now be characterized as an inordinate craving to "deify natural selection." *Evolution and Christians* (London: Longmans, 1961), p. 201.

38. S. J. Gould, *Ever since Darwin: Reflections in Natural History* (New York: W. W. Norton, 1977), p. 107.

39. Such as Sir Charles Bell's monograph mentioned in note 8 above.

40. See *Animal Life Encyclopedia*, ed. B. Grzimek (New York: Van Nostrand and Reinhold, 1974), pp. 419-20.

41. W. H. Thorpe, *Purpose in a World of Chance: A Biologists' View* (Oxford: Oxford University Press, 1978), p. 18.

42. Ibid.

43. *Time*, Feb. 25, 1985, p. 70.

44. Ibid. A statement of the entomologist, Thomas Eisner, of Cornell University.

45. R. Boyle, *A Disquisition about the Final Causes of Natural Things* (London: 1688), p. 157.

46. C. Sherrington, *Man on His Nature*, p. 78.

47. S. Mudd, "Spectroscopic Structure of the Bacterial Cell as shown by the Electron Microscope," *Nature*, 161 (1948), p. 302.

48. W. H. Thorpe, *Purpose in a World of Chance*, p. 21.

49. See D. L. Lack, *The Galapagos Finches (Geospizinae): A Study in Variation* (San Francisco: California Academy of Sciences, 1945) and its sequel, *Darwin's Finches* (Cambridge: University Press, 1947; Harper Torchbook, 1961).

50. Thus, for instance, the Nobel-laureate biochemist, Max F. Perutz, *Is Science Necessary? Essays on Science and Scientists* (New York: E. P. Dutton, 1989), p. 56.

51. See W. H. Thorpe, *Purpose in a World of Chance*, p. 20.

52. Ibid., p. 21.

53. E. B. Wilson, *The Cell in Development and Inheritance* (New York: Macmillan, 1896), p. 330.

54. It is, of course, a gross exaggeration to say as Barrow and Tipler do, that "there has developed a general consensus among evolutionists that the evolution of intelligent life, comparable in information-processing ability to that of *Homo sapiens* is so improbable that it is unlikely to have occurred on any other planet in the entire visible universe." *The Anthropic Cosmological Principle*, p. 133.

55. S. J. Gould, *Wonderful Life: The Burgess Shale and the Nature of History* (New York: W. W. Norton, 1989), p. 43.

56. T. Hardy, "The Last Chrysanthemum," in *Collected Poems of Thomas Hardy* (New York: Macmillan, 1926), pp. 136-37.

57. His two most important works are *The Fitness of the Environment* (1913), reprinted with an introduction by G. Wald (Gloucester, Mass.: Peter Smith, 1970) and the distinctly more philosophical *The Order of Nature* (Cambridge, Mass.: Harvard University Press, 1917).

58. *The Order of Nature*, p. 204.

59. Ibid., p. 192.

60. Ibid., p. 204.

61. For details, see *Studies in the Philosophy of Biology*, ed. F. J. Ayala and T. Dobzhansky (Berkeley: University of California Press, 1974).

62. *The Order of Nature*, p. 203.

CHAPTER FOUR

1. B. Carter, "Large Number Concidences and the Anthropic Principle in Cosmology," in M. S. Longair (ed.), *Confrontation of Cosmological Theories with Observational Data* (Dordrecht: D. Reidel, 1974), pp. 291-98.

2. The vastly enlarged 2nd edition (1989) of the *Oxford Dictionary of the English Language* refers (vol. 1, p. 511) to Carter's paper as the first appearance of the expression "anthropic principle." The remark of P. C. W. Davies in his *The Accidental Universe* (Cambridge: Cambridge University Press, 1982, p. 133), that "although the words 'anthropic principle' are not new, they appear to have been used in a modern context by Brandon Carter," is either a verbal muddle or a plain error.

3. R. H. Dicke, "Dirac's Cosmology and Mach's Principle," *Nature* 192 (Nov. 4, 1961), pp. 440-41.

4. Symposium I dealt with questions of the history of science relating to Copernicus.

5. Carter, "Large Number Coincidences," p. 291.

6. See, for instance, P. C. W. Davies, *The Accidental Universe*, p. 115, and B. J. Carr, "On the Origin, Evolution, and Purpose of the Physical Universe," *The Irish Astronomical Journal*, 15 (1982), p. 238.

7. J. Kepler, *De stella nova in pede Serpentarii* (1606) in Johannes Kepler, *Gesammelte Werke*, ed. M. Caspar, vol. I (Munchen: C. H. Beck, 1938), p. 21.

8. Carter, "Large Number Coincidences," p. 291.

9. See my translation, *The Ash Wednesday Supper* (*La cena de le ceneri*) (The Hague: Mouton, 1975), pp. 28-31.

10. A remark of Frances A. Yates in her *Giordano Bruno and the Hermetic Tradition* (Chicago: University of Chicago Press, 1964), p. 297.

11. See my translation, J. H. Lambert, *Cosmological Letters on the Arrangement of the World Edifice* (New York: Science History Publications, 1976), p. 73.

12.   He did so in his *Original Theory and New Hypothesis of the Universe* (1750). For details, see ch. 6, "Wright's Wrong," in my *The Milky Way: An Elusive Road for Science* (New York: Science History Publications, 1972), pp. 191–92.

13.   See my translation, with introduction and notes of I. Kant, *Universal Natural History and Theory of the Heavens* (Edinburgh: Scottish Academic Press, 1981), pp. 154–57.

14.   For details, see my Gifford Lectures, *The Road of Science and the Ways to God* (Chicago: University of Chicago Press, 1978), pp. 115 and 378.

15.   As is clear from Kant's sundry endorsements of the Enlightenement. For quotations, see my *Angels, Apes and Men* (La Salle, Ill.: Sherwood Sugden, 1983), p. 32-43.

16.   The topic of ch. 8, "The Myth of One Island," in my *The Milky Way*.

17.   For a documentation on Luther's abuse of Copernicus and its various interpretations, see A. Koyré, *La Révolution astronomique* (Paris: Hermann, 1961), p. 77.

18.   A point to which H. Butterfield called attention in ch. 2, "The Conservatism of Copernicus," in his *The Origins of Modern Science 1300-1800* (1949; New York: Macmillan, 1960).

19.   A fact discovered by Pierre Duhem in his monumental studies on the medieval origins of Newtonian science. For details, see ch. 10, "The Historian," in my *Uneasy Genius: The Life and Work of Pierre Duhem* (The Hague: Martinus Nijhoff, 1984).

20.   Quoted from the English translation of Copernicus' *De revolutionibus* in *Great Books of the Western World*, vol. 16, p. 508.

21.   Ibid., p. 510.

22.   Koyré, *La révolution astronomique*, p. 19.

23.   See translation quoted in note 20 above, p. 508.

24.   Even in his discovery of it by choosing the right one out of a total of 120 possible combinations, Kepler saw a finger of Divine Providence. For details, see my *Planets and Plan-*

etarians: A History of Theories of the Origin of Planetary Systems (Edinburgh: Scottish Academic Press, 1978), pp. 15-19.

25. Quoted ibid., p. 16.

26. Its first major installment came in Eddington's *Theory of Protons and Electrons* (Cambridge: University Press, 1936), although as early as 1919 Eddington indicated interest in the subject.

27. As recounted in Eddington's standard biography by A. Vibert Douglas, *The Life of Arthur Stanley Eddington* (London: Thomas Nelson, 1956), pp. 146 and 170.

28. This came to a climax in Eddington's posthumously published *Fundamental Theory* (Cambridge: University Press, 1946).

29. The concluding note in Eddington's *Space, Time and Gravitation: An Outline of the General Theory of Relativity* (Cambridge: University Press, 1920), p. 201.

30. P. A. M. Dirac, "Letter to the Editor," *Nature*, 139 (Feb. 20, 1937), p. 323; "A New Basis for Cosmology," *Proceedings of the Royal Society* (London), A165 (1938), pp. 199-208; "Cosmological Models and the Large Numbers Hypothesis," ibid., A338 (1974), pp. 439-48.

31. Dicke, "Dirac's Cosmology and Mach's Principle," p. 440.

32. Ibid.

33. Quoted in *The Accidental Universe* (p. 118) by P. C. W. Davies, from an unpublished University of Cardiff preprint entitled, "The Universe: Some Past and Present Reflections" by Fred Hoyle.

34. C. B. Collins and S. W. Hawking, "Why Is the Universe Isotropic?," *The Astrophysical Journal* 180 (1973), p. 334.

35. For details, see chs. 1 and 2 of my *God and the Cosmologists* (Edinburgh: Scottish Academic Press; Washington D. C.: Regnery Gateway, 1989).

36. I. Kant, *Critique of Pure Reason*, tr. N. K. Smith (1929; New York: St Martin's Press, 1960), pp. 432-39.

37. B. Carter, "Large Number Coincidences," p. 291.

38. J. D. Barrow and F. J. Tipler, *The Anthropic Cosmological Principle* (Oxford: Clarendon Press, 1986), p. 16.

39. D. V. Nanopoulos, "Bounds on the Baryon/Photon Ratio Due to Our Existence," *Physics Letters* B91 (1980), p. 67. Nanopoulos' paper, which ends with the remark that "to a greater extent than was imagined, things simply must be as they are" (p. 71) is aimed at showing the limitations put on grand unified theories by that ratio. In particular it demands the existence of quarks with six flavors.

40. B. J. Carr and M. J. Rees, "The Anthropic Principle and the Structure of the Physical World," *Nature* 278 (1979), p. 612.

41. See their paper quoted in note 34 above, p. 334.

42. Ibid.

43. See the first chapter, "Chance or Reality: Interaction in Nature versus Measurement in Physics" (1981), in my *Chance or Reality and Other Essays* (Lanham Md.: University Press of America, 1986). A more elaborate version of the same subject is my essay, "Determinism or Reality," to appear in *Great Ideas Today 1990* (Chicago: Encyclopedia Britannica, 1990), pp. 56-81.

44. Carter, "Large Number Coincidences," p. 294.

45. J. Silk, "Cosmogony and the Magnitude of the Dimensionless Gravitational Coupling Constant," *Nature*, 265 (Feb. 24, 1977), p. 711.

46. J. A. Wheeler, "Beyond the Black Hole," in H. Woolf (ed.), *Some Strangeness in Proportion: A Centennial Symposium to Celebrate the Achievements of Albert Einstein* (Reading, Mass.: Addison-Wesley, 1980), p. 354.

47. Ibid., p. 359.

48. B. J. Carr, "On the Origin, Evolution and Purpose of the Physical Universe," pp. 247-49.

49. Ibid., p. 250.

50. See ch. 44 in *Gravitation* by C. W. Misner, K. S. Thorne, and J. A. Wheeler (Freeman: San Francisco, 1973).

51.   Originated by B. S. De Witt in the late 1960s. For an ensemble of studies on it, see B. S. De Witt and N. Graham (eds.), *The Many World Interpretation of Quantum Mechanics* (Princeton: Princeton University Press, 1973.

52.   P. C. W. Davies, *The Accidental Universe*, pp. 127–28.

53.   Insistence on this well-nigh impossibility from the viewpoint of engineering is possibly the only sound part of *The Anthropic Cosmological Principle* (see note 38 above). Its authors fail to see that the piling up of vast amounts of materials relating to philosophy and the history of science does not make an expert in either of them.

54.   For a history of their inept theorizing, see my Fremantle Lectures, *The Origin of Science and the Science of Its Origin* (Edinburgh: Scottish Academic Press, 1978; Washington, D.C.: Regnery Gateway, 1979), ch. 4.

55.   For details, see ch. 2, "The Birth that Saved Science," in my *The Savior of Science* (Washington D.C.: Regnery Gateway, 1988; Edinburgh: Scottish Academic Press, 1989).

56.   The basic philosophical problems involved in speculating about extraterrestrials were once more ignored when in early 1990 Congress provided $10 million for constructing a multichannel listening device to detect "intelligent" signals from outer space. In a most unphilosophical way, Frank D. Drake, a chief proponent of the project, defended it with a confusion of logical simplicity with psychological complexity: "You can theorize forever. But intelligent life is so complicated, as we know from ourselves, that it's quite impossible to psych out the extraterrestrials and deduce by logic how they might behave. The only way we can really learn the truth is to search." *The New York Times*, Feb. 6, 1990, p. C12. No more philosophical depth was displayed by Robert T. Rood, an astronomer at the University of Virginia, sceptical about the project on the ground that "maybe we're a fluke," ibid.

57.   Tellingly, the first unequivocal assertion of a physical universe, in which no part was subject to disorder or illogi-

cality, came through Athanasius' defense of the divinity of the Incarnate Logos as the maker of the universe.

58. *Report of the Eighty-Fifth Meeting of the British Association for the Advancement of Science, Manchester 1915 September 7-11* (London: John Murray, 1916), p. 23.

59. A. France, *The Opinions of Jérôme Coignard*, tr. W. Jackson, in *The Works of Anatole France*, IV (New York: Wells, 1924), p. 114.

60. "All of sport is about the initial movement and if you interfere with that you are in trouble." Bob Simpson, captain of the Australian cricket team, quoted in *The Times* (London), Aug. 31, 1989, p. 36, col. 4.

CHAPTER FIVE

1. Seton Hall University, South Orange, N.J., named after Elizabeth Bayley Seton (1774-1821), foundress of the Catholic parochial school system in the United States and the first native-born American to be canonized.

2. E. Du Bois Reymond, "Die Sieben Welträtsel" (1880), in *Reden* (Leipzig: von Veit, 1886), pp. 381-411. It was an elaboration on an earlier, and no less famous, address of his, "The Limits of Our Knowledge of Nature," (tr. J. Fitzgerald, *The Popular Science Monthly* 5 [1874], pp. 17-32). On the one hand Du Bois Reymond insisted on the futility of understanding mental events in scientific terms, that is, quantities, he seemed also to suggest that whatever is not understood in those terms is not really understood.

3. The way was memorable both because of Socrates' readiness to die and because of his adverse impact on the prospects of science among the Greeks of old. On the latter point, see my article, "Socrates, or the Baby and the Bathwater," in *Faith and Reason*, 16 (1990), pp. 64-78.

4. For details, see ch. 14, "The Ravages of Reductionism," in my Gifford Lectures, *The Road of Science and the Ways to God* (Chicago: University of Chicago Press, 1978).

5.   B. Magee, *Men of Ideas: Some Creators of Contemporary Philosophy* (London: British Broadcasting Corporation, 1978), p. 131.

6.   For if all was futility, as Camus claimed by portraying the absurdity of reasoning, of man, and of creation, there could be no purpose in his writing *The Myth of Sisyphus*, in which the word purpose is conspicuously missing.

7.   Reliance on that Hegelian procedure assures that a problem soon ceases to be recognized as one. Thus while early Marxists still tried to show that there was no contradiction in their purposeful promoting the inevitable, their 20th-century successors no longer felt qualms on that score.

8.   A point made by the distinguished economist, D. K. Rangnekar, *Poverty and Capital Development in India* (London: Oxford University Press, 1958), p. 81, as well as by the well-known novelist, V. S. Naipul, *An Area of Darkness* (London: André Deutsch), pp. 216-17. The latter yielded to the lure of using a big word, creation, instead of saying simply 'purpose' as he wrote that Indian history's "only lesson is that life goes on. There is only a series of beginnings, no final creation."

9.   R. Doumic, *Discours de reception de Bergson à l'Académie Française, 24 mars 1918*, p. 51.

10. Ibid. See also, P. A. Y. Gunter (ed.), *Bergson and the Evolution of Physics* (Knoxville: University of Tennessee Press, 1969), p. 4.

11. H. Bergson, *Creative Evolution*, authorized translation by A. Mitchell, (1911; New York: The Modern Library, 1944), p. 295.

12. Ibid., p. 294.

13. Ibid., p. 203.

14. Ibid., p. 279.

15. B. Russell, *A History of Modern Philosophy* (New York: Simon and Schuster, 1945), p. 793.

16. J. Huxley, *Essays of a Biologist* (London: Chatto and Windus, 1926), p. 34.

17. B. Russell, "Free Man's Worship" (1902), in *Mysticism and Logic* (1917; New York: Anchor Books, 1957), p. 45.

18. J. Huxley, *Knowledge, Morality, and Destiny* (1957: New York: Mentor Books, 1960), p. 37.

19. *Creative Evolution*, p. 269.

20. H. Bergson, *The Two Sources of Morality and Religion*, tr. R. A. Audra and C. Brereton (1935; Garden City, N. Y.: Doubleday, 1954), p. 317. A strange conclusion of a book which so many have taken for a proof that Bergson came to believe in the Creator of the universe.

21. Ibid., p. 101.

22. Ibid., p. 264.

23. J. Maritain, *La philosophie bergsonienne* (1913), which appeared in English translation in a much enlarged form, *Bergsonian Philosophy and Thomism*, tr. M. L. Andison, and J. G. Andison (New York: Philosophical Library, 1955).

24. Ibid., p. 327.

25. S. Alexander, *Space, Time and Deity* (1920; New York: Humanities Press, 1950), vol. 1, pp. xii, 36, 44.

26. Ibid., p. ix. The essay was reprinted as ch. xiv in S. Alexander, *Philosophical and Literary Pieces*, edited with a memoir by his literary executor (London: Macmillan, 1939).

27. *Space, Time and Deity*, vol. 2, p. 346.

28. Ibid., p. 347.

29. Ibid., pp. 366-8.

30. Ibid., vol. 1, p. 58.

31. See ch. 2, "Universe Regained," in my *God and the Cosmologists* (Edinburgh: Scottish Academic Press; Washington D.C.: Regnery Gateway, 1989).

32. J. W. McCarthy, *The Naturalism of Samuel Alexander* (New York: Columbia University Press, 1948), pp. 106-7.

33. What made this possible was the application of four-dimensional geometry, as first suggested in 1871, and most explicitly, by J. F. K. Zöllner, professor of astrophysics in Leipzig.

34. As discussed in detail in the preceding chapter.

35. *Philosophical and Literary Pieces*, p. 95.

36. See *The Chief Works of Benedict de Spinoza*, tr. R. H. M. Elwes (1893; New York: Dover, 1951), vol. 2, pp. 408-9. The one who posed this incisive question to Spinoza was Tschirnhausen, a gentleman-philosopher from Heidelberg.

37. *Space, Time and Deity*, vol. 2, p. 424.

38. Ibid., p. 400.

39. *Philosophical and Literary Pieces*, p. 95.

40. Its first two volumes, constituting its First Series, were devoted to the "Foundations of a Creed."

41. G. H. Lewes, *Problems of Life and Mind* (Boston: James R. Osgood and Company, 1875), vol. 2, p. 370.

42. C. L. Morgan, *Emergent Evolution* (London: Williams and Norgate, 1923), p. v.

43. Ibid., p. vi. For Mivart's remark, see his *On the Genesis of Species* (London: Macmillan, 1871), pp. 186, 209, and 215.

44. Morgan, *Emergent Evolution*, p. vi.

45. Ibid., p. vii.

46. That chapter is important in that it reveals the impossibility to relate "emergence" as understood by Morgan, to a causal process. Much less then can it be purposeful, except as a purely verbal assertion.

47. C. L. Morgan, *Life, Mind and Spirit* (London: Williams, 1926), p. 145.

48. C. L. Morgan, *The Emergence of Novelty* (London: Williams and Norgate, 1933), p. 197.

49. Ibid., p. 201.

50. Ibid., p. 204.

51. See, for instance, the papers read at the Alpbach Symposium 1968, *Beyond Reductionism. New Perspectives in the Life Sciences*, ed. A. Koestler and J. R. Smythies (London: Hutchinson, 1969). See also references given in notes 2 and 4 above.

52. D. Emmett, "Whitehead, A. N." in *The Encyclopedia of Philosophy* (New York: Macmillan, 1967), vol. 8, p. 293.

53. *Modes of Thought* (1938; New York: Capricorn, 1958), p. 139.

54. *Adventures of Ideas* (1933; New York: Mentor Books, 1955), p. 273-4.

55. *Modes of Thought*, p. 74.

56. As set forth with particular force and incisiveness by E. Gilson in his *Being and Some Philosophers* (1949; 2nd enlarged edition, Toronto: Pontifical Institute of Mediaevel Studies, 1952).

57. *Process and Reality: An Essay in Cosmology* (1929; New York: Harper Torchbooks, 1960), p. 169.

58. *Modes of Thought*, p. 229.

59. *Adventures of Ideas*, p. 209.

60. Ibid., p. 294.

61. Ibid., p. 264.

62. Ibid., p. 295.

63. *Dialogues of Alfred North Whitehead*, as recorded by Lucien Price (1954; New York: Mentor Books, 1956), p. 239.

64. P. Teilhard de Chardin, *Writings in Time of War*, tr. R. Hague (New York: Harper and Row, 1968). Its subject index contains such entries as polyvalence of cosmos, superhumanity, biological threshold, and ontological drift.

65. Gathered from the subject index of *The Phenomenon of Man* and of *The Future of Man*.

66. P. B. Medawar, "Critical Review of *The Phenomenon of Man*," Mind 70 (1961), pp. 99-106.

67. See his introduction to *The Phenomenon of Man*, tr. B. Wall (New York: Harper and Brothers, 1959), pp. 18-19.

68. *The Future of Man*, tr. N. Denny (New York: Harper and Row, 1964), p. 318.

69. That "Teilhard accepted the notion of an evolving God" is claimed by J. D. Barrow and F. J. Tipler, *The Anthropic Cosmological Principle* (Oxford: Clarendon Press, 1986), p. 168, though with no documentation whatsoever, a circumstance rather revealing in a book overloaded with references.

70. *The Future of Man*, p. 15.

71. *Letters from a Traveller*, (New York: Harper and Row, 1962), p. 354.

72. *Letters of Etienne Gilson to Henri de Lubac*, annotated by Father de Lubac, tr. M. E. Hamilton (San Francisco: Ignatius Press, 1988), p. 136.

73. Such as P. de Lubac in his *The Religion of Teilhard de Chardin*, tr. R. Hague (New York: Desclee Company, 1967).

74. J. W. McCarthy, *The Naturalism of Samuel Alexander* (see note 32 above), pp. 106–07.

CHAPTER SIX

1. J. C. Maxwell, "Paradoxical Philosophy" (1878), in *The Scientific Papers of James Clerk Maxwell*, ed. W. D. Niven (Cambridge: University Press, 1890), vol. 2, p. 759.

2. V. Bush, "Science Pauses," *Fortune*, 71 (May 1965), p. 115.

3. Those essays were reprinted in A. Gray, *Darwiniana: Essays and Reviews Pertaining to Darwinism* (New York: D. Appleton, 1876), and reprinted with an introduction by A. H. Dupree (Cambridge, Mass.: Harvard University Press, 1963). The last article there is entitled, "Evolutionary Teleology."

4. *The Life and Letters of Charles Darwin*, ed. F. Darwin (London: John Murray, 1887), vol. 2, p. 371.

5. Ibid., p. 370.

6. Ibid., p. 378.

7. Ibid., p. 382.

8. Especially in his *The Arians of the Fourth Century*, first published in 1833.

9. See *The Life and Letters of Charles Darwin*, vol. 1, p. 316.

10. In his letter of May 22, 1860, to A. Gray, ibid., vol. 2, p. 312.

11. H. Spencer, *An Autobiography* (London: Williams and Norgate, 1904), vol. 2, p. 470.

12. J. B. S. Haldane, *Possible Worlds and Other Essays* (London: Chatto and Windus, 1927), p. 209.

13. Translated from his address, "Objets et résultats de paléo-neurologie," given in Paris, April 1955. See *Annales de paléontologie*, 42 (1956), p. 99.

14. From an early notebook of Darwin. See *Darwin on Man: A Psychological Study of Scientific Creativity*, by H. E. Gruber, together with *Darwin's Early and Unpublished Notebooks*, transcribed and annotated by P. H. Barrett, with a foreword by J. Piaget (New York: E. P. Dutton, 1974), C notebook, p. 451.

15. C. Darwin, *The Descent of Man and Selection in Relation to Sex* (new ed.; London: John Murray, 1901), pp. 123-26.

16. The Duke of Argyle (George D. Campbell) set forth this view in his *Primeval Man: An Examination of Some Recent Speculations* (New York: Routledge and Sons, 1869), pp. 145 and 147.

17. Darwin, *The Descent of Man*, p. 125.

18. On this and similar characterizations by Darwin of his ways of reasoning, see ch. 18 in my Gifford Lectures, *The Road of Science and the Ways to God* (Chicago: University of Chicago Press, 1978).

19. W. Köhler, *The Mentality of Apes*, tr. from the second revised edition by E. Winter (New York: Harcourt, Brace and Co., 1927), pp. 267 and 272.

20. Quoted in *Time*, March 10, 1980, p. 57.

21. See *Nim* by H. Terrace (New York: Knopf, 1979) and the collection of essays, *Speaking of Apes* (New York: Plenum, 1980).

22. W. E. Le Gros Clark, *The Antecedents of Man: An Introduction to the Evolution of Primates* (Edinburgh: Edinburgh University Press, 1959), p. 351.

23. Since its first publication in 1959, it has seen numerous reimpressions. References will be to the fourth reimpression (Chicago: University of Chicago Press, 1964). Oakley's definition of man as a tool-maker is a variation on Benjamin Franklin's dictum, "man is a tool-making animal." See also Oakley's long essay, "Skill as a Human Possession," in *A*

History of Technology, ed. C. Singer *et al* (New York: Oxford University Press, 1954), vol. 1, pp. 1-37.

24. Oakley, *Man the Tool-maker*, pp. 1-2.

25. *The Autobiography of Charles Darwin 1809-1882*, with original omissions restored, edited with appendix and notes by his granddaughter, Nora Barlow (New York: W. W. Norton, 1969), p. 119.

26. Most notably by William Whewell, and most succinctly by A. de Morgan: "What are large collections of facts for? To make theories *from*, says Bacon; to try ready-made theories by, says the history of discovery." *A Budget of Paradoxes* (1872; La Salle Il.: Open Court, 1915), vol. 1, p. 88.

27. In Bacon's characterization of final causes as "barren virgins" lies indeed hidden the barrenness of his method. See ch. 4, "Empirical Scouting," in my Gifford Lectures, *The Road of Science and the Ways to God* (Chicago: University of Chicago Press, 1978).

28. In a more acid style, Sir Edward Cooke, chief justice during Bacon's later years, called Bacon's *New Organon* an instrument "fit only for the Ship of Fools." *Brief Lives Chiefly of Contemporaries Set Down by John Aubrey between the Years 1669 and 1696*, ed. A. Clark (Oxford: Clarendon Press, 1898), vol. 1, p. 299.

29. Descartes, *Discourse on the Method*, Part VI. See *The Philosophical Works of Descartes*, tr. E. Haldane and G. R. T. Ross (Cambridge: University Press, 1931), p. 119.

30. See T. Sprat, *History of the Royal Society*, edited with critical apparatus by J. I. Cope and H. W. Jones (Saint Louis: Washington University Press, 1958), pp. 61-2, 77-8, 436-8. The reliability of that purposeful effort was reflected in the trust placed in the effectiveness of "a *Design*, which endeavors to give aid against all the infirmities and wants of *human Nature*," which, though "so great an *Attempt*, may be plentifully indow'd by a small part of what is spent on any one single Lust, or extravagant Vanity of the Time," and all the more so as it brings "so neer Mankind to its happinness" (p. 437).

31. See C. Becker, *The Heavenly City of the Eighteenth-Century Philosophers* (New Haven, Conn.: Yale University Press, 1932).

32. As claimed, for instance, by R. Feynman in his *QED: The Strange Theory of Light and Matter* (Princeton: University Press, 1985).

33. For a reconstruction of Anaxagoras' work from references to it in subsequent Greek philosophical literature, see D. E. Gershenson and D. A. Greenberg, *Anaxagoras and the Birth of Physics* (New York: Blaisdell, 1964).

34. The oversight of three such disparate thinkers as I. D. Stone, K. R. Popper, and R. Guardini is discussed in my article, "Socrates or the Baby and the Bathwater," *Faith and Reason* 16 (1990), pp. 64–78.

35. Especially in sections XLVI and LVII–LX.

36. In *On the Heavens* (274a) Aristotle states that if two bodies, one with the weight twice of the other, are dropped from the same height, the heavier would reach the ground twice as fast.

37. In order for this to happen, the Greek mind should have also broken out from the bondage of pantheism which heavily influenced Plato and Aristotle to see in the universe an animated entity capable, in its entirety and all its parts, of striving for a purpose. For details, see ch. 6, "The Labyrinths of the Lonely Logos," in my *Science and Creation From Eternal Cycles to an Oscillating Universe* (1974; reprinting of the 2nd enlarged edition of 1986, Lanham, Md: University Press of America, 1990). See also ch. 2, "The Birth that Saved Science," in my *The Savior of Science* (Washington D.C.: Regnery Gateway, 1988).

38. See *Leibniz Selections*, ed. P. P. Wiener (New York: Charles Scribner's Sons, 1951), pp. 69 and 320.

39. Maupertuis' mathematical elaboration of the principle of least action preceded by seven years his mainly philosophical *Essai de cosmologie* (1751) devoted to teleology with an eye on that principle.

40. W. Heitler, *Man and Science*, tr. R. Schlapp (New York: Basic Books, 1963), p. 97.

41. W. Heitler, "The Departure from Classical Thought in Modern Physics," in *Albert Einstein: Philosopher-Scientist*, ed. P. A. Schilpp (1949; New York: Harper and Brothers, 1959), vol. 1, p. 197.

42. For instance, J. Needham, who compounded the confusion by taking the organismic world view of the Chinese of old for an anticipation of General Relativity! See his *Science and Civilization in China, Vol. 2, History of Scientific Thought* (Cambridge: University Press, 1962), pp. 503–5 and 543–5.

43. W. Heisenberg, "Development of the Interpretation of Quantum Theory," in *Niels Bohr and the Development of Physics*, ed. W. Pauli (New York: McGraw-Hill, 1955), pp. 12–29.

44. *Electrons et Photons. Rapports et discussions du Cinquième Conseil de Physique tenu à Bruxelles du 24 au 29 Octobre 1927 sous les auspices de l'Institut International de Physique Solvay* (Paris: Gauthier-Villars, 1928), p. 264.

45. As claimed in particular in *The Tao of Physics: An Exploration of the Parallels between Modern Physics and Eastern Mysticism* by F. Capra, originally published in 1975. More of the same is offered in *Mysticism and the New Physics* by M. Talbot (New York: Bantam Books, 1980). For a good exposure of the misguided efforts to introduce Tao into physics courses, see E. R. Scerri, "Eastern Mysticism and the Alleged Parallels with Physics," *American Journal of Physics*, 57 (1989), pp. 687–92.

46. A most misleading aspect of that symbol is the distinct curved line that separates *yin* from *yang*, or dark from bright, or dry from moist. Actually the symbol stands for the continual fusion into one another of any of those two opposites, including being and non-being. Bohr presented his interpretation of quantum theory as having for its chief consequence the fact that "even words like 'to be' and 'to know' lose their unambiguous meaning." N. Bohr, *Atomic Theory*

and the Description of Nature (Cambridge: Univerisity Press, 1934), p. 19.

47. See ch. 2, "The Lull of Yin and Yang," in my *Science and Creation*, quoted in note 37 above.

48. Originated with J. E. Lovelock's *Gaia: A New Look at the Earth* (Oxford: University Press, 1979).

49. Letter of July 3, 1881, to W. Graham, in *The Life and Lettres of Charles Darwin*, vol. 1, p. 316.

50. C. Bernard, *Leçons sur les phénomènes de le vie communs aux animaux et les végétaux* (Paris: J. B. Baillière, 1878), p. 344. Quoted in E. Gilson, *From Aristotle to Darwin and Back Again: A Journey in Final Causality, Species, and Evolution*, tr. J. Lyon, with an Introduction by Stanley L. Jaki (Notre Dame, In.: University of Notre Dame Press, 1984), p. 30.

51. C. Bernard, in *Revue des Cours scientifiques*, 13 février 1875. Quoted in P. Janet, *Final Causes*, tr. W. Affleck (Edinburgh: T. and T. Clark, 1878), p. 124.

52. See, Gilson, *From Aristotle to Darwin*, p. 28.

53. C. Bernard, "Définition de la vie," in *La science expérimentale* (Paris: J. B. Baillière, 1878), pp. 210-11. Quoted in P. Janet, *Final Causes*, p. 263.

54. J. Rostand, *Les grands courants de la biologie* (Paris: Gallimard, 1951), p. 198.

55. B. Fellman, "An Engineer's Eye Helps Biologists Understand Nature," *Smithsonian*, July 1989, p. 98.

56. A statement of O. Ellers, quoted ibid., p. 101.

57. J. Monod, *Chance and Necessity: An Essay on the Natural Philosophy of Modern Biology*, tr. A. Wainhouse (1971; New York: Vintage Books, n.d.), p. xi.

58. Ibid., p. 9.

59. Ibid., p. 144.

60. Ibid., p. 145.

61. Ibid., p. 180.

62. R. Dawkins, *The Blind Watchmaker* (New York: W. W. Norton, 1986), see especialy the diagrams in ch. 3, "Accumulating Small Change."

63. Ibid., p. 318.

64. Ibid., p. 12.

65. See especially ch. 2, "Nebulosity Dissipated," in my *God and the Cosmologists* (Edinburgh: Scottish Academic Press; Washington D.C. Regnery Gateway, 1989).

66. R. Dawkins, *The Selfish Gene* (Oxford: Oxford University Press, 1976), p. 215. A similar ruse is evident in M. Ruse's claim in his *Taking Darwinism Seriously* (Oxford: Blackwell, 1986) that freedom is but our seeing from "inside" what from the "outside" is known to be fully programmed with epigenetic rules (pp. 143-47). Such ruses have, of course, found a most fertile breeding ground in behaviorism and sociobiology.

CHAPTER SEVEN

1. Quoted from *The Marx-Engels Reader*, ed. R. C. Tucker (New York: W. W. Norton, 1972), p. 124.

2. Ibid.

3. The lectures, which had "Values of Western Civilization" for their general theme, were given at the All-Union Cinema Center, Moscow, June 17-23, 1989.

4. Quoted from *The New York Times*, April 17, 1966, p. E2.

5. See E. Fromm, *Escape from Freedom* (New York: Rinehart, 1941).

6. And since such a condition is illusory, the only option that remains for those existentialists is a cavorting in momentary choices for the sake of making choices. A graphic description of this is Simone de Beauvoir's comment, in her *Little Women*, on Jo March "who was always making choices and sometimes they were neither well reasoned nor good. The idea of choice must have frightened me a little, but it was

exhilarating as well." Quoted by A. Quindlen, "Heroine Addiction," *The New York Times*, April 29, 1990, p. E21.

7. Voltaire, *Le philosophe ignorant* (1766), in *Oeuvres complètes de Voltaire* (Paris: Garnier Frères, 1877-85), vol. XXVI, p. 55.

8. Ibid., p. 56.

9. Ibid., p. 78.

10. See note 2 in ch. 1.

11. Quoted in A. M. Wilson, *Diderot* (New York: Oxford University Press, 1972), pp. 576-77. Diderot's letter was a reply to Mme de Vaux' inquiry about the influence of a comet, visible at that time, on events on earth.

12. A. S. Eddington, *The Philosophy of Physical Science* (London: Macmillan, 1939), p. 182. Five years earlier Eddington compared human freedom to "that of the mass of 0.001 mg which is only allowed to stray 1/5000mm in a thousand years" *The New Pathways in Science* (Cambridge University Press, 1934), p. 88.

13. A. S. Eddington, *Space, Time and Gravitation* (1920; New York: Harper and Row, 1959), p. 201.

14. See ch. 1 "The Universe Regained" in my *God and the Cosmologists* (Edinburgh: Scottish Academic Press; Washington DC: Regnery Gateway, 1989).

15. For a detailed discussion, see my essay, "Determinism and Reality," *Great Ideas Today 1990* (Chicago: Encyclopedia Britannica, 1990), pp. 276-302.

16. A. Einstein, Foreword to *Spinoza Dictionary*, ed. D. Runes (New York: Philosophical Library, 1951), p. vi.

17. See U. Tal, "Jewish and Universal Social Ethics in the Life and Thought of Albert Einstein," in *Albert Einstein: Historical and Cultural Perspectives: The Centennial Symposium in Jerusalem*, ed. G. Holton and Y. Elkana (Princeton: University Press, 1982), p. 318.

18. See his "Physics and Reality" (1936), in A. Einstein, *Out of My Later Years* (New York: Philosophical LIbrary, 1950), p. 60.

19.   A. Einstein, Introduction to *Spinoza: Portrait of a Spiritual Hero*, by R. Kayser (New York: Philosophical Library, 1946), p. xi.

20.   A. Einstein, Letter of April 11, 1946, to O. Juliusburger, in *Albert Einstein: The Human Side: New Glimpses from His Archives*, ed. H. Dukas and B. Hoffmann (Princeton: University Press, 1979), p. 81.

21.   Ibid., p. 82.

22.   Ibid., pp. 26-7.

23.   Ibid., p. 92.

24.   Most memorably in two addresses on science and religion, delivered in Princeton in 1939 and 1941. See A. Einstein, *Out of My Laters Years*, pp. 25-32.

25.   *The Ethics*, Part I, Definitions I, 7.

26.   G. K. Chesterton, *St. Thomas Aquinas* (New York: Sheed & Ward, 1933), p. 231.

27.   H. Poincaré, "Sur la valeur objective des théories physiques," *Revue de métaphysique et de morale*, 10 (1902), p. 288.

28.   A. H. Compton, *The Freedom of Man* (New Haven: Yale University Press, 1935), p. 26.

29.   Ibid., p. 54.

30.   Ibid., p. 59.

31.   Ibid., p. 60.

32.   See G. S. Kirk and J. E. Raven, *The Presocratic Philosophers: A Critical History with a Selection of Texts* (Cambridge: University Press, 1962), p. 413.

33.   *Protagoras* 361a. Quoted from *The Collected Dialogues of Plato*, ed. E. Hamilton and H. Cairns (New York: Pantheon Books, 1963), p. 351.

34.   *The Republic* 617a. Quoted from ibid., p. 841.

35.   619d, p. 843.

36.   That the most intellectual part of the soul may not perish with death is stated in *De anima* (430, 22a) and that it comes

"from the outside" into the body is stated in *On the Generation of Animals* (736, 28b). Aristotle never as much as hints that the soul, once separated from the body, is individual.

37. *Nicomachean Ethics* 1113b3-5. Quoted from W. D. Ross, *Aristotle* (London: Methuen, 1923), p. 201.

38. Thus, according to Ross, Aristotle's statement, just quoted, "is not so much an assertion of free will as a reply to those who would avoid responsibility for wrong actions while taking credit for good ones" (ibid.). In his *Aristotle's Theory of the Will* (London: Duckworth, 1979) A. Kenny observes that "no Aristotelian expression corresponds to the English expression 'freedom of the will' " (p. vii) and recalls approvingly the view of Ross on the subject.

39. *Politics*, Bk. VII, ch. 7.

40. *Thucydides. History of the Pelopponnesian War*, tr. R. Warner, with introduction and notes by M. I. Finley (Harmondsworth: Penguin Books, 1976), p. 145.

41. *Meteorologica* 339b, *On the Heavens* 270b.

42. *Metaphysics* 1074b. For further details, see my *Science and Creation: From Eternal Cycles to an Oscillating Universe* (1974; 3d edition).

43. *Politics* 1329b, Bk. V. ch. 12.

44. See M. Pohlenz, *Freedom in Greek Life and Thought: The History of an Ideal*, tr. C. Lofmark (Dordrecht: D. Reidel, 1966), p. 131.

45. *Stoicorum veterorum fragmenta*, ed. J. von Arnim (Leipzig: B. G. Teubner (1903-24), vol. II, pp. 189-90.

46. Ibid., p. 190.

47. Letter to Menoeceus 134, in *Epicurus: The Extant Remains*, ed. and tr. C. Bailey (Oxford: Clarendon Press, 1926), p. 91.

48. As amply shown in *The Origins of Stoic Cosmology* by D. E. Hahn (Ohio State University Press, 1977).

49. Horace, *Satires* II, 8, in *The Complete Works of Horace*, edited with an introduction by C. J. Kraemer, Jr (New York: Modern Library, 1936), p. 78.

50. Quoted by Pohlenz, *Freedom in Greek Life*, p. 177.

51. Ibid., p. 134.

52. Seneca, *De vita beata*, 15, 7.

53. Deuteronomy, 30:19-20. This and subsequent passages, unless noted otherwise, are quoted from *The New American Bible*.

54. Sirach, 15:11-20.

55. Quoted from *The Grail Psalms* (1963; London: Collins, 1987), pp. 237-38.

56. See especially John 8:31-32.

57. Paul's most activist behavior and consciousness certainly bespeak his conviction about having a genuinely free will at his disposal. There is, in addition, his deep awareness of his own moral responsibility to live up to the demands and standards of God's grace given to him.

58. Rom. 1: 28-30.

59. "Paulatim docuit pedetemptim progredientes," *Lucreti de rerum natura libri sex*, ed. C. Bailey (Oxford: Clarendon Press, 1898), Lib. V, linea 1452.

60. Quoted in the translation of R. E. Latham, *Lucretius: The Nature of the Universe* (Baltimore: Penguin classics, 1951), p. 215 (Bk V, lines 1450-53).

61. Ibid., p. 94.

62. *Physical Science in the Times of Nero: Being a Translation of the Quaestiones Naturales of Seneca* by John Clarke (London: Macmillan, 1910), p. 298 (Bk VII, ch. 27).

63. Ibid., p. 307 (Bk. VII, ch. 32).

64. Ibid., p. 153 (Bk. III, ch. 29).

65. Seneca's admiration for Berossos was shared, among other prominent Romans, by Vitruvius, the famed architect of early Imperial times, who repeatedly refers to Berossos in his *De architectura*.

66. *Augustine: Concerning the City of God against the Pagans*, tr. H. Bettenson (Baltimore: Penguin Books, 1976), pp. 499-500

(Book XII, ch. 21). For further details on Augustine's opposition to the idea of Great Year, see my *Science and Creation: From Eternal Cycles to an Oscillating Universe* (1974; 2nd ed., Edinburgh: Scottish Academic Press, 1986), pp. 177-82.

67. Ibid. p. 1072 (Bk XXII, ch. 24).

68. N. Fustel de Coulanges, *La cité antique. Etude sur le culte, le droit, les institutions de la Grèce et de Rome* (11th ed.; Paris: Hachette, 1885), pp. 462-3.

60. See M.-D. Chenu, *Nature, Man, and Society in the Twelfth Century: Essays on New Theological Perspectives in the Latin West*, with a Preface by E. Gilson, selected, edited, and translated by J. Taylor and L. K. Little (Chicago: University of Chicago Press, 1968), pp. 43-45, and R. W. Southern, "Aspects of Historical Tradition of Historical Writing. 2. Hugo of St. Victor and the Idea of Historical Development," *Transactions of the Royal Historical Society*, 21 (1971), pp. 159-79.

CHAPTER EIGHT

1. "La Ruta Maya," *National Geographic*, Oct. 1989, p. 447.

2. Ibid., p. 446.

3. D. Gabor, *The Mature Society* (New York: Praeger, 1972), p. 51.

4. Ibid. Gabor obviously had in mind the scene where Pinetree, a Neanderthal, lets his finger be axed off by Tuami, another Neanderthal. The incident is more fatalistic than voluntary: "Tuami struck hard and there was now a glistening stone biting into the wood, Pinetree stood still for a moment or two. Then he removed his hand carefully from the polished wood and a finger remained stretched out on the branch. He turned away and came to sit with the others." W. Golding, *The Inheritors* (New York: Harcourt, Brace & World, 1955), p. 147.

5. Ibid., p. 51.

6. The same is true of the remark of B. F. Dick, author of

William Golding (New York: Twayne Publishers, 1967), that while "H. G. Wells confidently proclaimed that man cannot penetrate the Neanderthal mind, Golding replies that, on the contrary, one could do so; and he brilliantly proved his point" (p. 98).

7. J. S. Mill, *Three Essays on Religion* (London: Longmans, Green, 1875), p. 58.

8. Quoted by R. Reinhold, "Fault Lines: California Struggles with the Other Side of Its Dream," *The New York Times*, Oct. 22, 1989, Section 4, p. 1.

9. As reported in *The New York Times*, Oct. 14, 1990, p. C1.

10. Gabor, *The Mature Society*, p. 51.

11. G. Stent, *The Coming of the Golden Age* (Garden City, NY: The Natural History Press, 1969), p. 74.

12. *Education at Berkeley: Report of the Select Committee on Education* (Berkeley: University of California, Academic Senate, March 1966), p. 20.

13. Stent, *The Coming of the Golden Age*, p. 79.

14. Ibid.

15. *Education at Berkeley*, p. 32.

16. Ibid., p. 30.

17. Ibid., pp. 30-31.

18. Thus Stent takes the open-endedness of fundamental-particle research and of mathematics (in virtue of Gödel's theorem) for an elusiveness of rationality (*The Coming of the Golden Age*, p. 113).

19. See *The New York Times*, Aug. 7, 1989, p. A10.

20. S. Mydans, "AIDS Patients' Silent Companion is Often Suicide, or Thoughts of It," *The New York Times*, Feb. 25, 1990, p. 1.

21. As claimed by Stent, *The Coming of the Golden Age*, p. 135.

22. S. Freud, *The Ego and the Id*, in the *Standard Edition of the Complete Psychological Works of Sigmund Freud*, ed. J. Stratchey (London: 1953-75), vol. 19, p. 50.

23. P. Gay, "Freud and Freedom," in A. Ryan (ed.), *The Idea of Freedom: Essays in Honour of Isaiah Berlin* (Oxford: Oxford University Press, 1979), p. 55.

24. Ibid. Freud's reference is to Paul Julius August Moebius (1853-1907), author of books on human psychological evolution.

25. "Among all my patients in the second half of life—that is to say over thirty-five—there has not been one whose problem in the last resort was not that of finding a religious outlook on life." C. Jung, *Modern Man in Search of a Soul* (London: Routledge and Kegan Paul, 1933), p. 264.

26. As abundantly clear from ch. 11, "On Life After Death," in C. G. Jung's *Memories, Dreams, Reflections*, recorded and edited by A. Jaffe, tr. from the German by R. and C. Winston (1961; London: Collins, 1982), especially pp. 351-53.

27. T. B. Macaulay, "Ranke's History of the Popes" (1840), in *Critical and Historical Essays* (London: J. M. Dent and Sons, 1907), vol. II, p. 42.

28. Rom. 8:33-39.

29. A variation on the statement of P. Viereck, who in his *Shame and Glory of the Intellectuals* (Boston: Beacon Press, 1953), wrote: "Catholic-baiting is the anti-Semitism of the liberals" (p. 45).

30. A point engraved particularly sharply on my memory, following a chance encounter, in an early afternoon in September 1974 in Jerusalem's Old Town with a Jew of German origin who kindly volunteered to give me directions. One word led to another. After recalling his days in Berlin in the early 1930s he remarked: "In the apartment house where I lived at that time, there were several Catholics, one of them a member of the Centrum Party. They were the first ones to have been deported. We Jews followed only afterwards."

31. He did so in a lecture given on March 6, 1927, in London. For its text, see B. Russell, *Why I Am Not a Christian and Other Essays on Religion and Related Subjects* (1957: New York: Simon and Schuster, n.d.), pp. 3-23.

32. B. Russell, *The Impact of Science on Society* (New York: Simon and Schuster, 1953), p. 92.

33. Rom. 8:28-32.

34. As concisely put already by St. Augustine in his *De dono perseverantiae*, one of his latest works, written in 429: "We do not think that grace is given to anyone because of his own merits, nor do we suppose that anyone is punished except on his own desserts" (11, 25).

35. The illogicality of denying ontological causality on the basis of quantum mechanics is the topic of my essay, "Determinism and Reality," *Great Ideas Today 1990* (Chicago: Encyclopedia Britannica, 1990), pp. 276-302.

36. Here the meaning of contingency is the very opposite to what is usually denoted as randomness. Rather it means that a reality is contingent insofar as its concrete existence is contingent upon a rational choice independent of it. For further details, see my *God and the Cosmologists* (Edinburgh: Scottish Academic Press; Washington D. C.: Regnery Gateway, 1989), pp. 87-8.

37. For an example of that well meaning but unconvincing bravery, see the work quoted in note 51 to ch. 5.

38. Quoted in W. Ward, *The Life of John Henry Cardinal Newman* (London: Longmans, Green and Co., 1912), vol. 2, pp. 342-3.

39. The friend was William Froude (1803-79), a prominent civil engineer. For further details, see my essay, "Newman's Assent to Reality: Natural and Supernatural," in *Newman Today*, ed. S. L. Jaki (San Francisco: Ignatius Press, 1989), pp. 193-4.

40. This distinction is capital in Newman's argumentation whose weakness lies in his inability to come to grips with the question of universals. See ibid., pp. 200-2.

41. *Meditations and Devotions of the Late Cardinal Newman* (New York: Longmans, Green, and Co., 1893), p. 301.

42. From his immortal poem, "Lead Kindly Light," written in 1833.

43. J. H. Newman, *Discourses Addressed to Mixed Congregations* (New York: Longmans, Green, and Co., 1902), p. 111.

44. Ibid., p. 122.

45. The stature of Whittaker, the scientist, may best be gauged from the opening statement of W. H. McCrea in his obituary of Whittaker in *The Journal of The London Mathematical Society*, 32 (1957), pp. 234-56: "The name of Sir Edmund Whittaker will always hold a unique place in the history of British mathematics. It may reasonably be claimed that no single individual in this century or the last had so far-reaching an influence upon its progress." The various aspects of Whittaker's scientific achievements were amply treated by D. Martin, G. Temple, R. A. Rankin, A. C. Aitken and J. L. Synge in *Proceedings of the Edinburgh Mathematical Society*, 2 (195859), pp. 1-55. J. McConnell's study there (pp. 57-68) of Whittaker's thoughts on the relation of physics, philosophy, and theology hardly does adequate justice to the subject. Whittaker's achievements as a historian of physics are still looking for an expert investigator. Last but not least, a more than cursory portrayal of Whittaker's life is still to be written.

46. First published in 1910, it came out in a vastly enlarged two-volume second edition in 1951 and was reissued as a Harper Torchbook in 1960. Whittaker's convincing documentation of the pioneering contributions of Poincaré, Lorentz, and others to the Special Theory of Relativity was the cause of unjust undervaluation of his masterpiece in circles where almost all credit on that score is given to Einstein.

47. E. T. Whittaker, *The Beginning and End of the World* (London: Oxford University Press, 1942), p. 41.

48. Ibid., p. 42.

49. Ibid.

50. *Man and His Future: A Ciba Foundation Volume*, ed G. Wolstenholme (London: J. A. Churchill, 1963).

51. Ibid., see, for instance, pp. 295-6 and 380.

52. See Viereck, *Shame and Glory of the Intellectuals*, p. 45.

53. *Man and His Future*, p. 292.

54. *Macbeth*, Act II.

55. I. Domb, *The Transformation: The Case of the NETUREI KARTA* (1958; 2d ed; Brooklyn, N.Y.: Hachomo, 1989), p. 12.

56. From H. Hoover's letter to Senator W. H. Borah, Feb. 28, 1928. In view of the now proverbial rowdyism of British soccer fans, one may doubt the unrestricted validity of George Herbert's statement, "The Englishman never enjoys himself except for a noble purpose."

57. W. Heisenberg, *Physics and Beyond: Encounters and Conversations*, tr. A. J. Pomerans (New York: Harper and Brothers, 1972), p. 217.

58. *The Collected Poems of W. B. Yeats* (2nd ed.; London: Macmillan, 1950), p. 211.

59. G. K. Chesterton, *What's Wrong with the World* (New York: Dodd, Mead, and Co., 1910), p. 48.

60. Definitive edition, New York and London, 1923, p. 244.

61. C. S. Lewis, *The Case for Christianity* (New York: Macmillan, 1948), p. 45.

62. C. S. Lewis made no secret of the fact that in advocating the idea of "mere Christianity" he tried to modernize the ideas of Richard Baxter, a notable 17th-century Puritan preacher.

63. *The Mind at the End of Its Tether*, discussed in ch. 2.

64. This statement, which I have found in an unpublished paper of Prof. Charles Dunn of Clemson University, is not reported in biographies of H. G. Wells by L. Dickson, G. West, and N. and J. MacKenzie, all of whom are in obvious sympathy with their hero's anti-Christian sentiments.

65. Quoted in Time, June 1, 1981, from a review of *The Intimate Sex Lives of Famous People* by A. and S. Wallace and D. Wallechinsky (New York: Delacorte, 1981). No less decadent is Anatole France's dismissal of God's love as mere onanism. See M. Corday, *Anatole France d'après ses confidences et ses souvenirs* (Paris: André Delpeuch, 1928), p. 190.

66. See L. Huxley, *The Life and Letters of Thomas Henry Huxley* (London: Macmillan, 1900), vol. 1, p. 218.

67. B. Dobrée, *Modern Prose Style* (Oxford: Clarendon Press, 1934), p. 220.

68. Quoted in *Time*, November 6, 1989, p. 87. It was not mentioned there that already as a schoolgirl she was ready to give anything for recognition. Thus she recalls that in order to gain the attention of the older girls in the school, she openly disagreed with the religion teacher, a priest, on the possibility of a rational proof of the existence of God. See her *Memories of a Catholic Girlhood* (New York: Harcourt, Brace and Company, 1957), pp. 120-21. See also, p. 107.

69. See C. Lehmann-Haupt's review in *The New York Times*, May 22, 1989, p. 18.

70. Ibid.

71. See Mel Gussow's obituary of Beckett in *The New York Times*, Dec. 27, 1989, p. 1.

72. T. S. Eliot, *The Family Reunion*, Part I, Scene II.

73. Susan Cohen, "My Only Child Dead a Year," *The New York Times*, Dec. 21, 1989, p. A31.

74. *The New York Times*, March, 15, 1990, p. A16.

75. D. Gabor, *The Mature Society*, pp. 51-2.

76. Quoted from C. Lehmann-Haupt's review in *The New York Times*, Feb. 1, 1990, p. C21.

77. Aug. 25, 1989, p. 20.

78. Ibid.

79. A. S. Eddington, *The Nature of the Physical World* (Cambridge: Cambridge University Press, 1928), p. 165.

80. See *Pascal's Pensées*, tr. W. F. Trotter, with an introduction by T. S. Eliot (New Yor: E. P. Dutton, 1958), p. 61 (#206).

81. Rev. 1:5.

82. Christ did so especially in His great debate with the Jews as recorded in ch. 8 of John's Gospel.

INDEX OF NAMES

285

INDEX OF SUBJECTS

least action, principle of, 161–2, 269
lesbianism, 199
life, origin of, 38, 84; carbon based,
  90–1, 107; non-carbon based, 96,
  123; extraterrestrial, 123; as
  mechanism, 166; unobservable, 166
Lisbon earthquake, 71–2
logic, Hegelian, 119
logical positivism, 118
love, 135; Christian, 219

machine guns, 18
machines, 165
man, and evolution, 43, 47; biological
  future of, 50; privileged position of,
  92; as toolmaker, 155–8, 267–8;
  dehumanized, 162, 178
Marxism, 175–7
Maya sacrifices, 206
mechanism, biological, 165–7
mechanistic philosophy, 162, 180
medieval technology, 4–5, 239
metaphors, Teilhardian, 141–2
metaphysics, 79
method of science, 83, 145–6, 158,
  184
Milky Way, 94–5
mind, mistrust in, 151–2; as mere
  byproduct of matter, 153
monkeys and tools, 155–6
morphology, 48
multiworld theory, 112

natural selection, 38, 40, 50, 77, 79,
  147–8, 172, 253–4
naturalism, 130
nature, non-causal, 19
Neanderthals, 207, 277–8
necessity, 186–8
neo-Kantianism, 167
neutrinos, 102
Newton's first law, 114
Newtonian physics, and free will,
  184–6
nisus, 127–30
non-conformism, 213
novelty, 137

observer and reality 107–9
oceanic feeling, 216

Omega Point, 142
ontological argument, 64
ontology and causality, 242
optimism, 71–2, 252
order, principle of, 61
organisms, their goal-seeking, 167

pantheism, 122
Paradise on earth, 5, 11, 14, 16
pattern, 64; versus purpose, 64,
  88
personal identity, 131–2, 140
phenomenology, 119
physico-theological proof, 63
physics, mechanistic, 160–2;
  organismic, 161
Pleasure Principle, 200, 205–10
prayer, 192–3
predestination, 191–2, 220–1
prehistoric man, 205–8
primeval soup, 84
process, cosmic, 46; Whiteheadian,
  137–40
progress, necessary, 13 122; technical
  versus moral, 12–15; as ambivalent,
  15, 22–4; merciless, 18, 22–3; idea
  of, 19–21; and evolution, 20–1; and
  war, 22–3; as religion, 24; its
  bankruptcy, 26; and neocapitalism,
  27, 30; and science, 27;
  Sakharovian, 28–9; and the sacred,
  30, 290–1; as economic
  productivity, 178; its origin, 200–4
protoplasm, 254
Providence, divine, 223–5
purpose, sense of, 18; its Socratic
  sense, 117, 161; and logical
  positivism, 118; and existentialism,
  118–9; and phenomenology, 119;
  and Muslim creed, 120; and soul,
  125–6; cosmic, 137; and beauty,
  140; and quantum mechanics, 162–
  3; its analogical realizations, 169; as
  God's will, 225–6; its scientific
  witness, 228–32; despaired of, 235–
  7; see also *suffering*
psi-function, 163
psychoanalysis, Freudian, 216;
  Jungian, 216
psychoanalysts, unhappiness of, 236–7

(continued from p. ii)

By the same author

The Savior of Science
(Wethersfield Institute Lectures, 1987)

Miracles and Physics

God and the Cosmologists
(Farmington Lectures, Oxford, 1988)

The Only Chaos and Other Essays

Catholic Essays

*Cosmos in Transition:
Studies in the History of Cosmology*

Olbers Studies

★ ★ ★

Translations with introduction and notes:

The Ash Wednesday Supper (Giordano Bruno)

*Cosmological Letters on the Arrangement
of the World Edifice* (J. H. Lambert)

Universal Natural History and Theory of the Heavens (I. Kant)

Note on the Author

Stanley L. Jaki, a Hungarian-born Catholic priest of the Benedictine order, is Distinguished Professor at Seton Hall University, South Orange, New Jersey. With doctorates in theology and physics, he has for the past thirty years specialized in the history and philosophy of science. The author of thirty books and over eighty articles, he served as Gifford Lecturer at the University of Edinburgh and as Fremantle Lecturer at Balliol College, Oxford. He has lectured at major universities in the United States, Europe, and Australia. He is honorary member of the Pontifical Academy of Sciences, *membre correspondant* of the Académie Nationale des Sciences, Belles-Lettres et Arts of Bordeaux, and the recipient of the Lecomte du Nouy Prize for 1970 and of the Templeton Prize for 1987.